D. H. B. Brower

Danville, Montour County, Pennsylvania

a collection of historical and biographical sketches

D. H. B. Brower

Danville, Montour County, Pennsylvania
a collection of historical and biographical sketches

ISBN/EAN: 9783337193416

Printed in Europe, USA, Canada, Australia, Japan

Cover: Foto ©Andreas Hilbeck / pixelio.de

More available books at **www.hansebooks.com**

A COLLECTION OF

HISTORICAL AND BIOGRAPHICAL SKETCHES.

BY

D. H. B. BROWER.

*Founder of the MONTOUR AMERICAN and the
DANVILLE RECORD.*

HARRISBURG, PA.:
LANE S. HART, PRINTER AND BINDER.
1881.

TO

MY WIFE AND CHILDREN,

WHOSE EARNEST AFFECTION

THROUGH ALL THE CHANGING SCENES OF LIFE

HAS MADE THE SUNSHINE OF HOME

THIS VOLUME IS AFFECTIONATELY INSCRIBED BY

THE AUTHOR.

Introduction.

In the list of secular studies history is among the most interesting and the most important. Indeed, there seems to be an almost universal desire to lift the misty veil of the past, and to note the changing scenes that mark the progress of Adam's family through all the centuries past and gone. Not alone to satisfy the cravings of a curiosity that is commendable, but because the richest lessons of wisdom are drawn from the experience of the past. Still more interesting and important is the general, and, especially, the biographical history of our own locality. Here, with emotions of strange delight we trace the stern, heroic lives of the pioneers, and with ever-increasing interest watch the growing fields succeed the forest, pleasant homes supplant the rude log cabin, and the development of society as it joins the onward march to a higher civilization. On the other hand, there is a desire no less universal to be remembered by those who come after us. Thus prompted, men have sought out the most enduring material by which to transmit their names and achievements down the ages. They have reared monuments of granite, carved their deeds on the solid marble, and written their names on the everlasting rocks. But all those have yielded to the corroding power of Time, and their moldering remnants become the subjects of uncertain speculation to the antiquarian. Written history is the great conservator of the past and the most enduring memorial for the ages to come. The wondrous tower on the plains of Shinar is leveled with the dust from which it rose, and the glory of Babylon is shrouded in darkness. The pomp and pride of Pharaoh, the armies of Amalek, the power of Moab, the Syrian, the Chaldean, with all the heroes and nations of antiquity, are known only through the written chronicles kept by the scribes of Israel—chronicles that point the student to the dim and broken fragments of crumbling monuments that strew the track of finished centuries. Written history will be faithful to its mission. It will " not perish from the earth." Its universality, its vast capabilities of reproduction and translation into all languages, insure its duration to the end of time.

But apart from the history of the world, apart from the discovery and history of our own country, Danville has a history all its own—a history of deep and absorbing interest, not only to the descendants of the old pioneers, but to all who have found a home within its borders. Let it be understood, however, that I make no pretension to a consecutive history of Danville in these pages ; and as every author in his work presents some characteristic of himself, so let it be in this. Never having been trained to methodical action or the minutiæ of business tactics, a mental metamorphosis will not be expected. I have no ambition to tread the beaten path by tracing and connecting every link in order more exact than the real occurrence. As Comstock says in his unique Tongue of Time, "We have heard a thousand times that the sun arose in glory and sat in gold." Now let us hear something else. There are a thousand books, with chapter, verse, section, and paragraph, stately and uniform as the cogs of a wheel. Now let us have something else. But neither the local historian nor the oldest inhabitant can gather many reliable facts from the dim and misty past. As they grope amid the deepening shadows, they may find here and there an isolated fact : but the opening pages of Danville are shrouded beneath a dusty veil that can never be lifted. Its general outline may be traced or imagined by those who are personally interested in certain genealogies, or who have been schooled in the wild experience of frontier life, but the life record of those who first surveyed this scene is buried forever in the tomb of the past. What hopes and fears, what daring projects or great resolves, once animated the village fathers and mothers, we shall never know. They are gone to the realms where " the rude forefathers of the hamlet sleep."

The main object in these pages is to note the history of Danville and mark its progress during the last quarter of a century, or during the twenty five years it has been under my own personal observation.

Although without special order, these random sketches may be presented, yet they are all true to life. Not like the stately pile that science builds, but like the landscape view from a railroad car. I care not a straw for professional critics. The constitutional grumbler is in the same category. No doubt some sap-heads will say they could have gotten up a better work, and who will perchance condemn the entire volume, because there is no mention of them or theirs, or of some occurrence in which they or a relative was the lion of the occasion. All this must be expected, for a certain tribute must always be paid to the wiseacres of the day. No doubt some village Solomon will shake his head and say that he knew all that himself. "Everybody knows the business houses on Mill street, and where the court-house stands Why tell us what we know?" Not so fast, sir; I am not writing for the present only, but for the future. I am telling other generations away in the days to come, how and by whom Danville affairs were conducted before they were born. It is the duty of the historian to present the situation just as it is around him in his own day. So don't be selfish and scold because some things are described that you know as well as the writer. Those very items may be of the deepest interest to your grand-children. I have availed myself of all the sources of information within my reach. I am, however, chiefly indebted to J. Frazer, Esq., of Cincinnati. His careful research has contributed much to this volume. Many thanks to him for his valuable aid in rescuing important facts from the shadows of forgetfulness. With this introduction, this book is placed before the public, with the earnest hope that it may meet a kindly reception, and, in some degree, serve the purpose of its creation.

THE AUTHOR.

Location.

DANVILLE is situated on the right bank of the North Branch of the Susquehanna river, and about eleven miles above its confluence with the West Branch at the town of Northumberland. It is surrounded by the most charming and picturesque scenery, and is nestled in a narrow valley, between Blue Hill and Montour Ridge. Tall hills, in their wild grandeur, and clad in their native robes of emerald, rise on every side, and down the pleasant vale, beyond the river, the beautiful white cottages of South Danville and Riverside dot the landscape. In the north-west, and close at hand, Bald-Top rears its barren crown above the stately furnaces at its base, whilst dense volumes of smoke and clouds of steam roll slowly up its rugged steep. A view from the summit is one of the grandest imaginable, if you delight in wild and varied scenery—pine-clad hills and broad majestic rivers. The whole town from that point, from Sidler's Hill to Sageburg, and from Swampoodle to Frogtown, like a vast panorama, is spread out before you. Drowsy Mnemoloton looms up beyond the river, whilst almost beneath your feet railroad trains, like huge serpents with fiery breath, traverse the scene. The asylum, the opera house, the great iron works, almost a score of churches, and two thousand dwellings, are all before you. From below, Bald-Top seems like a frowning fortress on the line of Montour ridge, and, although its slopes are covered with spruce and pine, its crest is bald and bare, where scarce a shrub has grown within the memory of man. Half a mile below is the "dark ravine" and the precipice known as "lover's leap." It is true that almost every locality boasts a "lover's leap," but the title to this is derived from a veritable Indian legend well known among the Delawares, and often rehearsed among the early settlers of Danville. It is said that the daughter

of an Indian chief, related to the renowned Tamenund, whose wig-
wam stood in the village, on the banks of the "Crooked river," at
the confluence of Mahoning, was given to a young brave of the war-
like but waning *Leni Lenape :* but the dusky maiden had chosen a
lover of her own whom she loved with all the deep and deathless
devotion of her passionate race.   A short time previous to the proposed marriage with " Big Turtle," she met her Huron lover near
the precipice, and as her tribe was on the war-path against the Hu-
rons, she was discovered by a scout and confronted by her father.
The old sachem, with a thunder-cloud on his brow, demanded of
his daughter the final renunciation of her chosen lover.   True to
the impulse of her woman's nature she refused, and with one pierc-
ing cry sprang from the rock and sacrificed her life on the altar of
a deathless passion.   There, in that dusky glen, she sleeps a dreamless sleep in her virgin purity, where now the careless feet of another
race and another generation tread upon her lowly mound, and where
the merry voices of a strange people have long since broken the
solitude of her lonely grave.   The gladsome voices of the young and
the gay now mingle with the music of the brooklet as it rushes to
the river ; and as they spread their dainty fare on the mossy rocks,
or dance upon the green, do the votaries of pleasure ever think of
the dark-eyed maiden that quietly sleeps beneath their feet?

Altogether the scenery around the town of Danville is not surpassed in this portion of the State, and in its wild romantic beauty
can only find its rival among the Alleghenies.   It is true, the rest-
less enterprise of a growing population is here and there slowly
working a change, but the silver sheen of the river will continue to
sparkle in the morning sun, and there will stand forever Blue hill,
around whose hazy brow, in misty veils, still hang the legends of
Indian lore.

Land Titles.

The land embraced in the corporate limits of Danville was originally within the boundary of Northumberland county, and its inhabitants were involved in all the horrors of border warfare with the
French and their Indian allies, and afterwards with the English and
the same bloody savages.   The Shawanese, the Senecas, and the
Delawares were in the neighborhood.   The latter were the most

numerous, and, for the most part, the least troublesome. The Iriquois, who made frequent and murderous raids on the white settlements, often acted the part of incarnate devils. The Delawares had a village of considerable importance at the mouth of the Mahoning creek, just below the present town of Danville, and the boys of today still find arrow-heads and other warlike implements fashioned by the rude skill of "old Nakomis," or some other dusky arrow maker of the forest. The same spot is now frequently occupied by the semi-barbarous Zingari—the wandering gypsies—the decendants of Egypt.

In 1772, Northumberland county was taken from Berks, Lancaster, Northampton, and Bedford. It then included Columbia county, of which Montour was a portion. Columbia county was taken from Norhumberland and organized as a new county on the 15th of March, 1813, and Danville was made the county seat of Columbia county. But the county seat, by a popular vote, authorized by the Legislature, was moved to Bloomsburg in 1845. The people of Danville, and those of the lower end of the county, were not satisfied, and demanded a division of the county. Accordingly, on the 3d day of May, 1850, an act was passed by the Legislature erecting the county of Montour, and making Danville the county seat of the new county. The writer of this volume was then a member of the State Legislature, from Butler county, and cast his vote in that body in favor of the new county.

The ground occupied by the town of Danville belonged to several tracts, and it is exceedingly difficult, if not impossible, to trace the various transfers previous to the purchase and settlement of Gen. William Montgomery. By the old parchment deeds and surveys, in the office of George W. West, Esq., present surveyor of Montour county, it appears that one of these tracts, containing one hundred and twenty acres, extending from Chestnut to Church street, and from the river to the base of Montour ridge on the north, was surveyed to George Jewel, on the 3d of April, 1769, and transferred to Turbet Francis on the 16th of December, in the same year, and on the 2d of May, 1782, sold to John Simpson, and by John Simpson and his wife, Ann Grimes, sold and conveyed to William Montgomery, for £600, on the 15th of April, 1783. The tract below Chestnut street, including the mouth of Mahoning creek, containing one hundred and eighty acres, was known as a Proprietary Manor, and was patented to Rev. Richard Peters. Another account says that the Proprietor, John Penn, patented the same tract to John Lukens, the State Surveyor at the time. A. F. Russell, Esq., in his biography of General William Montgomery, says that William Montgomery purchased land here of J. Cummings, and also that he bought a tract of one hundred and eighty acres of J. Simpson, on which the town of Danville was laid out, by a deed bearing date November 26, 1774. If the reader can get the precise facts, by studying the old records, he is wiser than the writer of this book. It is certain that the land occupied by the greater portion of Danville was purchased by General William Montgomery, prior to 1776, the period of his location in this place. There may have been conflicting claims to the land, that were subsequently purchased by General Montgomery, and so to us confused the records. On the north of these tracts, the land belonged to John Montgomery : on the north-east to Amos Wickersham, which afterwards became the property of the Frazers and the Yorks ; on the south-east, were the lands of the Sechlers, who were among the earliest settlers of this place.

This was known for some time as " Montgomery's Landing," and also as " Mahoning Settlement," until the town was laid out by General Daniel Montgomery, son of William Montgomery, in the year 1792, or that part of the town lying between Mill and Church streets, and from the river to the canal, which ground he had purchased from his father. As Daniel Montgomery was then the most enterprising business man in the place, whose store and mill were the centers of attraction to all the country around it, and as he was very popular and highly respected, the people, by general consent, began to call it " Danville," out of compliment to Daniel Montgomery. In 1776, General William Montgomery built the log house that still adjoins the stone mansion he afterwards erected, and there his youngest son Alexander was born, in 1777, and died in the same room in 1848. The widow of Alexander resided there until her death, which occurred only a few years ago.

At an early day Jacob Gearhart established a ferry across the river. The ferry house stood above Ferry, at Pine street. John Sechler, father of Jacob Sechler recently deceased, laid out that part of the town above Church street. Between the Montgomerys and Sechlers, they made something of a muddle near where the planing-mill now stands in not properly joining the streets.

General William Montgomery, after Daniel had laid out his land in town lots, laid out that part lying below Mill street, down to Chestnut, donating at that time thirty-one lots for the endowment of an academy, stipulating that it should be under the control of the Presbyterian church, and that one of his descendants should always be on the board of trustees.

Amos Wickersham donated to the Presbyterians the ground on which the Grove church is built, and also the adjoining burying ground.

The court-house ground was donated by General William, and that on which the jail stands by General Daniel Montgomery.

General William Montgomery.

General William Montgomery was the most notable settler of this region. He came from Chester county, where he was born on the 3d of August, 1736, and was a prominent actor in the Revolutionary war, and also in civil life before he came to this place. He first located in Northumberland, and moved to Danville in 1776. He immediately began to make improvements, but on account of the murderous raids of the Indians, he took his family to a place of safety until the campaign of General Sullivan gave security to the settlers. General Montgomery himself was inured to the hardships of war, having been schooled in the camp, the field, and the forest. During his lifetime, he was called by the people to a variety of responsible positions, both civil and military. He was a representative in Congress and president judge of the courts in Northumberland county. But chiefly does he claim the gratitude of posterity for his constant efforts for the material and moral welfare of Danville, for his devotion to the physical comfort and religious training of the growing community of which he was the founder. He occupied many positions of public trust during his long and useful life, and always with honor to himself and to the advantage of the public. He died in 1816. This note is brief, but his life-work will, in a measure, appear in these pages, as we trace the various movements and enterprises that gave birth, life, and character to the town of Danville.

The Indians.

We have no special record of the terrible ordeal through which the early settlers of Danville had to pass. Enough to know that it was like the hard experience of others on the frontier. The danger from the merciless savage was constant, day and night. The farmer was suddenly struck down by the bullet of the stealthy foe ; the assemblies for worship or social enjoyment often terminated in a bloody tragedy ; "the darkness of midnight glittered with the blaze of their dwellings, and the war-whoop of the savage awoke the sleep of the cradle." The settlers of Danville were surrounded by the Six Nations, including the Tuscaroras that had been driven out of North Carolina. The Five Nations adopted the Tuscaroras into their confederacy, by which they became the Six Nations. The renowned Shikellimy was, at that time, the grand chief of all the tribes. His lodge was at Shamokin. The Delawares were spread from the Hudson to the Potomac, but were conquered by the Six Nations. The Shawanese came from Florida, and were allies of the Delawares. The most northern village of the Shawanese was at Chillesquaque. The Delawares were divided into three tribes—the Turkeys, the Turtles, and the Wolfs or Munci. The latter tribe was the most fierce and warlike : and the most *gentle*, if that term may be applied to savages, were those whose emblem was the Turtle. The Delawares called themselves the *Leni Lenape*, or original people. The settlers called the Six Nations " Mingoes," "Maquais." The French called them "Iroquois."

The great Shikellimy was the grand ruler of the conquered Delawares and Shawanees, though he himself belonged to the Oneidas, of the Six Nations. But there was constant war among the savages ; treachery circumventing treachery : torture and murder succeeding torture and murder. The condition of civilized society brought into contact with the bloody savages may well be imagined, and without any special record of their individual suffering, a glance at their surroundings will teach us to know how much we owe the settlers of Danville for the peaceful homes we now enjoy. Shikellimy was the father of Logan, whose celebrated speech you have doubtless read in the school books of to-day. The speech in which he bids adieu to his home and turns towards the setting sun, and in which he says that not a drop of his blood coursed in the veins of any relative. He was alone, and yet had always been a friend to the white man. This sad farewell to the scenes of his youth and the graves of his fathers will ever remain on our records as the grandest model of Indian eloquence. Logan was a Mingo chief. His lodge was at the mouth of Chillesquaque; afterward, he lived further up the valley. In 1774, the expedition of Lord Dunmore was the occasion of Logan's departure and of his celebrated farewell address. It is said that he was at the Indian town, at the mouth of the Mahoning creek, now within the borough limits of Danville, about the year 1772. He is said to have been six feet high, well proportioned, and straight as an arrow—a perfect model of manhood. He went to Michigan in 1774, and was cruelly assassinated there. While sitting at a camp fire, with his blanket over his head, a hostile Indian stole up behind him and tomahawked him, thus putting out the light of life from as much nobility as the Indian is capable of possessing.

The Post-Office.

The Danville post-office was established in 1806, General William Montgomery being the first postmaster at this place. He and Daniel Montgomery served until 1813, when Rudolph Sechler was appointed, April 3 of that year. He held the office until James Loughead was appointed, on the 24th of November, 1820. David Petrikin succeeded him, on the 1st of February, 1834. Next John Best was appointed on the 21st day of March, 1837, who served until the appointment of Sharpless Taylor, on the 25th of March, 1841. He was followed by Alexander Best, who was appointed on the 9th of November, 1842. Gideon M. Shoop was appointed on the 11th of April, 1849. During his term the new county of Montour was created. On the 26th of November, 1852, Thomas C. Ellis was appointed, and on the 21st of September, 1853, Thomas Chalfant received the appointment. During his term, in 1856, the Danville post-office became a Presidential appointment, and Mr. Chalfant was re-appointed by the President, on the 21st of February, 1856, and served until the 28th of May, 1861, when he was succeeded by Andrew F. Russel, who was re-appointed on the 14th of July, 1865, and served until Ogden H. Ostrander was appointed, on the 16th of

April, 1867. Charles W. Eckman was appointed on the 5th of April, 1869, and re-appointed on the 18th of March, 1873, and again re-appointed on the 7th of April, 1877. Colonel Charles W. Eckman is the present incumbent. Under his administration there have been great improvements, both in the arrangements and appointments of the office and in its management, giving the highest degree of satis-faction to the department and to the public. In September, 1874, he moved the post-office to the opera-house, a central location, fit-ting it up with seven hundred and fifty-six Yale boxes. These boxes, with the handsome casing, give a stylish appearance to the office, where every desired convenience is afforded. There is not a country town in the State that can boast a better-conducted, better-arranged, or more elegant post-office than that of Danville.

In every country town the post-office is a good place to study human nature. See that individual who only gets one letter in six months, who always struggles to be first at the delivery. At last he gets a letter! See how he turns it over and over, looks at the ad-dress, examines the stamp, and seems astonished to find himself in possession of the prize. He looks up at the crowd with an air of importance, whilst the crowd is silently reading him. Next look at that spruce young clerk, who gets a dozen or more for his employer. How wise he looks, and seems to say to the crowd, "Look at *my* correspondence." Then comes the indignant individual, who won-ders why he got none, and thinks there must be something wrong in the management of the mail. He calls on the postmaster to know why it didn't come. Now comes the bashful young man, who ex-pects a letter from his lady love. He looks as if the postmaster and everybody else knew the nature of the precious epistle, and slips away to enjoy it by himself. There comes a big man, carelessly treading on other folks' corns. He gets a dun from his wash-woman, and tries to pass it off for a draft on the bank. Do you see that booby on the side-walk, or, in cold weather, backed against the inside wall, just to see who comes and goes, or to glance at what others get. There comes Miss Sweet Sixteen. She expects a letter from "somebody," but, seeing the crowd, she retreats until the coast is clear. She does not choose to let all the world see her blushes as she receives the prize. But now make room for the man from the rural district, who inquires for the whole neighborhood. He at last gives way to the confident chap, who gets mad when he fails to get a letter, because he is sure it was mailed. So if you want to take a good lesson on human nature, just go to the post-office at mail time. And don't forget to take a quiet smile at the fussy man, who rushes in, peeps into half the boxes, then peers down the schute where the drop letters go. What he sees there, has never been revealed.

Grove Presbyterian Church.

The Grove Presbyterian, or, as it was originally called, Mahoning Presbyterian Church, is the oldest religious organization in Danville. While this place was still known as "Mahoning Settlement," Rev. John Bryson was the first Presbyterian minister. He preached at first in Gen. Montgomery's dwelling house, and when the congregation became too large services were held in the barn. The first, or the old log, church was built 1778 or 1779. The logs for the church were nicely prepared. They were scored by George Maus and Isaac Boudman. They were hewn by Thomas Hughes. This church stood until 1826, when a plain brick church was built. This modest structure was the sacred temple in which the generation worshipped that is now passing away. Though services had been held with some degree of regularity as early as 1777 the congregation was not organized until 1785. Unfortunately there exists at the present time no complete record of the church in those early days. Our sketch must, therefore, of necessity, be very brief in relation to a subject so full of interest to many who are now living here and elsewhere.

Among those who contributed to the preaching of the Gospel in "Mahoning Settlement," previous to the organization of the church, were William Montgomery, Peter Blue, Gilbert Vorhes, David Goodman, John Emmitt, John Wilson, John Irwin, Peter Mellick, Robert Henry, Benjamin Fowler, John Ogden, Lemuel Wheeler, David Carr, John Clark, John Black, Daniel Kelly, Garret Van Camp, William Gray, Joseph Barry, Martin Todd, John Evart, Peter Rambo, Andrew Cochran, Charles McClahan, James Grimes, William Lemon, William Montgomery, Jr., Robert Giles, Joseph Rosenberry, and David Subingall.

At a later period, namely, in 1793, the salary to be paid to the pastor by Mahoning church was fixed at seventy-five pounds per an-

2

num, said pastor to divide his services between Mahoning and Derry congregations. The salary was guaranteed by Joseph Biggers, Hugh Caldwell, Thomas Gaskins, James Stephenson, William Donaldson, John Emmett, Sr., Robert Donaldson, John Donaldson, Joseph Williams, John Woodside, George Caldwell, John Jones, William Colt, John Montgomery, Daniel Barton, Christian Campbell, Robert Williams, Alex. McMunigal, William Montgomery, Jr., John Moore, Daniel Montgomery, Robert Montgomery, John Carr, James Loughead, Robert Campbell, Thomas Best, James Consart, Gilbert Vorhees, James Curry, Peter Blue, Andrew Cochran, M. Gulick, Richard Robinson, Jacob Gearhart, Jr., Frederick Blue, John Emmett, Jr., John Young, Elias Harrison, Isaac Woodruff, Stephen Hunt, Albert Ammerman, and Philip Young. This congregation, as stated, was organized in 1785. Gen. William Montgomery was chosen an elder at the same time, and continued an active and faithful officer until his death, which occurred in 1816.

The brick church built in 1826 was a neat and plain structure, presenting quite a picturesque appearance, embowered as it was in a grove of forest trees. The new church is a massive and handsome structure of artistic stone-work in the Gothic order of architecture, and was dedicated in 1875. It occupies the site of the old brick church on the Knoll, surrounded by the remaining forest trees and a grove of beautiful young maples that were planted to take the place of the ancient oaks that are rapidly passing away. The building of this magnificent temple was superintended by Mr. Joseph Diehl, a master mechanic and builder, whose handiwork is seen on many a public and private building in this region. As previously stated Rev. Bryson was the first pastor of Mahoning, now the Grove Presbyterian church, and with the aid of the old pioneers he laid the foundations deep and strong for a lasting church, a religious home to bless the passing generations for centuries to come. Rev. Patterson was a worthy successor. His ministration was long and abundantly blessed. Greatly beloved by his people, his name is still a household word among their descendants. Rev. Dunlap succeeded him in the pastorate of Mahoning church, and he was followed by Rev. Halliday.

Then came Rev. Doctor Yeomans, who, as a scholar, a preacher, and pastor, will be long and gratefully remembered. He died in this place, universally lamented, as every christian knew that a good man and a strong leader had been called away. During his pastorate, about 1849 or 1850, the question of a new church edifice was agitated. There was some division of sentiment in reference to its location. A portion favored the erection of the new church on the south side of the canal, and others adhered to the old site in the grove, now rendered doubly dear as the place where their fathers and mothers had worshipped. The former succeeded. A new church was built on Mahoning street, and Rev. Doctor Yeomans continued his ministry in the new church. The adherents to the Grove were without a regular pastor, as the organization, with the pastor, had gone with the new church. In 1855, however, Presbytery organized a new congregation in the old church, and called it "Mahoning Presbyterian Church, North." But this title was considered too cumbrous, and through the efforts of Rev. C. J. Collins and others it was changed to the more convenient and more euphonious name of "The Grove Presbyterian Congregation." Rev. C. J. Collins was the first pastor. He remained some ten years and resigned to assume the duties of an educator in an institution of learning. Rev. Collins was somewhat austere, an excellent scholar, and an eloquent preacher, but not remarkable for his knowledge of human nature, and, consequently, less a pastor than a preacher. He had a deep bass voice—sanguine in temperament and full of patriotism, he preached some flaming war sermons, as well as many eloquent discourses on the christian warfare. He was succeeded by Rev. Doctor J. Gordon Carnachan, a graduate of Scotland's most celebrated university, and a profound scholar. For close logical reasoning and theological attainments, he has few equals in this country, and his impassioned perorations touched the finest chords of the human heart. Dr. Carnachan is not only an eloquent preacher but a man of commanding ability, unexcelled in this country as a Greek and Hebrew scholar, on whom the greatest university of Europe conferred its highest honor. He left this place to take charge of a congregation in Meadville, where he still remains. He was followed in the pastorate of the Grove church, by Rev. Reuben H. Van Pelt. Rev. Van Pelt was a good man, and an earnest preacher. If more limited in his mental power than his predecessor, he was more successful in his pastoral relations. Rev. W. A. McAtee was next called

to the charge of the Grove church. And whilst he engaged the
affection and confidence of his people, as a faithful shepherd and a
man of more than ordinary ability, there is some difficulty in correctly analysing his mind. A shade of sadness at times seemed to
fall on his most brilliant efforts, and a far-away expression succeeded
the moments of rapture. But none doubted his goodness, none
questioned his ability, nor did his people withhold their love and respect. After his resignation Rev. John B. Grier became the pastor
of the Grove congregation. He is the youngest son of M. C.
Grier, who was long an elder in that church, and lately deceased.
The Grier family has given the church a number of eminent preachers, and Rev. John B. Grier bids fair to maintain the high degree
of ability and usefulness to which they attained. His learning,
his aptness to teach, and his vivid imagination, inspired by the
spirit of religion, cannot fail to result in the accomplishment of
his mission. With a critical, and yet a comprehensive mind, cultured with care; a generous nature open to all; and, though young
in years, yet strong in the spirit and power of the Gospel; who will
say he is not destined to eminence in his high profession? Among
the families connected with the old church, and whose descendants
still worship in the Grove, mention is made of the Montgomerys,
Maus, Currys, Yorks, Diehls, Griers, McMahans, Magills, Walizes,
Cathcarts, Boudmans, Moores, Gearharts, and Russels.

The Grove church contains the largest organ in Danville, costing
some three thousand dollars.

Mahoning Presbyterian Church

This church was built in 1853, on Mahoning and Ferry streets,
the congregation, as before stated, retaining the name and the organization of the original church. The building is handsome and
well-arranged. It is surmounted by a steeple containing a bell and
a town clock. Some years ago a storm blew down the spire, which
was never replaced. There is a fine memorial window in the rear
of the pulpit. The designs in colors are elegant and appropriate,
having been placed there by E. B. Reynolds, in memory of his
mother, who had been a member of the congregation for many
years. Rev. Doctor Yeomans, who was the pastor in the old church,
continued his ministrations in the new for a number of years, and

died greatly lamented by the community, as well as the members of his own religious household. Rev. Doctor Yeomans was a man of very superior powers of mind : in truth, he was a great as well as a good man. He may not have been fully appreciated at home, but he ranked with the most eminent divines of the Presbyterian Church in the United States. His reputation extended all over the country, and his great ability was not only acknowledged by making him Moderator of the General Assembly, but in according to him the deference that exalted merit demands on all occasions.

Rev. Ijams succeeded to the pastorate of Mahoning Presbyterian church, after the death of Dr. Yeomans. He was something of a sensationalist ; eloquent he was, and, withal, rather dramatic. Of course a sermon would be dull and lifeless without it : yet it should not be all drama, nor yet the most prominent feature of a discourse. His imaginative powers were good, and as an orator he stood deservedly high, but the people missed the solid, glowing force of truth they were wont to hear from Dr. Yeomans. Rev. Ijams resigned, and Rev. A. B. Jack was called to the charge of Mahoning Presbyterian church. He was distinguished for originality, for a wide range of thought and power of language. His descriptive powers are something remarkable, his oratory peculiar, startling, and effective. For sublimity of conception and beauty of expression, some of his discourses were unsurpassed. After officiating for several years, he resigned to take charge of a congregation in Hazleton, where he still remains. Rev. F. R. Beeber succeeded him in this place, and if not as brilliant as his immediate predecessor, he is a solid thinker, a good speaker, and an excellent pastor. In his earnest life-work, Rev. Beeber endeared himself to the hearts of many ; his faithfulness as a minister, his ability as a teacher, and his fidelity as a friend, will not be forgotten. Rev. R. L. Stewart, the present pastor, has just entered upon his work in this place, and the indications point to the best results.

Climate and Longevity.

In glancing at the climate of Danville and the longevity of its people, I again copy from the memoranda of Mr. J. Frazer. He says, the climate of Danville is exceedingly favorable to the health and longevity of its inhabitants. Epidemics seldom prevail. Its near proximity to 41° north latitude, approximates that of the insalubrious cities of Pekin, Constantinople, Naples, and Barcelona. Yet the isothermal line shows that it corresponds with the more salubrious regions of New Jersey, Long Island, England, Ireland, Belgium, Southern Germany, the Crimea, China, Japan, Washington Territory, Montana, Nebraska, most of which are several degrees north of its parallel of latitude, and showing a divergence between that and the isothermal line.

The peculiar and admirable location of Danville is most favorable. The description of the mountain in a far remote geological period, caused by the bursting through its barriers by the pent-up waters of an ancient lake or primeval ocean on its northern side, or by some other stupendeous convulsion of nature, scooped out a gateway through Montour Ridge to effect an outlet for the Mahoning, and thus afford a most admirable site for the town. It reminds us of the Blue Ridge, cloven asunder to yield a passage for the Potomac below its confluence with the Shenandoah, at Harper's Ferry, which Jefferson so graphically described, and to see which, he asserted, was worth a voyage across the Atlantic. And thus Danville is in a favorable situation to receive the sunshine of early spring, the balmy and invigorating breezes of summer, which reach it from the Susquehanna, and the prolonged and delightful autumn. Few places are so highly favored. The extreme old age of many of its people corroborates this, extending, as they do, much beyond the three score and ten years of the Psalmist. From memory we can recall the names of the following ancient residents of the place and vicinity who attained a great age: Robert Finny, ninty-five years; Mrs. Jane Montgomery, ninty-three years; John Sechler, ninty-three years; Peter Baldy, ninty-two; Sarah Lloyd, ninty-one; Joseph Maus, Rudolph Sechler, William Philips, each ninety; Charles M. Frazer, eighty-nine; George A. Frick, eighty-six; Michael Blue, eighty-four; William Donaldson, the Revolutionary patriot, eighty-two; Thomas Woodside, John

Deen, John Moore, each eighty ; and the following beyond the seventy years : Paul Adams, John Frazer, John Russel, John Reynolds, John Cooper, John Montgomery, John Yerrick, Daniel Frazer, Daniel Woodside, Dr. David Petrekin, William Whitaker, William Yorks, Samuel Yorks. To this list scores, now living or recently deceased, could be added. Among those still living, are the following octogenarians : Jacob Sechler, ninty years ; Dr. William H. Magill, eighty-six ; Judge William Donalson, now of Pottsville, in his eighty second year. Many others of a good old age could be enumerated who are " natives to the manor born," or who resided here for many years. Among these is Rev. Samuel Montgomery, now of Oberlin, Ohio, in his seventy-fifth year.

The health of a people is a desideratum of the first importance. Without it, all the temporal blessings lose much of their value. This is painfully apparent in the South, and in some places in the great West. Surrounded by regions of exuberant fertility, yet so unhealthy that the valitudinary inhabitants would gladly exchange their luxurious homes for those of less productiveness, if they could thereby have their impaired health restored. The people of Danville should duly appreciate the great blessing they enjoy in having so favorable a climate.

Prominent Men.

It is a source of deep regret that no reliable record can be obtained of such prominent men in the past history of Danville, as Reverend John B. Patterson, Doctor Alexander C. Donaldson, Rudolph Sechler, William G. Hurly, and many others. Moreover, what record we have of others is meager and unsatisfactory. From a few notes made by Mr. F., and what could be gathered from other sources, the following brief notes are presented :

ALEM MARR graduated at Princeton in 1807, and was admitted to the bar in 1809. He represented this district in Congress from 1829 to 1831, and spent his whole professional life in Danville.

SAMUEL KIRKHAM, the grammarian, succeeded D. C. Barrett in the Danville school, about 1819 to 1821. He was a competent teacher, but not so successful as Mr. Barrett. His " Lectures on English Grammar " was one of the most popular school-books of the day, and almost as generally used as Webster's spelling-book.

It went through one hundred and twenty-nine editions. His "Essay on Elocution" was a valuable treatise, but never attained a tithe of the popularity of his grammer. President Lincoln obtained his grammatical knowledge from the latter treatise, and there is yet in the hands of one of his admirers in Iowa, the identical volume in which the great emancipator studied. His signature is on a fly-leaf, with the homely caution, "Steal not this book, &c."

Dr. DAVID PETRIKIN was a native of Bellefonte. He studied medicine and practiced his profession in Danville. He represented this district in Congress two terms, from 1837 to 1841, and died on the 3d of January, 1849.

DANIEL FRAZER was born May 2, 1755, and married Sarah Wilson in 1772. She died in 1775. He was again married. His second wife was Isabella Watson, whom he married on the 6th day of February, 1777. He died in Danville on the 26th of March, 1828. His children were Charles, Emma, Margaret, James, Alexander, Sarah, Jane, William, Christiana M., Agnes, Daniel, and Thomas; all of whom are dead, except Christiana, who married Enos Miller, who died in 1870. All deceased except Mrs. Miller. His descendants reside in Montour county, New York, and Michigan. gan. He came to this place about 1790, and purchased of John Frazer one hundred acres of land in the south-west part of his two hundred and eighty-four acre tract. On this land he resided thirty-eight years, until his death, in the seventy-third year of his age. He was an honest and industrious farmer, enjoying the respect and confidence of his fellow-citizens. For a long time he resided at the base of the hill, near the site of an old Indian trading post, and a very short distance north of the spring. In 1824, he built the substantial stone residence which is still standing. All the southern portion of his farm is now within the corporate limits of Danville.

ELLIS HUGHES came to this place from Catawissa, about 1820. He was a school teacher and surveyor. He was also appointed register and recorder by the Governor, and served with great satisfaction to the people. He taught school for some years in a school-house that stood near where the *Record* office now stands. He was a good teacher, and was universally respected by the community. He also took care to see that his children were all well educated. Ellis Hughes was a faithful member and an efficient officer in the Methodist church, and died in the faith of the christian, in the year 1850.

DANIEL MONTGOMERY, a brother to Gen. William Montgomery, lived in the old frame house now occupied by Mr. Bentzbach, near the river. He kept a store, but was chiefly known as a painter—in fact, an artist of no mean pretensions. He was the father of Judge Montgomery.

WILLIAM HARTMAN was one of the old-time citizens of Danville. He was a chairmaker, and resided on the premises now occupied by his son, Joseph Hartman, on Mill street. William Hartman came to Danville in 1814. He was a class-leader in the Methodist church, and was one of the six members formed into the first class in this place in 1815. He was an honest, industrious citizen, and a true christian. He died in 1851.

Master Gibson and the Mahoning School.

To rescue from oblivion the name and services of Master Gibson, a worthy school-master of the days of yore, is the object of the present chapter.

The picturesque eminence, the site of the Grove church and school-house, and the cemetery, comprising in all two acres, was the donation of Amos Wickersham to John Simpson and others, trustees for a church, school-house, and burial place, in 1776. In shape it was a parallelogram carved out of the hundred-acre tract, afterwards the farm of Daniel Frazer, which bounded it on three sides, the fourth being the farm of Gen. Montgomery, extending thence to the river.

The three-fold but congruous purpose to which that beautiful and prominent eminence was appropriated—for a house of christian worship; for a *God's acre*, a place of sepulture, where the forefathers of the village sleep the sleep which knows no terrestrial awakening; and for a place of learning, where the children of the adventurous founders of the settlement would acquire the elements of an education to qualify them to become useful and respectable members of society. This union gave to this venerated spot a sacred character, which all future time cannot fail to cherish, respect, and honor.

The old log school-house was built about 1785, probably two years anterior to the erection of the old Presbyterian church edifice, and was thirty yards east of it. It was a most unpretentious building; the logs were not even " rough hewn." It was twenty feet square, one story, and that of only sufficient height to allow the teacher to stand erect. An only door, fronting the church, afforded means of ingress and egress. The chimney was at the opposite end, and admitted fuel eight or ten feet long, whereby rousing fires were maintained on cold winter days. A window at either side, two or three times the width of its height, admitted light. There was a rude puncheon floor, and the seats were of the same material. Desks were made of a single board along the sides, so as to enable the student to face the window, and afforded facilities for writing to the more advanced students.

This rude structure, and the church hard by, had a vigorous and flourishing grove of primitive forest trees around them, which were of much protection in shielding them from the summer's heat and winter's cold. Their luxuriant foliage was pleasing to the eye and gratifying to the taste of the admirer of natural scenery. It is to be regretted that the absence of groves immediately around such buildings should prevail to so large an extent in this enlightened age. The poet tells us " the groves were God's first temples," but we show very little appreciation of them.

For a few years, this rustic school-house was occupied by school-masters and their little schools of twenty scholars. The teachers were without families, and, as the custom of that day was, boarded around with their employers in rotation, thus getting remuneration, in part, for the tuition. At that primitive day, this was a convenient arrangement for both parties. Tradition fails to hand down to us the names of these peripatetic pedagogues. During the most of the decade following, up to the close of the last century, Master Gibson, " the village master, taught his little school," but, unlike his predecessors, he had a family, and did not make his home with his patrons. Of this worthy, traditionary history affords us many interesting particulars ; quite as many as could be expected through so unreliable a medium, after the lapse of a century. He was probably a Scot, like his successor, but he may have been a countryman of Goldsmith's, possibly the original from which the character in his celebrated poem was drawn,

> " While words of learned length and thundering sound
> Amazed the gazing rustics ranged around;
> And still they gazed, and still the wonder grew,
> That one small head could carry all he knew."

Many anecdotes verify this. At that period the opinion prevailed that a boy with a large head was a blockhead. One of the boys—no favorite with the master—had a capacious head, and nicknamed "chuckle-head:" to ridicule the boy's great caput, the master wrote in his copy-book for him to copy, "Big head, little wit," which the boy copied, adding "Little head, less yet." Surprised at this retort, the master very discreetly passed by the offense in silence lest he should publish his own discomfiture. The copies for writing were all written by the master in a legible hand, and generally in rhyme. These are examples:

> By diligence and care, you may write fair.

> Many birds of many kinds,
> Many men of many minds.

> Command you may your mind from play.

> All work and no play, makes Jack a dull boy.

The books used in his school, were the New England Primer, embellished with a quaint likeness of the *Honorable* John Hancock, *Esq.,* President of the American Congress, and numerous wood-cuts of rude appearance; Dilworth's Spelling Book, Fenning's Spelling Book and New Guide to the English tongue, Dilworth's Arithmetic, a useful book entitled The Young Man's Companion, a kind of sequel to the others, well calculated to qualify the older boys for business. Those more advanced read the Bible, Milton's Paradise Lost, Goldsmith's Histories abridged. In this brief course, many of the pupils were very thorough, and acquired a good practical education which would compare, not unfavorably, with that obtained in the common schools of to-day. Owing to the multiplicity of studies in the latter, many of the scholars attain only an imperfect and superficial knowledge of the course of study taught in them.

During the time Mr. Gibson taught in this school he was quite successful, and the size of his school was much larger than of his predecessors. His pay was by voluntary subscription. For the smaller scholars, he received eleven shillings three pence, for the larger ones, fifteen shillings, Pennsylvania currency, per quarter, of three months, equivalent to $1 50 and $2 00 Federal money, as it was then termed.

During his mastership, most of the leading citizens contributed to the support of the school. Legendary history has preserved the names of the following patrons of the school: Gen. William Montgomery, John Montgomery, John Sechler, John Frazer, Daniel Frazer, Thomas Osborne, William Sheriff, Thomas Stevenson, John Gulick, George McCulley, Edward Morrison, Murdo Morrison, John Simpson, Paul Adams, John Evans, Philip Maus, Joshua Halleck, John and James Emmitt, Alexander, Ewing, Dr. Forest, John Hill, and the Sanders, the Blues, the Moores, the Woodsides, the Cornelisons, the Colts.

The pupils, as has been stated, attended school only about one fourth of the year, few of them for more than two or three winters: at different periods they were John, Jacob, Samuel, and Harmon Sechler, Archibald, John, James, and Robert Woodside, Jacob, Isaac, James, Ann, and Mary Cornelison, Jesse Simpson, Mary, Margaret, and Charles M. Frazer, and their cousin Charles Frazer, Samuel and John Huntington, Isaac, Peter, Samuel, and John Blue, Asa, Samuel, and Charles Moore, Abie, Josiah, Griffith, and William Phillips, Joseph and Jacob W. Maus, Charles Evans, John McCoy, Jefferson and Robert Montgomery, from Tennessee. Except the Frazers's, Sechler's, and Montgomery's, the pupils were too remote from the school to go home for dinner, and were obliged to bring their dinners with them. There was but one intermission during the day, from twelve to one o'clock, but the students were permitted to withdraw one at a time. A triangular block about the size of a spelling book with the word *in* painted on one side, and *out* on the other, suspended to a nail on the back of the door: the student going out turned the *out* to the school, and on his return the *in*, when another might enjoy the same privilege.

The fuel for the school was supplied from the windfalls in the two-acre lot, and was chopped by the school boys. During the noon hour, they amused themselves by swings formed by bending down the small saplings, by quoits, shindy, ball, running, jumping, and wrestling. Marbles and kites had not yet reached the rural settlement, and they were rare thirty years subsequently.

If the temperature permitted sugar-making in February, many of the larger boys left the school to engage in it before the expiry of their three months' study. The demand for labor at home often

shortened the term of study at school, and the want of the fifteen
shillings for the payment of tuition not unfrequently forbade their
attendance for the winter.

Mr. Gibson was the last teacher in the old log school-house.
General Montgomery having donated a lot in his plat of Danville,
west of Mill street and north of Market street, in 1802, a new
frame school-house was erected. Mr. Andrew Forsyth, eminent for
his scholastic acquirements and his virtues, became principal of the
school. He was succeeded by Mr. John Moore, who afterward became one of the principal merchants of the place. Mr. Thomas
W. Bell, the skillful penman, was the next instructor; and he was
succeeded by Colonel Don Carlos Barrett, the most popular and
successful educator that ever presided over the school. He subsequently became an eminent lawyer and statesman in Texas, and,
with Austin and Huston, constituted the triumvirate, with dictatorial
powers, during the Texan Revolution. After him came Samuel
Kirkham, the distinguished and successful grammarian; and after
him, Ellis Hughes, a cultured and most competent teacher. Simultaneously with these latter, were John Richards, Thomas Grier, and
Stephen Halff. Soon after, the public schools superseded the private
institutions, and their history can be traced up more satisfactorily
than that of the latter, left almost wholly to tradition, not always
reliable.

Master Gibson taught seven or eight winters. He was a rigid
disciplinarian, with European ideas of control of his school, and,
without hesitancy, used the birch freely, in accordance with the
precept of the wise king. Nevertheless, he was honored and revered by his pupils. He was a good and useful man in his day and
generation. Little is now known of his family. The writer met
his daughter in 1822, then the wife of a respectable farmer on the
Chillisquaque.

The last survivor of Master Gibson's pupils has recently passed
away. The venerable Jacob Sechler, one of the first white children
born in Danville, and a nonogenarian, died on Christmas day, 1880.
A year or two since, Mr. George S. Walker, with courteous civility,
submitted to him the data from which this notice was written, and
he stated they were substantially correct, but, from impaired memory, he could give no further facts whereby the account could be
rendered more perfect.

Union Hall Hotel.

Union Hall Hotel, near the court-house, was built by Philip Goodman, in 1818. He had previously kept the "old Pennsylvania House." His card in the town paper was inserted as follows:

" NEW TAVERN

PHILIP GOODMAN

informs his friends and the public that he has commenced keeping tavern in his new brick house, sign of the

GOLDEN GLOBE

Mill street in the town of Danville, two doors south of the Court House, where by his attention and superior accommodation as to house room and stabling, he hopes to merit a share of the public patronage.

DANVILLE, *July 9th, 1818.*"

The house was kept by Mr. Goodman for several years; but it seems that its building, together with a line of stages to Pottsville, swamped him, financially, and he moved to Owego, New York, where he died some years ago. Several persons kept the house from that time until 1836, when it was purchased by William Henrie. He made several improvements and also changed its name to " Union Hall Hotel," which was suggested by his son Arthur, a brave young soldier, who died soon after the war. Mr. Henrie successfully conducted Union Hall Hotel for thirty-five years. It enjoyed great popularity under his administration. Some years ago it was nearly destroyed by fire, after which it was re-constructed and enlarged. It was afterwards kept by Alem M. Sechler, and others.

Fifty Years Ago.

The recollections of Mr. John Frazer, now of Cincinnati, are so interesting and so admirably detailed, that I copy them entire, exactly as written by himself, as I also copy many other sketches in relation to the olden time. In kindly replying to my request for sketches on various points, historical and biographical, he has given them, not only more correctly, but in better style than my own, that

I felt bound, in justice to the reader, to insert them without the change of a syllable.

Random Recollections of Danville as it was half a Century since.

" This is my own, my native land."

It is half a century this day since the writer bade a final adieu to Danville as a place of residence. He was then a youth, and regretfully parted from kindred and friends, to whom he was attached by the closest ties of consanguinity and friendship. His reminiscences of that period are very distinct : he proposes giving you a brief summary of them.

The population of the village was then seven hundred and forty: the buildings numbered eighty ; most of these were dwelling houses on Water, Market, and Mill streets. They were bounded by the river, Church street, Sechler's run, and Factory street ; these limits were very much less than the present area of the borough. They were chiefly frames, but many of the primitive log buildings yet remained. The brick buildings were the court-house, Goodman's tavern, Dr. Petrikin's and Mr. Frick's residences, and Mr. Baldy's store. Subsequently many brick structures were erected, all, or nearly all of which remain.

The pursuits of the citizens were confined to the ordinary mechanical trades, the professions, and for so small a population, a large amount of merchandising. There was scarcely a germ of the manufacturing interest which has grown to be of such vast importance since that day. About 1817, on Market street, near Pine, William Mann manufactured nails in a primitive way, by hand. The bars or hoops of nail iron were cut by a machine worked by a treadle with the foot, and by a second operation, the heads of the nails were formed by a blow or two with a hammer : by unremitting industry, I suppose a workman could only produce as many nails in a month, as one can now, by the aid of machinery, in a single day. And this simple, modest manufacture was the precursor of the immense iron manufactures of the present time, which has earned for the place a high reputation excelled by few in that industrial pursuit, and it has been the cause of the rapid increase of the population of the place, so that it now more than equals all the residue of the county.

The nucleus of the settlement, around which the accretion of population was subsequently gathered, was American, originating during the last two decades of the last century, by emigration from south-eastern Pennsylvania, southern New Jersey, Sunbury, and Northumberland. To these were added, from time to time, European emigrants—chiefly Germans, British, Irish, and Swiss, a few French and Dutch, possibly some Danes and Swedes. Of British emigrants up to that date, I do not recollect a single Welshman, although they soon after became a most important element of population employed in the iron manufacture. These apparently discordant elements soon yielded to the potent attraction of association, so that early in the present century, the homogenity of the young and vigorous community was assured. Seldom did any people enjoy a more happy harmony. This uniformity extended both to religion and politics. They derived their revealed theology from the Bible, as expounded by the followers of Calvin and Knox; their moral theology from the Presbyterian pulpit, the Westminster catechism, and, to no inconsiderable extent, from Milton's Paradise Lost, which was received as a commentary by some, as a supplement by others. With what awe they read,

> "Of Providence, foreknowledge, will, and fate;
> Fixed fate, free will, foreknowledge absolute."

Bunyan's Pilgrim's Progress was also a work of great authority. The libraries were very limited; neither Aristotle, nor Pliny, nor Buffon were in demand; but Æsop's Fables, Weem's Life of Washington, Cook's Voyages, and Riley's Narrative were among the most popular books for miscellaneous reading. Shakspeare's Plays were placed on the *index purgatorius* by some, and few advocated their general use. The venerable Doctor Nott, who was president of Union College for the unprecedented term of sixty-two years, used to say to the students: "If you want to get a knowledge of the world and human nature, read the Bible; but if you will read any other books, read Homer and Shakspeare. They come nearer Moses and Paul than any others I am acquainted with." Fox's Book of Martyrs was esteemed a much more suitable book for youthful readers than the great English bard; they were also allowed that most captivating of boys' books, Robinson Crusoe.

All were not Calvinists; yet, under the wise and judicious pastorate of that good and faithful shepherd Reverend John B. Patterson—ever honored for his blameless life and unostentatious piety—they were kept within one fold and one baptism until the close of his long ministry. He was occasionally aided by pastors from neighboring towns. I can now recall the names of Reverend Messrs. Dunham, William Smith, Nicholas Patterson, Isaac Grier, John Bryson, and Hood.

The Reverend William B. Montgomery and his wife, *nee* Jane Robinson, of the Presbyterian church, the devoted missionaries to the Osage Indians, had recently departed for Union Station, the scene of their labors, which then seemed to us tenfold more remote than Japan does now, and took a longer time in journeying thither. For more than thirty years they labored there, under great privations, until they both fell victims to epidemic cholera.

For a number of years, the followers of Wesley increased in number, and through the zeal and labors of William Woods, William Hartman, William Whitaker, of the village; Judge Jacob Gearhart, of Rush township, and others, a church was established about 1815. It was supplied by itinerant preachers. Of these, I can now only recall the name of Reverend George Dawson. There was a local preacher, Simons by name, who occasionally exhorted and preached at his own house, on Market near Church street. I well remember the appearance of these devoted itinerant preachers in their journeys around the circuit, with their jaded horses, their portmanteau and umbrella tied on behind their saddle, and hat covered with oil cloth to protect it from the storms, and their extremely plain garb, such as I saw Lorenzo Dow wear at a subsequent date.

The Catholics, now so numerous, were scarcely known as sectaries, Michael Rafferty and Francis Trainor being the only two I can recollect. The Reverend Mr. Kay, a Socinian or Unitarian, preached at times, but without making proselytes. The Reverend Mr. Shepherd, a Baptist of the Campbellite portion of that sect, preached occasionally. He was an eloquent and popular divine. There were a number of Lutherans, to whom Reverend Mr. Kesler, from the vicinity of Bloomsburg, preached at long intervals. The Episcopalians were not numerous, and it was suggested that they

3

and the Lutherans unite and form a union church; but this was impracticable, and the former erected, own, and occupy the church edifice on Market street, on ground included in what, at an early day, was called Rudy's woods. These sectaries were all destitute of church buildings, except the Grove church. This was the spacious log church, built more than forty years before the time of which I write, in the form of a T, and was amply large for the congregation. Besides the sects named I can recall none others of that date.

The old log church had recently been demolished and F. Birkenbine was building a brick church edifice under a contract with James Donaldson, Robert Curry, Robert C. Grier, Herman Sechler, and John C. Boyd, the trustees, for the consideration of $1,775.

The social relations of the community were eminently pacific and cordial, doubtless promoted by the matrimonial unions between members of the several very large families of some of the early emigrants. The Montgomerys, of whom there were two brothers, Daniel Montgomery the elder; and his brother; General William Montgomery, whose sons were General Daniel, Colonel John, and Alexander. The son of the senior Daniel Montgomery was Judge William Montgomery. The Woodside family was a large one, consisting of Thomas, Archibald, John, James, Daniel, William and Robert. Of the Moores: Asa, John, Abner, Burrows, Samuel, Charles, Andrew Y., Edward S., and several daughters. Of the Mauses: George, Elizabeth, Philip, Susan, Samuel, Lewis, Charles, Joseph, and Jacob W. Of the Sechlers, I recollect Rudolph, George, John, Jacob, Samuel, and Harmon. At a later date came Mrs. Cornelison and her children, Joseph, William, Jacob, Isaac, Cornelius, James, Ann, and Mercy. Of the Whitakers, John, Thomas, William H., Irwin, Jane, Elizabeth, Polly, Nancy, Fanny, and Juliana: William Wilson, the long time justice of the peace, with a large family of eleven children and their descendants, now numbering about one hundred. There were also the Clarks, Gearharts, Gaskinses, Blues, Rishels, Phillipses, Diehls, Sanderses, Fousts, Frazers, Donaldsons, Willitses, and Brewers.

Many of the pioneer customs still prevailed. Manufactures of the most pressing necessity were found in almost every household. The spinning-wheel for tow and flax; the big wheel, as it was called, for woolen yarn. These were woven in the place, and made into

clothing at home, and most of the villagers and their children were
clad in these domestic suits. The tailor and shoemaker itinerated
here and in the vicinity and were almost constantly employed. A
dwelling without a detached bake-oven would have been deemed incomplete; there were no bakers by profession, and of necessity each
housewife was her own baker. The Franklin stove and the six-
plate stove were still in use : the ten-plate stoves had recently been
introduced and were a great improvement on the former, as much
so as the Palace Cook and Heater are upon the latter. Our stoves
were then manufactured by Mr. Hauck, and bore the legend, " JOHN
HAUCK, *Catawissa Furnace;*" and it was one of the mysteries that
troubled the brains of the boys, how it ever got there in iron letters,
as much as did the effect of the music of Orpheus, which "drew
iron tears down Pluto's cheek."

By industry and frugality the people lived in comparative comfort, paid their preacher and school-master promptly, and their
printer as soon as convenient, thereby preserving a good conscience
and securing peace of mind.

The school-master was abroad. Thomas Grier taught a classical
school and prepared boys for college. Stephen Halff also taught
a private school, and Reverend Mr. Painter was principal of the
Danville Academy, then a new institution. The predecessors of
these were Master Gibson who taught in the old log school-house
near the first edifice of the Grove church ; Messrs. Andrew For-
sythe, John Moore, Thomas W. Bell, Don Carlos Barret, an eminent teacher, John Richards, Samuel Kirkham, the distinguished
grammarian, and Ellis Hughes, a most competent and successful
educator, favorably remembered by many of his pupils still living.
In all these schools the girls and boys recited in the same room,
which I then thought contributed much to the decorum and good
order of the schools, and think so still.

The houses were then chiefly on Water, Mill, and Market streets,
and with scarcely an exception had gardens attached to them,
with a portion of each allotted to flowers. The damascene rose,
guelder rose, flowering almond, peony, narcissus, lilac, lily, pink,
and other familiar floral productions were wont to ornament it and
make it "unprofitably gay." The boys, after school hours, often
reluctantly, tried their 'prentice hands at horticulture, and the most

onerous part of their labor was the removal of the water-worn stone,
rounded by attrition in by-gone antediluvian ages, in fluviatile or
oceanic currents.   They abounded on Market street lots and other
elevated portions of the village.   Doubtless by this time a succession of youthful gardeners have removed them all and made
horticultural pursuits less laborious.

Amongst other amusements the boys enjoyed skating, sledding,
sleighing, nutting, trapping, fishing, playing ball, bathing in the
river and in the Mahoning : in the latter, west of Factory street,
hard by a buttonwood or sycamore, was a famous bathing-place.
Flying kite and playing marbles in the spring were not forgotten.
All these afforded them the needed recreation from study and labor.

But I must not omit the muster days of the military.   The old
Rifle Blues was one of the oldest, if not the oldest, volunteer military organization of the county.   The Light Dragoons, Captain
Clarke, were the admiration of all the boys of the place and their
parades were gala days.   The Columbia Guards was a fine company
of infantry, numbering over sixty, commanded by Captain James
Carson.   The train band, Captain Yorks, was also one of the institutions of that day.   The regimental musters were generally held
at Washingtonville, and drew together crowds of spectators to witness their grand maneuvers, discuss politics and tavern dinners.

The *Watchman* was then the only newspaper.   George Sweeny,
the veteran editor, was its proprietor.   He had published the
Columbian Gazette in 1813 ; which was succeeded by the *Express*,
by Jonathan Lodge in 1815, and afterwards by Lodge & Caruthers.
The *Watchman* was established in 1820.   It was published on
Market street, east of Ferry, and had a sign in front of the office
upon which was painted the head of Franklin with the legend from
Milton, " Where liberty dwells, there is my country."   There were
then few painted signs in the place, and this one was very con-
spicuous.   Although the *Watchman* was not half the size of the
American it was esteemed a grand journal and had great influence
in the politics of the county.   It was made up chiefly by copy from
other papers and seldom contained editorial articles.   Readers were
not so exacting then as in these latter days.

The politics of the village like those of the county were largely
Democratic.   What Democratic principles were I had no very

definite idea, but had a vague impression that they were just the reverse of Federal principles, and I suppose that this negative definition quadrated with the ideas of the dominant party. State politics absorbed the attention of politicians and banished from their minds national politics to an extent that must have gladdened the hearts of those stolid politicians, the States' rights men. I remember how a villager pertinaciously urged the nomination of General Jackson for Governor, and he honestly believed that the gubernatorial honor was the highest that could be conferred upon the old hero.

The members of the bar were few in number. Ebenezer Green ough had recently removed to Sunbury. Judge Grier, from his profound legal attainments and fine scholarship, stood at the head of his profession. Alem Marr, the pioneer lawyer, was a good classical scholar and a graduate of Princeton. He represented the district in Congress in 1829. LeGrand Bancroft was district attorney. The other members were George A. Frick, William G. Hurley, John Cooper, James Carson, and Robert McP. McDowell. A short time subsequently John G. Montgomery, Paul Leidy and Joshua W. Comly were added to the number. All of them are deceased, except the latter.

The medical men were not numerous. The first in the place was Doctor Forrest, the grandfather of Mrs. Valentine Best. His successor, Doctor Barrett; his, Doctors Petrikin and Daniels. At the period of which I write there were also Doctors McDowell and Magill. The latter was then a young practitioner in the beginning of his long and successful career, and now remains, beyond the age of four-score years, the honored head of the profession which has increased fourfold since he became a member of it. And now Danville began to rear medical men of her own. Herman Gearhart and Alexander C. Donaldson were initiated into the profession, under the tuition of Doctor Petrikin. At the same time Samuel Montgomery and Matthew Patterson were divinity students. John Martin was a law student in Mr. Marr's office, and subsequently practiced in Clearfield county.

General Daniel Montgomery was the first merchant, but, having acquired a fortune, was now residing on his fine farm a mile or two above town. His cousin, Judge William Montgomery, an old citi-

zen, was now the oldest merchant, with his store corner of Mill and
Market streets and his residence on the opposite corner. He bore
his full share in the burden of improving and bettering the condition of his fellow-men ; was one of the pillars of the church and
founder of the first Sunday school ; when many others, if not opposed to it, aided it only in a prefunctory way, and he lived to see
it permanently established. Peter Baldy, though still a young
merchant, was engaged in an extensive business and dealt largely
in grain. He commenced in the old log building which had been
occupied by King & Hamilton ; from thence, he removed to his
well-known store on Mill street where he continued his business
for half a century, when he retired having accumulated a fortune.
The other merchants were John Moore, John Russell, and William
Colt, all old and esteemed citizens : and William Bickley, Boyd &
Montgomery, John C. & Michael C. Grier, and Michael Ephlin
who had more recently engaged in business. Mr. Loughead had
retired from business to devote his time to the post-office, and Jeremiah Evans had recently moved to Mercersburg.

The old Cross-Keys tavern, kept by Mrs. Jemima Donaldson was
the best in the county and it is doubtful whether it has been surpassed to this day. The Union hotel, the first three-story brick
building and the best one in the place was built and kept by Philip
Goodman. John Irwin kept a tavern, corner of Market and Ferry
streets. And the most ancient hostelry of them all, the Rising Sun,
the old red house at the foot of Mill street with the walnut tree at
the door, and its crowd of the devotees of Bacchus who made it
resound with

> " Midnight shout and revelry,
> Tipsy dance and jollity."

The Ferry tavern, by George Barnhart where I often hurried by,
fearing the sound of the fiddle, judging that old Satan could not be
far distant from the violin, thus condemning that first of musical instruments, from its association with much that is vile. Then there
was the Jackson tavern, Mill street near Mahoning, by William
Clark, a soldier of the revolution, with the likeness of General
Jackson painted on its sign, thus superseding that of Washington,
as the latter in its day had replaced that of George III: *tempori
parendum*. The taverns then had a monopoly of retailing intoxi-

eating liquors dealing them out by the gill; and rye whisky was the chief liquor used, and doubtless was less hurtful than the villainous compound now sold under that name. Some who then indulged in "potations pottle deep" nevertheless attained a great age; when one of them was warned against indulging too freely in it, as it was a slow poison, replied that he was aware of that for he had been using it sixty years and it must be *very slow*. The coffee-houses, now destitute of coffee, the saloons, groceries and other refined modern drinking places were then unknown.

In addition to these taverns, Mrs. Spence kept a boarding-house, and had for her guests some of the most respectable people of the place.

Amongst the active and industrious citizens were the blacksmiths. John Lunger was one of the earliest, and had a shop on Ferry street. John Deen's smithy was on Market near Ferry street, where by many and well-directed blows he hammered out a fortune. Joseph Cornelison's was on Mahoning near Mill street.

George McCulley was one of the pioneer carpenters and removed to Ohio, near Wooster where some of his descendants still reside. Daniel Cameron, a worthy Scot and the great pedestrian who walked from Harrisburg to Danville in a day without deeming it any great exploit was a skilfull carpenter and builder. Adam Schuyler and George Lott were also engaged in that business.

The chairmakers were William Hartman who was also a wheelwright, and the brothers Kirk. William Mann was also engaged in that calling for a year or two.

Shoemakers—William Woods, Gideon Mellon, Henry Sanders, Thomas Wiley.

Tailors—William M. Wiley, who removed to Harrisburg, William Whitaker, Amos E. Kitchen. William Ingold was a vagrant workman who plied his needle at the houses of his employers, and was noted for his quips and quirks and idle pranks whereby he amused and often astonished the boys of the village.

Honest John Reynolds, from Reading, was the veteran hatter, who for long years supplied men and boys with hats. Martin McCollister was a more recent and very skilfull workman.

Thomas Blackwell carried on the fulling-mill and saw-mill near what is now the junction of Mill and Bloom streets.

The first brewer was Richard Matchin. The citizens of that day were not, as we now phrase it, educated up to a due appreciation of that beverage, consequently it proved less profitable than brewing lager, weiss, and buck beer at the present time.

George Wilson was the first cabinet-maker, and some of his substantial old-style furniture has survived to the present days. Burrows Moore was long engaged in the same business.

The Scotch weavers had been famous in the early days of the settlement. Of those who were engaged in the business fifty years since I can now only recall the names of Christopher Smith and Peter Goodman. The latter was a most respectable and industrious German from the Fatherland.

Coppersmiths and tinners—Alexander Wilson, James Wilson, John C. Theil.

Watchmaker and jeweler, Samuel Maus.

There were several saddlers—Alexander Best, Hugh Flack, Daniel Hoffman, and possibly others.

Rifles were in demand, and had always been much used by the pioneers. These were supplied by Samuel Baum and George Miller : the son of the latter succeeded him and still continues the business.

Of public functionaries, we had but few, and their removals were few and far between. In the language of an eminent statesman it might then have been truly said: " Few die and none resign." Judge Seth Chapman was long the presiding judge of our courts. He was a man of moderate legal attainments, yet he made a good presiding officer. He was assisted by his associates, Judges Montgomery and Rupert. George A. Frick was prothonotary, having been appointed to that office by Governor Snyder in 1813.

William Wilson, Rudolph Sechler and Joseph Prutzman were the justices of the peace : Andrew McReynolds, sheriff : Daniel Cameron, constable. Mr. Sechler was also register and recorder. James Loughead, a dignified yet popular gentleman of English origin, was postmaster, and held the office for the long term of fourteen years, twice as long as any other, with one exception. The office was first established in 1806, Judge Montgomery being the first one appointed, and held his commission from President Jefferson, and filled the office for seven years. This just and pious man discharged this trust, as he did all others, to the entire satisfaction of the Government and the community. He was succeeded by that other faithful public servant, Rudolph Sechler, who held it for a like term of seven years, until Mr. Loughead's appointment. I never knew a more honest man than Mr. Sechler. With him it was innate. He could not be otherwise than honest. His countenance, his actions, his words, in short, everything about him proclaimed his sterling integrity : and what gave a charm to it he was quite unconscious of his being more honest than other men. Of his large number of connections I never knew one whose integrity was called in question. It is highly gratifying to know that in the seventy years the office has been in existence, there has never been a defaulter to the National Government, and that all of the thirteen incumbents of the office have diligently and faithfully discharged the trust reposed in them. Had the same care and discrimination been exercised in making appointments elsewhere the nation would not have been disgraced by the peculations and plunderings of the people's money by unfaithful officers.

One of the eccentric characters of the vicinity was Mr. Finney, who died ten or twelve years subsequently to the period of which I write, almost a centennarian. He was a man of gallantry, a kind of Beau Nash of more than eighty, with a peculiar child-like tenor voice, who delighted to play the gallant with the young ladies of the village, and drive them around the place and vicinity in his old style chaise. Robin Finney, as he was always called, from his great age and attention to the fair sex was a great favorite with them, and was well-known to the people of that day. His chaise and one owned by General D. Montgomery and one by Judge Montgomery, were the only pleasure carriages of that kind in the county. The old time carriage of Philip Maus which attracted the attention and excited the wonder of the village urchins and the more modern carriage of General Montgomery were the only pleasure carriages of that style. Traveling on horseback was then the proper thing for both sexes, old and young, gentle and simple, and its general disuse is to be regretted. But it was too slow a mode of locomotion for this fast age.

Abe Brown was an African, or an American of African descent, and the only one in the place. He had been a mariner, and after he came here was a servant to Mr. Loughead. He emigrated to Mahoning county, Ohio, where by industry and frugality he ac-

quired a competency and enjoys the respect of the community where
he resides. Jack Harris was an octoroon, a fine looking lad, and
so nearly white that he might pass for an Anglo-American. Though
not darker than a brunette, the rude boys persisted in calling him
Black Jack. These boys attended the schools, and were treated with
more justice and consideration than fell to the lot of their race after
the *dictum* that black men had no rights which the whites were bound
to respect.

The members of Congress resident in Danville were as follows:
General Daniel Montgomery, in 1810. This eminent citizen was
one of the leading pioneers, and enjoyed the confidence and respect
of the people. He was the Nestor of the community and resided
in dignified retirement on his fine farm a mile or two up the river.
Mr. Alem Marr who had from the organization of Columbia
county been one of the leading lawyers, represented the district in
1830. Doctor Petrikin, a man of great energy, with strong attach-
ments and equally strong resentments, was a member from 1837 to
1843. Although no great orator, he was a man of influence in the
House. I met him at Washington during the exciting times in
which he served and was impressed with his power as a politician.
Mr. John G. Montgomery, an able lawyer and member elect to the
Thirty-fifth Congress died in 1857 before the time arrived to take
his seat. Mr. Leidy, his successor, served in 1858-9. Doctor
Strawbridge was the last resident who represented the district in
Congress.

The great flood of 1817, usually called the August flood, surrounded the place so that, for the time, it became insular. The
only approach was by boats. I saw the bridge over the brook on
the road, then an extension of Church street, float away with a
man on it who secured it before it reached the river.

The inhabitants were supplied with flour from the mills of John
and Alexander Montgomery and Joseph Maus all propelled by the
water of the Mahoning. Farmers in the vicinity took their grain in
sacks to the mills; the miller ground it for a toll of one tenth.
Except for the Baltimore, Philadelphia, or Reading markets, it was
seldom put up in barrels. Steam power had not been introduced
in the place or neighborhood, except at Boyd's mill which was then
a new one on the left bank of the river above town.

Whiskey was the Archimidean lever that moved the world. Contracts could not be made or performed without its potent aid. The merchant kept it on his counter, for his customers would not purchase goods without it. It was indispensable at musters and elections. The farmer's fields could not be cultivated without its use as a motor. Mr. Robinson, in the vicinity, offered the laborers who were employed in his harvest fields extra pay if they would dispense with it, but they refused. The temperance cause was advocated by its friends, but its opponents, numerous, defiant, and violent, determined that their liberties should not be subverted by a few fanatics who were worse than the Federals.

The Mormon delusion was in its incipiency. Joseph Smith, Sidney Rigdon, and Pearly B. Pratt were its chief apostles. Through their zeal it was introduced in Palmyra, Kirtland, Jackson county, Missouri, Nauvoo, and, finally, at Salt Lake City, at which latter place its most revolting feature of polygamy was introduced. The present revelator and prophet boasts that he has more control over his people than Moses had over the Israelites, yet he claims more credit for having produced ninety-three bushels of wheat from one acre than for any other of his deeds.

Slavery was acquiesced in under its constitutional guaranty. It was to be let alone, but *no more* slavery. Slaves were to be given up, but the area of slavery was not to be extended.

The first half century of our Independence was at its close. On the 4th of July, its two powerful advocates, Adams and Jefferson closed their long and eventful lives just fifty years after they had signed our great Charter of Liberty.

At that time, John Quincy Adams was President and J. Andrew Shulze, Governor. Stealing the public moneys was not then disguised under the mild terms of defaults and discrepancies.

The half century just closed has been an eventful, almost a marvelous one. In 1826, we had no railways, telegraphs, type-writers, gas, petroleum, no canals, iron furnaces, forges, rolling-mills ; no bridge over the river, no fire engines of any kind, nor many other indispensable improvements, deprived of which we would speedily retrogade to what we were at that period. The population has increased more than tenfold, and Danville has kept pace with the rest of the world, and shown an energy and perseverence worthy of

her, notwithstanding the many depressions and conflicts incident to
her position as a great manufacturing center. Her numerous sons,
dispersed throughout the great West, and in other portions of our
vast Republic, now in exile from her borders, look with pride upon
her onward course in material prosperity, and her commendable
progress in religion, morals, and science, the social virtues and the
amenities of life, which they trust may continue, and enable her,
for all future time, to maintain her elevated position in the good old
Commonwealth.

Susquehanna Floods.

There was an old tradition, or rather a prophecy, among the Indians that roamed about the Susquehanna, that great floods in this
river occurred at regular intervals of fourteen years; and this in
some degree proved true in the days of our fathers. The first great
flood of which we have any account was in 1744; the second in
1758; the third in 1772, and that which is known as the great
" pumpkin flood " was in 1786. There being just fourteen years
between each of these floods. The " pumpkin flood " was in the
month of October and was so designated on account of the immense
number of pumpkins that floated down the stream from the fields
above. It began to rain on the 5th of October, 1786, and rained
incessantly for several days. The water rose rapidly and swept
all before it. Several persons were drowned near the place now
called Rupert, and at Sunbury houses were overflowed and many
people were lost. Northumberland was also flooded and much damage was done. This flood was long remembered and known among
the old settlers as " the great pumpkin flood." In the spring of
1800, just fourteen years after the " pumpkin flood," another great
freshet occurred. It rained three days and three nights, carrying
off a deep snow and doing much damage. In 1814 there was
another destructive flood that caused much loss of life and property.
Here the old Indian tradition that floods occurred every fourteen
years failed; for the next was in 1817, after an interval of only three
years. The next flood of note was in 1847. If there were any from
1817 to 1847 we have no record of them. Many of my readers
will remember that of 1859 which also raised the water in the
North Branch over eight feet above high water mark. Still more

vividly do they remember the extraordinary flood of March, 1865. The exciting scenes in Danville on the 17th and 18th days of that month will never be forgotten. The river began to rise on Friday, and on Saturday the water rose to four feet above the highest flood on record. A great portion of Danville was overflowed and many families were compelled to leave their homes in haste. Women and children were taken from their houses in boats. The whole district from Sageburg to Mill street was covered with water reaching up Mulberry street and to the scales in front of the Montgomery building. The low lands along the Mahoning were also under water. On Mulberry as well as on Mill street boats and rafts were moving among the houses and gliding high over the gardens. The river bridge was much injured but withstood the onset. Many stables and other buildings floated about and found new and strange foundations as the water receded, without any regard to the side that was up or down. Only one man, Peter Green, was drowned at this place. He fell into the Mahoning from a small raft while attempting to supply his family with coal. His body was recovered and properly cared for. Another great flood in the North Branch in 1875 took the river bridge that had so long withstood the assaults of the angry torrent, but when the Catawissa bridge came down and struck it broadside it had to yield. It has since been rebuilt more substantially than before. We had very high water on the 12th of February, 1881.

Olden Habits and Customs.

The habits and customs of the last generation, it is true, may have been less refined in some respects, but they were more wholesome and more favorable to longevity. A thousand inventions of the present day, then unknown, invite to ease, indolence, and luxury; but they are at the same time effeminating, and minister not only to new forms of bodily ailments but tend to shorten life. The *physique*, at least, of the last generation was superior to this, and as the full exercise of the mental powers depends on the proper development of the body, the palm of intellectual superiority and force of character may also be claimed. This is due to the habits and customs of the past and the changes that have been wrought in the last half century.

The boy who is reared in the lap of luxury grows up like a cryptogamous plant, and withers like Jonah's gourd in the strong light of the meridian sun. But he who from early youth is inured to toil, accustomed to simple diet, and taught by experience the lesson of self-reliance, will grow up strong and vigorous like the oak of the forest. Hence it is that not only the hardy athletes, but the solid thinkers and leading men of the times so often come up from the lower ranks of society and outstrip those who enjoyed every external advantage in the start. The habits and customs of the last generation were more favorable to the development of both mind and body. If not, why is it that the race of far-seeing and almost prophetic statesmen is passing away? Those now in the front ranks of political power are but pigmies in contrast with the leading spirits of the nation in the early history of the country. True, it is sometimes said they were only comparatively great, as others around them were small—just as the pedagogue is great in the midst of his pupils. But, "by their fruits ye shall know them." Their works and the fruit of their planting not only remain as memorials of wisdom and of human greatness, but the highest glory of the present statesman is to approach as near as possible to the excellence of those who have gone before.

But let us look at some of the customs and habits of the past, and whilst we may find much to amuse us, there is also much to challenge our more serious attention.

Pure air, exercise, and simple diet will produce a hardier people, stronger physically and intellectually, than impure air, close houses, feather-beds, indolence, and luxurious living. If the nourishment of the physical system consists of highly-seasoned dainties, and that of the mind, the no less poisonous aliment of the novel, both will become dyspeptic.

Now let us go back for half a century and take a look at the old folks. What are our grandfathers and grandmothers doing? See that rude pile of stones from which the smoke slowly arises. And what means that "rap, rap, rap?" Sometimes it is muffled, and then again it rings out quick and sharp. The man is breaking flax, and in the early winter you hear the sound of the "brake" echoing all over the country. Near the barn, the women folks, with wooden paddles, are "swingling" and preparing it for the "heckle." Then,

in the long winter evenings they ply the spinning-wheel whose
whirr is heard far in the night. See, that mischievous boy has got
his fingers in the "flyers!" Ah! that was the fate of many a
youngster. The yarn thus spun was woven into cloth, and little
else than "homespun" was worn in the family. The finer portions
were bleached and made into underclothes and bedclothes, and the
coarser into pantaloons, &c. There was too some taste about it.
The thrifty housewife with hickory bark dyed it yellow, and this,
warp-woven with the natural woof, made what was called "sham-
baree;" or it was striped and barred with the same, white and yellow.

When the sheep were sheared, the wool was cleansed and "picked,"
made into rolls with a pair of hand-cards, spun on a big wheel, dyed,
woven and made into winter garments, all within the family. Don't
you remember the big wheel? What a whirr the spinner would give
it, and then step backwards to extend the thread as it took the twist,
and forwards again as it wound on the spindle. Then she gave it
another whirl that made it buzz and hum all over the house. A
young lady who was a good spinner was respected accordingly in
those days. Some went out to spin among the neighbors, and it was
no uncommon thing to meet a woman on the road with a spinning-
wheel on her shoulder, "going out to spin" by the day or by the
dozen. Of course this passage from family to family was rather
favorable to "gossip," and then we heard of "spinning yarns,"
but spinners generally married in due time. A few who did not
were called "spinsters," and now all old maids are designated in
the same way.

When a young lady was married, no matter how humble the circumstances of her parents might be, she always got an outfit of a
bureau, a bed, a cow, and a spinning-wheel. If she had no parents
to provide them, she went to work industriously until she earned
them herself, or she was "bound to work" in a richer family until
she was eighteen years old, and the bed, the cow, the bureau, and
spinning wheel were provided for in the indenture. In all cases the
wedding was postponed until she had the outfit, as it was a lasting
disgrace to marry without it. The more wealthy added a horse and
a side-saddle, but the spinning-wheel was no less essential. We may
hereafter take a look at a wedding in the olden time. At present
we shall only glance at some items tending to establish the proposition in hand.

Again we listen to the regular sounds of a ceaseless hammering in yonder barn. Like the stroke of the flax-brake it is muffled at times, and again it rings out sharp and clear as it strikes the floor. They are threshing with the flail. These flails were sometimes called "poverty sticks," because the poorer day laborers went round among the farmers in the winter time and flailed out the grain for the tenth bushel. There were generally two in company, and the precision with which they kept stroke in striking the same spot and flinging the "suple" end of the flail round their heads would astonish you at this day. Each man could earn a bushel or more of wheat or rye in a day. Another mode of threshing grain then in vogue was to lay it on a floor and then drive a team of horses over it in a circle, until the grain was tramped out. Corn was threshed in the same way, for there were no machines to do the work.

Wheat and rye were harvested with the sickle, and as many as fifty reapers could be seen together in an oblique line gathering the golden grain. Good reapers were highly prized, and the best was generally made the leader for the day. It was considered mean for the owner to take the lead, as the number and the length of the rests under the trees, as well as the number of drinks, was regulated by the leader. Hence it was considered proper to have one who was disinterested. Of course, they looked for a full bottle of whisky and plenty of fresh water every "through," or oftener, if the field was long. These were usually supplied by little urchins, called "bottle boys." These "bottle boys," for small pay, were bound to have fresh water and the whisky at the proper time and place, as ordained by the leader. This was generally under the shade of a tree nearest the next resting place. Each reaper, in turn, seized the bottle by the neck and took a draught, as they said, "by the word of mouth," amid the songs and jokes of the gay reapers assembled for a brief respite under the wide-spreading walnut tree. At last the welcome sound of the dinner horn is heard, when a two hours' rest was taken. At four o'clock the lunch arrived and was often spread in the shade on the green sod, and never were the substantial dishes of the good lady better appreciated nor were ever rosy cheeked girls more heartily welcomed than those who brought them to the field.

It may seem strange, but it is true, that there was but little drunkenness, notwithstanding the workingmen drank from ten to twenty times a day, and the diseases that now choke the life out of habitual drinkers were unknown. The only solution is in the fact that the liquor was pure. Compounders of liquors had not been born, and it was free from the poisons now often decocted. This fact in addition to the constant exercise of drinkers in the open air, prevented injurious results. To drink was more common then than now. Scarcely a family was without at least a jug in the house, and many families bought it by the barrel. The boys could drink when they pleased, and whisky was always set out to visitors, and especially when the pastor called; and the writer remembers well with what a bland smile some of these walked up to a decanter and seized it by the neck. It was then considered no less respectable to swallow spirits than it was to take a glass of water. It was cheap, too. Pure rye whisky was retailed at all the stores, at from eight to ten cents a quart. In public houses it was sold for three cents for half a gill. When a drink was called for at the bar the bar-tender always set out a half-gill stem glass and filled it himself. The customer himself never got hold of the bottle at all. But this was then regarded the same as it is for a saloon-keeper to measure out a glass of lager. Who knows but the world may continue to improve until, under its civilization, it will become the fashion to roll a keg of beer to a customer, to take his fill, and call it a drink?

All in all, as we rummage amid the memories of the olden time we find more to approve and less to condemn than we do when we look abroad on the boasted wisdom, light, and knowledge of the present day.

Christ's Episcopal Church.

On the 28th day of October, 1828, the corner-stone of the Protestant Episcopal church was laid in Danville. Previous to that period a number of early settlers who had wandered beyond the reach of their respective congregations found themselves deprived of the privileges and ordinances in which they had been reared. Actuated by a common impulse they began to meet together for religious worship. Under these circumstances the prejudices of early life speedily gave way, and soon the flock was characterized by a oneness of heart and mind. For some time they had occasional

4

services in the court-house, under the ministration of Reverend James Depuy, of Bloomsburg, who also became their regular pastor for two or three years, after the church was built. The lot on which the church and parsonage are erected is situated in a central location, on Market street. The building originally cost about $6,000, the chief burden of which was borne by a few individuals. The following gentlemen composed the vestry at the period when the corner-stone was laid: Joseph Maus, John Reynolds, Jacob Swisher, Peter Baldy and Michael Sanders, George A. Frick and B. Appleman. But, strange as it may seem, there was not a single communicant of the Episcopal church among them. Peter Baldy and Michael Sanders were members of the Evangelical Lutheran church at that time. Mr. Sanders adhered to the Lutherans subsequently, but Mr. Baldy became an Episcopalian. Some of the founders proposed to devote the new church building to the use of both the Lutherans and Episcopalians; but they soon discovered its impracticability, and all finally agreed that the church should be devoted to the exclusive use of the Protestant Episcopal service. On the 25th day of October, 1829, just one year after the corner-stone was laid, the first communicants of the church, ten in number, were confirmed by the Right Reverend Henry W. Onderdonk. Reverend James Depuy labored faithfully among them, and under his pastoral charge the foundations of a permanent congregation were laid. He is still remembered as a man of learning, of eminent piety, and deep devotion to the responsible duties of his position. He is described as rather tall and slender in personal appearance, light complexion, amiable countenance, and a good speaker. He was very acceptable to his people. He was last heard of in Nebraska. Reverend Mr. Drake, of Bloomsburg, supplied the pulpit occasionally after the departure of Reverend Depuy. Reverend A. Landerback was the next rector. He remained for about five years. He at the same time had charge of the church at Sunbury. He is, also, affectionately remembered by the older members. He removed to Iowa. The next in order was Reverend R. M. Mitchison, who remained only about six months and was succeeded by Reverend Milton C. Lightner who assumed the charge in 1842. He officiated in Christ's church for about seven years with great acceptance. He removed to Manayunk, and Reverend Mr. Elsegood, formerly a minister in the Methodist denomination, took his place in Danville. At the end of two years Reverend Mr Elsegood removed to Easton and was succeeded here by Reverend Mr. Page of New York, who also remained two years. In February, 1855, Reverend Edwin N. Lightner, brother to Reverend Milton C. Lightner. succeeded to the charge of Christ's church, and continued its rector until May, 1870, when the loss of health compelled him to resign the charge. Reverend Edwin N. Lightner occupied a high place in the affection and confidence of the community, as well as in the hearts of the people to whom he ministered for about fifteen years. He resides in Riverside. In September, 1870, Reverend J. Milton Peck was called to the rectorship of Christ's church, in which he still continues. His ministration seems very acceptable to his people and the church is prospering under his care.

In 1845, some improvements were made in the church buildings, and in 1856 the congregation spent nearly $3,000 in improving and beautifying both the interior and the exterior of the building. It now presents a very handsome appearance with its stylish architecture, its brilliant stained glass and general ornamentation. It is surmounted by a double cross rising in solemn grandeur amidst a beautiful grove of forest trees, and an excellent bell calls the worshipers to the sanctuary. The interior is ornamented in appropriate style and is furnished with an excellent organ. A pleasant parsonage adjoins the church. It is proper to say that Mr. Peter Baldy, Sr., one of the founders of the church, has been its main support for more than half a century up to the time of his death in 1880, and left to the church $50,000 in his will.

Indiantown.

In the lower portion of Danville borough there is a lovely tract of level ground near the mouth of the Mahoning. This beautiful and picturesque locality with all its charms of scenery and with all its inspiring associations is still known by the unpoetic name of the '' Creek's Mouth.'' Other localities with far less pretention to romance or historical importance rejoice in names that in some measure give expression to their beauty or recall the scenes that mark their history. But no, our people are a plain folk, and are but little impressed with the spirit of romance. So we must accept the situation and continue to call it the "Creek's Mouth." There was an Indian village on this spot, and I give the savages some degree of credit for their taste in selecting this site for their village home. It was inhabited by a tribe of the Delawares, with a few of other names. The Delawares professed neutrality during the French war and continued their friendly relations, but like all others of their race they smarted under the impression that they were wronged out of their lands by the pale faces, and this made them sullen and treacherous. So we find the Delawares doing their terrible and bloody work at the massacre of Wyoming and in many of the murderous forays that mark with fiendish cruelty the annals of frontier life.

The village at the mouth of the Mahoning was the home of the maiden, "nameless here forever more," that now sleeps in the dark ravine. Ah, yes, however rude the life, however wild and savage the surroundings, love will enter the heart, and nature will assert her claims in all conditions of human society. Here, too, within the limits of our town, for a season, tarried the renowned Tamenund, an old and venerated prophet of the Delawares, whose counsel was wisdom and whose judgment was law. He was more than one hundred years old at the time of the French war, and died among the remnant of his people in the State of New York. In this region we have one uncertain memorial of the great chief, and that is the name of a railroad station, (Tamanend,) on the Catawissa railroad. But Tammany hall, in the city of New York, which is named for the wise, old counselor, Tamanund, will long perpetuate his name if it does not always exemplify his wisdom.

Robert C. Grier.

The venerable Justice Grier, late of the United States Supreme Court, died at his residence, No. 1428 Spruce street, Philadelphia, at the advanced age of seventy-six years, having been born in Cumberland county, Pa., March 5, 1794. His father was the Reverend Isaac Grier, who, shortly after the birth of his son Robert, removed to Lycoming county, where he taught school, preached to three separate congregations, and cultivated a farm. Young Grier was carefully educated by his father, and when old enough assisted him

in the school and on the farm until at the age of seventeen he was
sent to Dickinson College. Graduating in 1812 with the highest
honors he accepted the post of tutor for a year, at the end of
which time he removed to Northumberland, where his father had
established an academy that had gained a high character. Here
Robert assisted his father, and on the death of the latter, in 1815,
succeeded him as principal. He now, however, studied law and
in 1817 was admitted to the bar, and commenced practice at Bloomsburg, Columbia county. After remaining there a year he removed
to Danville, soon obtaining a large and lucrative business. After a
successful practice of about twenty years he was, in 1838, appointed
by the Governor of the Commonwealth to the position of president
judge of the district court of Allegheny county, and removed to
Allegheny city where he lived until 1848. In that year he went to
Philadelphia and continued a resident until his death. In 1846 he
was appointed by President Polk an associate justice of the United
States Supreme Court, to succeed Justice Baldwin. As a circuit
judge he also had charge of the circuit embracing Pennsylvania and
New Jersey. In this capacity he presided at the celebrated trial of
Castner Hanway, in Philadelphia, under the fugitive slave laws.
During the war, although a life-long Democrat, he was a rigid,
patriotic, and unfailing Union man, and loyally sustained the Government.

Judge Grier had resigned his position previous to his death, on
account of failing health. He was one of our most eminent men.
He was a brother to M. C. Grier, of Danville, who died a short
time ago in this place.

Reverend William B. Montgomery.

About 1821, Mahoning, from having been on the frontier, and
dependent, to some extent, for religious instruction on missionary
labors, began to send missionaries abroad. Of these were Reverend
William B. Montgomery, son of Colonel John Montgomery, one of
the prominent pioneers of Mahoning, and Jane, his wife, daughter
of Mr. Robinson, a devout and worthy pioneer of the same place.
Mr. Montgomery was a lineal descendant of Captain Montgomery,
born in 1666, and was an officer under William of Orange at the
battle of Boyne Water, and for bravery in that memorable conflict

was promoted to be a major in the British army. His son was
Alexander Montgomery, born about 1700, and died in 1746. His
son was William Montgomery, born 1736, O. S., and was the lead-
ing pioneer of Danville, and died here in 1816. His son was John
Montgomery, born in 1765, and died here in 1834. His son, the
missionary, was born here about the year 1788, and died in Indian
Territory, in 1834. He was the eldest of the nine children of John
Montgomery and Elizabeth, his wife, *nee* Bell. His brothers were
James, Daniel, and John ; his sisters, Jane, Margaret, Mary, Re-
becca, and Elizabeth.

William was a pious, studious youth, and his parents resolved to
educate him for the ministry. His academic education was obtained
at Nassau Hall, Princeton, where, it has been said, he was the class-
mate of Alem Marr, who resided in Danville in 1813, when Columbia county was organized, and was the first lawyer resident in the
county. As theological seminaries were not then established in the
country he studied divinity with that eminent divine Reverend
John B. Patterson, who for nearly a third of a century was the
pastor of the Grove Presbyterian church. His devotion to his religious duties and ardent zeal made him desirous to engage in missionary labors. Having been brought up on the border, where
most of the pioneers had imbibed strong prejudices against the
aborigines, with whom they had long feuds from the very beginning
of the Mahoning settlement, and were generally more ready to in-
jure or destroy them than to promote their temporal or spiritual
welfare, he was not influenced by the popular prejudice against the
savages, but, on the contrary, was elevated above it by his education and religion. He was accordingly appointed a missionary by
the Union Foreign Missionary Society, to the Osages in the valley
of the Arkansas. A few years later, this society was transferred to,
or merged in, the great A. B. C. F. missions, without any material
change in the relations of the missionaries.

He was married to Miss Robinson in 1820. His wife was well
educated and pious, possessed of every Christian grace, undaunted
courage and unbounded zeal in the cause of missions, and was
truly a *help meet* for him in the great work to which he had devoted
his life. But their friends looked upon their acceptance of this appointment as a great sacrifice on their part. Their mission was to

the Osages at Union Station, on the margin of Neosho river, west of the Mississippi, twenty-six miles north of Fort Gibson, Indian Territory. It seemed at that day to be as remote from Danville as Tangariyika lake in equatorial Africa does now, and required doubly as long a time to journey to it. And yet, that station is now not very far from the geographical center of the nation. Amidst the benedictions and sorrowing farewells of their many friends who with reason feared they should behold their faces no more, these devoted and devout missionaries departed on their errand of Christian love and mercy early in the month of April, 1821. Samuel Robinson, Mrs. Montgomery's brother, accompanied them. They, with a number of others, composing a considerable mission family, went *via* Pittsburgh, the Ohio, Mississippi, Missouri, and Osage rivers, enduring much exposure, suffering, and privation, and ended their toilsome journey of about four months August 2. Some idea of the hardships and exhaustion they endured may be learned from the fact that during their travels and within three months after their arrival the number of their family was diminished by the deaths of seven of them including Mrs. Montgomery and her infant child. Pious, noble, and heroic woman! Her sacrifices in the cause of her Divine Master, so far as visible to mortal ken, were unavailing for the promotion of the great cause to which she had dedicated her life and energies It was well. Her Father in heaven in kindness, mercy and love, removed her from the afflictions which are in the world to the Paradise of God.

After this afflicting bereavement Mr. Montgomery commenced his labors, but owing to his ignorance of the barbarous language of the Osages he found it extremely difficult to address them, as he was obliged to do, through the medium of an interpreter. He at once resolved to master their uncouth language. But it was only after long, persistent and laborious efforts he succeeded so as to address them in their vernacular tongue. He reduced it to writing, and with the aid of Mr. Requa, completed an elementary book, containing a translation of various portions of the Bible. This was the first book ever written in their language. After long delay it was ultimately published by the society in Boston. Thus following a similar course to that pursued by John Eliot, the apostle of the Indians, two centuries before.

The privations to which these devoted Christians were subjected was fatal to many of them, particularly to the female portion. About two years subsequently to the decease of Mrs. Montgomery, her husband was again married, to Mary Weller, his second wife, who lived only a few brief years, leaving him again bereaved. Nevertheless, he never faltered in his labors for the welfare of the Osages, though surrounded and almost overwhelmed with discouraging difficulties, which would have caused most persons to have despaired. His energies and life itself were consecrated to the cause, and his efforts ceased only with his life.

About 1831, he was married the third time to Harriet Woolley. The health of the missionary family began to be more promising, when that scourge of mankind, the Asiatic cholera, invaded this continent. In two short years it reached Union Station, in all its appalling virulence. On the 14th of July, 1834, it broke out at Hopefield Station, near Union. Mr. Montgomery, assisted by M. Beatt, with great care and solicitude nursed and cared for the sick Indians and assiduously ministered to their wants, but "the pestilence that walketh in darkness, and the destruction that wasteth at noonday," prostrated him on the 17th. His unremitting care for the poor Osages who were dying around him proved too much for his strength. In the midst of his Christian efforts for their temporal and spiritual welfare, he was removed from the midst of his earthly labors. The swift-winged messenger of death came without warning, yet found him with his lamp trimmed and burning. In twelve hours from the attack God took him to himself. Servant of God! Well done! His missionary brethren at Union hastened to him at Hopefield, but the vital spark had fled. From so pure and righteous a life as his the end could be none other than a triumphant one. Upon the first attack he exclaimed: "Can it be that in less than twenty-four hours I shall be walking in the streets of the New Jerusalem? I know in whom I have believed." And he peacefully passed away to the bosom of his Father and his God. He left messages of love to all his Christian brethren. He urged them not to abandon the Osages, and not to count any sacrifices too great for their salvation. His wife bore her irreparable loss with great fortitude, and placed her trust in the Lord who doeth all things well. A few days subsequently she returned to Union Station.

Beatt, the Frenchman, was the only assistant his wife had through his fatal illness. "Oh," said he, "I never saw a man die as happy as that man."

His devoted wife was a few weeks later attacked by a bilious remittant fever, which on the 5th of September proved fatal. It was reported she also died of cholera, but she died of the fever, as here stated.

Honor and praise to the memory of these devoted evangelists. Their labors and trials bring forcibly to mind those of the apostles, and especially those of St. Paul, who, leaving to others the conversion of the Judeans, labored long and successfully in Asia Minor, and ultimately extended his mission to the very pillars of Hercules in his efforts to supplant paganism by the light and power of the Gospel. So Mr. and Mrs. Montgomery, leaving their native homes and civilization behind them, and regardless of the perils which beset them, without hesitancy braved them to end their days amongst fierce and savage men. Yielding to the convictions of duty they zealously labored in their Master's vineyard and sealed their devotion to His cause with their lives. And no Christian hero ever rejoiced more than they when called to depart to their homes in the heavens. "Let me die the death of the righteous, and let my last end be like his."

Orchards.

After some interesting general remarks, Mr. Frazer observes in relation to the early orchards of this locality:

About 1785, some of the pioneers in Mahoning, then almost coextensive with the present county, planted small orchards. They were not deterred by the silly couplet, "He who plants pears, plants them for his heirs," for, with right-minded men, planting for heirs should be motive sufficient. Afterwards, during the last decade of the century, most of those who had large farms planted their orchards. By the year 1812, these began to yield abundant crops, and the people within the boundaries of the present county were supplied with fruit, but much of it of a very ordinary quality; the "crafte of graftynge, alterynge, and plantynge of fruites" not having arrived at the perfection it has since attained.

One of the first to plant an orchard was General William Montgomery. Possibly John Simpson, his predecessor in the ownership
of the town tract, may have planted a few trees. This orchard was
in the immediate vicinity of the old stone mansion-house, now north-
east corner of Mill and Bloom streets, and extended to Ferry street
or beyond it, and north beyond Centre street. It was composed
chiefly of apple trees, with a few peach, pear, and cherry trees;
when in bloom it presented an attractive appearance.

> "And many a vernal blossom sprung,
>   And nodded careless by."

At the corner of the orchard, near Ferry street, stood a cider-mill
and press, all of the olden style. The mill was composed of a
wooden wheel, six feet in diameter and a foot thick, with a shaft
through the center, the wheel revolving in a circular trough or groove.
In this groove the apples were placed, and by applying horse power
to the shaft, passed the wheel over and crushed them to pomace;
this was then placed in a press of rude and simple construction, and
the cider was expressed from it. This was the first mill of the kind
I ever saw, and the first in the county, I believe. It continued in
use until 1816 or later.

From the cider, apple brandy was distilled, which was more prized
by some than whisky. Cider-royal was made by adding a few gallons of whisky to a barrel of it. The London vintner, it is well
known, fortifies his weak wines with brandy. The cider-royal was
a favorite liquor with the young who had not yet been educated up to
the full appreciation of whisky. Cider, with the addition of apples,
was boiled down to apple-butter, an excellent article for the table,
still in use. To make this, required constant boiling for about
twenty-four hours. The services of a young lady and gentleman
were usually called into requisition on such occasions, and they
generally found stirring apple-butter to be no uncongenial employment, for the process of butter making and courtship could, not unfrequently, go on simultaneously.

Another early orchard was that of General Daniel Montgomery,
on the eastern side of Mill street, partly on the ground now occupied
by the Montour House. The trees bearing the choicest fruit were
plainly designated by the number of clubs lodged on their branches
by trespassers who took delight in stolen fruit. I have an indistinct

recollection of a Fourth of July celebration, probably in 1814, in the orchard, and from this I have since had forcibly impressed on my mind the propriety of celebrating that day in a grove. I may here be pardoned for relating a trifling incident connected with that celebration. Provision had been made for a kind of pic-nic entertainment for the villagers and their families. Mr. Thomas W. Bell showed his gallantry by serving the ladies with refreshments ; coming to one of more greed than manners, who emptied the tray of cakes into her capacious pockets, " Well," said Dominie Pell, " some take one, some take two, but you leave none."

Mr. Philip Maus had a large orchard on his farm, on the northern slope of an eminence between his homestead and the forks of the road to Mausdale. It contained good, but not the choicest fruit. It was one of the first planted in that vicinity. His son George devoted much attention to its care and culture, to

" Teach the trees with nobler loads to bend ; "

and by building fires at many places in the orchard at times of late frosts, supposed he several times saved the crop of fruit, or part of it from perishing with the cold.

Beyond this orchard, on the Mooresburg road, were the small orchards of Justus Strawbridge, Lewis Maus, and Colin Cameron, of young and vigorous trees, but probably now large and ancient.

The next in date, probably 1791, was that of Mr. John Frazer, on the north side of the Bloomsburg road, and extending back beyond Pleasant street, and between D and F streets. In this extensive orchard there was much choice fruit, all grafted, from the Burlington nurseries, then, or subsequently, famous under the management of William Coxe, the distinguished pomologist and author of " The Cultivation of Fruit Trees." It made a fine appearance, and was in full bearing in 1815. Several trees near the house were almost of forest size, and produced excellent crops. The Pennock was a large apple, with seven synonyms : the Newtown Pippin, a famous keeper ; the large and rich Vandervere, a native of Wilmington, with its eighteen aliases ; the luscious Harvest apple, earliest of them all ; the Rambo, a native of Delaware, a favorite, which, around Trenton, was popularly styled the bread-and-cheese apple ; the Romanite, a small apple, but a great keeper, of a dark cranberry

color : the golden-hued Porter apple ; the Maiden's Blush, a native
of Jersey, the most beautiful of them all : the Winesap, the Green-
ing, the Russet, the large and luscious Spitzenberg, the Pearmain,
the Doctor apple, which originated in Germantown, and doubtless
others which have escaped my recollection. The Priestley apple
had its origin in Northumberland, but was not very highly prized
here. In this fine orchard, in autumn

> " The wide projected heaps
> Of apples, which the lusty-handed year
> Innumerous o'er the blushing orchard spread,"

cheered those who, in pioneer days, had long been deprived of this
valuable fruit. On the eastern side of the orchard was a row of
cherry trees, which bore profusely, and afforded a good supply of
that fruit for the neighborhood. Near by there was also a number
of peach trees, bearing fine crops of that luscious fruit.

The cider-mill and press were of the best construction, built by
that skillful workman, Jacob W. Maus. The mill was composed of
double cylinders ; the press was worked with a powerful screw, a
foot in diameter. Eight or ten barrels of cider could be manufactured daily with them. I have seen none to excel them since.

Mr. Daniel Frazer had an orchard just east of his stone mansion ;
it was planted at a later period than the others : the trees were young
and thrifty, and bore good fruit, and were in good bearing in 1820.

These were all Philadelphians, who had in that fine market acquired a just appreciation of good fruit, and made laudable efforts
to procure it. Some of the trees were obtained in that city, some
at Burlington, and some at Northumberland. In the latter place
several English emigrants had introduced many choice varieties of
fruits, and devoted much care to their successful cultivation.

Mr. Paul Adams, a mile or two north-eastwardly from Danville,
had a small but prolific orchard, chiefly of winter apples. I well
remember at an early day seeing the trees bending under the burden
of a luxuriant crop, and some of the boughs breaking off, notwithstanding the props placed under them for their protection. Mr.
Adams was an elder in the Presbyterian church, a just man of most
venerable, and, I may with no impropriety say, apostolic appearance :
and this aspect was made the more impressive by his wearing a muslin
cap of pure white on his venerable head, which was wholly destitute
of hair.

Three generations have enjoyed the fruits of these orchards, planted on the borders of civilization by the provident early settlers, but several of them are now occupied by the dwellings of the citizens within the corporate limits of the borough.

In addition to these, John and Alexander Montgomery, the Sechlers, the Gaskinses, the Sanderses, the Diehls, the Rishels, the Fousts, and others, had orchards of which I knew so little, that I shall not attempt to describe them.

The apple is said by Professor Salisbury to be highly nutritious, and he claims to have demonstrated that it is superior to the potato in the principles that go to increase the muscle and *brain* of man. Doctor Johnson highly esteemed it for culinary purposes. He said : " If possible, have a good orchard. I knew a clergyman of small income, who brought up a family very reputably, which he chiefly fed on apple dumplings."

Before closing, I must mention the noted peach orchard of Mr. Michael Blue, two or three miles out on the hills. He was a Jerseyman, and they are said naturally to take to watermelons and peaches. It was congruous, therefore, that he should have the best peach orchard in the settlement. It was an extensive one, of natural fruit, consequently of small size, but much of it good flavor, yet not such as would compete with the large and luscious fruit from Delaware and New Jersey, now offered by the fruiterers in the Baltimore, Philadelphia, and New York markets.

General Daniel Montgomery.

General Daniel Montgomery was born in Chester county, Pennsylvania, and while yet a boy came to this place with his father, General William Montgomery. He was the most active and enterprising member of the family. To him, mainly, we are indebted for the town itself and the current of trade that nourished its young life and growth amid the struggles of its early days. For him the town was properly named, "Danville." He opened the first store in the place, where the Montour House now stands, and he also engaged in many enterprises, both in and out of the town, but all tending to build up and to give substantial importance to the place. Like his father, he was elected to Congress, and held many public trusts that will appear in the progress of this volume. He died in Danville, in 1831.

General Daniel Montgomery, from the universal testimony of his cotemporaries, was in all respects one of the best men that ever in his life work blessed the people of this place. He was not only active and enterprising, leading the way in every progressive improvement. but he was at the same time just, considerate, and generous, kind, and charitable. Daniel Ramsey says, that in times of scarcity, often experienced in frontier settlements, General Daniel Montgomery would never refuse a poor man a sack of flour. but freely give it without payment ; but no man could buy grain or flour from him at any price. only for his own use. Speculators were not allowed to make " a corner" in those days. His death, in 1831, was felt as a severe blow to the progress of the town, and he was sincerely mourned by many who had shared his bounty, as well as by the people in general. His funeral was one of the largest ever witnessed in this place. It was not the " hollow circumstance of woe," but the stern reality. His memory is still gratefully cherished by those who knew the sterling character of his mind and the everlasting goodness of his heart.

Items of Yore.

The fort or block-house nearest to Danville was at Washington-ville. It was erected at quite an early day on ground now partly owned by Joseph Hartman. The fort stood a little up the creek from the spot where Snyder's mill now stands. Very recently, musket balls and other war-like relics have been found on or near the site of the old fort.

Reverend Isaac Grier, father of Judge Grier and of M. C. Grier, late of Danville, deceased, was an eminent scholar, who graduated at Dickinson College in 1788 and entered the ministry in 1791. He taught as principal of the academy in Northumberland for some years. and died in that place on the 23d of August, 1814, in the fifty-first year of his age. He was not only a scholar, but a Christian in the full sense of the word.

The first Bible society of Pennsylvania was organized at Milton. in 1816. Reverend J. B. Patterson. long the beloved pastor of the Presbyterian church in Danville, was the first president of the society.

The old " Franklin Court " was located in the rear of the Mansion House, built by John Moore. It was a noted place of resort in the olden time. There are some still living who can remember the gay and jolly times they had in old Franklin Court in the days of *auld lang syne*. It has now disappeared, all but its crumbling foundation, and many of its old habitues like its ancient walls have gone into the shadows of the past.

There was a celebration of the 4th of July in Danville. in 1807, at which Daniel Montgomery was president. James Laird vice president, and Andrew Russell secretary. On this occasion James Boyd offered a very curious toast. Political parties at that time were those who called themselves " Democratic Republicans," the Federalists, and there was also an offshoot of the regular Democrats who opposed Simon Snyder and favored Spayd or some other Democrat for Governor. These were called " Quids." The toast referred to was as follows: " The Quids—a jackass a piece to them and a snail's horn for a spur, so that each mule may ride his own ass."

The Old Block-House.

The spirit of improvement has rudely laid its relentless hands on the time-honored memorials of *auld lang syne*. One by one the old, familiar objects that were wont to greet our eyes. are passing away. Among these cherished objects, is the old block-house. There in days gone by, the cheerful pop of ginger beer, enlivened the scene in the sultry summer time. Then how imposing the edifice stood when May became a squire and it became a temple of justice. The elements battered and the floods rolled into its cellar in vain. How the weather-beaten structure seemed to loom up among the loftier buildings reared around it, and how proudly it wore its chimney crown as the " Rangers " and the " Buglers " gathered beneath its ancient shingles when " court was called and the squire showed them that the " way of transgressors " is jailward. There too they concentrated their forces in the long winter evenings to while away the passing hours, as he of the ermine regulated the fitful motion of some quaint or crazy, old clock ; or stewed the bivalves on that curious little stove. And when the trying time arrived to choose town officers, how they probed the character and weighed the chances of each sovereign whose name was presented for office. Finally when the ticket was agreed upon, then they passed the hat around for contributions to meet the expense of printing. On one occasion the hat had an unfortunate hole in the crown; but the statesman was equal to the occasion. With solemn mien he held his open hand under the place where the hole was, and deftly caught the pennies as they sifted through. The next thing in order was to raise a unanimous boom for the candidates chosen and as a rule they were successful.

Venerable old building! you came down to us from a former generation. Where now will the Rangers congregate? I almost imagine I see them mournfully turning away, each with a chip as a memorial; for lo! the jack-screw was applied and the time of departure came. Farewell old block-house. The judge and the court may pass away, but a new legend shall be woven to charm a future coterie, when you have gone to kindling wood. In the palmy days of its glory the village statesmen assembled there and often displayed more solid sense than Congress or the cabinet. But it departed. It does not lie in ruins like Baalbec, Palmyra, or Pompeii; but it went away bodily by force of jack screws and rollers, and left not a chip behind. Even the kindly host, who once amid the cheerful voices and sage discussions of the aforesaid village statemen dealt out to them the steaming oysters and the popping, foaming small beer, he too with solemn mien took a bottle in one hand and a stew-pan in the other, and followed the venerable structure as it slowly rolled up Mulberry street.

Population.

The population of Danville, owing to its large manufactories, is somewhat fluctuating. Though of late years even the once floating element is becoming more permanent. The reason is found in the fact, that many of the workingmen have secured homes of their own, and have made this their settled residence.

In 1840 the population of Danville was about 2,000. In 1850 it was 3,333, and in the census taken by the writer of this book, under the town authorities in 1855, the population was 5,422, of whom 2,583 were females and 2,839 were males. In making this enumeration, I was assisted by Doctors Cromlish and Richter. In 1860 the official report of Doctor Caldwell, enumerator under the authority of the United States, was 6,580. In 1870 L. O. VanAlen was appointed to take the census. He reported the population of Danville to be 8,129. In 1880 H. B. Strickland, P. C. Murray, John K. Geringer and Charles H. Gulick were the Government enumerators. They reported a population of 7,698. First ward, 2,029 : Second ward, 1,392 ; Third ward, 2,276 : Fourth ward, 2,001.

Random Items.

The steam mill on Church street was built by P. Baldy, senior, in 1839. It is a solid, stone structure and is still in operation. Abram Sechler, the pioneer of band music, was for many years the engineer at the stone mill. It is at present idle.

The Cross-Keys was one of the early taverns in this place. It stood on the river bank, on the site now occupied by Robert Mc-Coy's residence. It was long kept by Mrs. Donaldson and was in its day the noted hostelrie of Danville. There the officers of the "Codorus," the pioneer steamer up the Susquehanna, were banquetted, on their ill-fated voyage ; and there on many a joyous occasion the villagers met in the olden time.

The old charcoal furnace, and the first in this place, was built by B. Patterson in 1838. It stood near where the Catawissa railroad crosses the street, just beyond the Mahoning steam mill. When anthracite coal began to be used, the old furnace was abandoned and suffered to fall into ruin. The last vestige of the old stack has long since disappeared.

Doctor Petrikin built a woolen factory near the present location of the co-operative rolling-mill, about 1830. After being in operation for some time it stood idle for many years, as a habitation for "the owls and the bats." Some time between 1856 and 1860 Duncan C. Hartman converted it into a planing-mill and did quite a lively business. It was afterwards used as a spike and bolt factory by the proprietors of the Rough and Ready ; but was swept away by fire in the winter of 1871.

There was a bank of discount and deposit opened in 1871 in the room now occupied by the "New York tea store," where Alex. M. Diehl presides, takes greenbacks and the "dollars of the daddies," on deposit, and issues fine groceries, fruits and notions on which there is no discount. The bank, after some time, paid its depositors and discontinued the business.

5

THE KEYSTONE BUILDING, an elegant structure adjoining the Opera House, was built by Colonel A. H. Brown in 1874. It is now occupied by Sheldon & Co.'s dry goods store. Colonel Brown, as he is familiarly called, is one of those jovial, cheerful and generous hearted men we meet only once in a while. He served in the One Hundred and Eighty-fourth regiment, Pennsylvania Volunteers, and was wounded in battle. He was a gallant soldier, a man among men.

There was a grist and plaster-mill, known as the John Montgomery mill, that occupied the site of the stone mill that was burnt a few years ago. The stone mill was built in 1825 and there was a woolen factory and a carding machine at one end. This establishment did an extensive business in its day. Just back of Daniel Ramsey's residence there was a woolen factory built by General William Montgomery, who left it to Daniel and Alexander, his sons; afterwards it was operated by Alexander alone, until 1839. The building has now entirely disappeared; but it was a great public benefit in early days.

There was also a saw-mill a little further south, in the rear of C. Laubach's residence. This is also gone without leaving a vestige to mark the place where it stood.

Some distance down the canal was General Daniel Montgomery's mill. The ruins are yet visible in the crumbling foundation of a building that was of so much benefit to the public, and the scene of so many acts of kindness to the destitute of that day.

In 1816 the ground occupied by the Montour House was an orchard, except the corner occupied by a small, two-story brick house, where Daniel Montgomery opened the first store in Danville. The ground from Mill street up the canal was a swamp extending up to General Daniel Montgomery's farm, which has since been known as the Pineo farm, and on which the asylum for the insane is now built. There in that extensive swamp the tall rushes grew and the bull-frogs held their evening concerts.

A meadow, between the canal and Mulberry street, extended from Mill street up to the Pineo farm. It was partly overgrown with tall rushes and low shrubbery through which the creek meandered in the tortuous channel chosen by itself, and the green sward was on a level with its banks. Large and beautiful willows stood where now the cinder covers the ground and has almost buried the stream that struggles through its narrow bed far below the bald and barren surface of to-day.

" Franklin Court " was an old time *cafe*, that stood in the rear of the Mansion House, and was the theater of many diversified scenes in the drama of human life. The foundation walls can still be seen among the accumulating rubbish ; but it has almost passed out of the memory of man.

JOHN C. BOYD came to Danville about 1820. He was a descendant of a prominent and patriotic family of Chester county, Pennsylvania. His remote ancestors were from Ireland. After he came to Danville he married a daughter of General Daniel Montgomery, and engaged in merchandising, in the room that had been occupied by his father-in-law. In 1824 he sold his stock of goods and located on a tract of land that had been given to Mrs. Boyd as a marriage portion, by General Montgomery, and since known as " Boyd's farm." It is some two miles up the river on the opposite shore. There he built a flouring-mill that is still in operation. He also enlarged the farm by purchase of adjoining lands, built the homestead and greatly improved the property. The snow-white and cheerful homestead affords a pleasant and beautiful view, with its surroundings, from the heights round about Danville. Mr. Boyd also joined with much energy in the various enterprises and public improvements of the day. Affable in his manners, generous, firm and enterprising, he won the respect of his fellow-citizens and made for himself an honorable record, and his children may be proud to bear his name through the world. But death came in the midst of his usefulness and closed his career while it was yet high noon. He died on the 18th day of August, 1849, in the fifty-sixth year of his age. His sons inherit much of the sterling qualities of mind and heart that characterized their honored father, John C. Boyd.

Montgomery Building.

Alexander Montgomery, who was born in the old mansion across the street from this building, and who died at the age of three score and ten, in the very chamber of his birth, was the founder of this edifice, as well as one of the early founders of Danville, and it still bears his name. The town received its name from his brother, General Daniel Montgomery, by whom its original foundation was

laid. Highly respected in their day, their memory is still gratefully cherished by their descendants and those with whom they
were associated in life. But to the building. The first wing, or
that on Bloom street, was erected in 1841, by Alexander Montgomery, and the other portion of the structure was erected in 1845.

On the 28th day of April, 1848, it was entirely destroyed by
fire, involving a loss of some $15,000. It was occupied at the time
of the fire by A. F. Russell's dry goods store; M. C. Grier's drug
store; the office of the *Danville Democrat,* published by Charles
Cook, Esquire; Mrs. Lenhart's dwelling; and J. G. Maxwell's dry
goods store. Mr. Russel lost about $4,000. Mr. Grier's loss was
near $3,000. Mrs. Lenhart's furniture and the office of the *Demo-
crat,* with the building, were all a total loss. During the same
season Mr. Montgomery contracted with A. G. Voris for its rebuilding, but Mr. Montgomery died before its completion. The
executors, Andrew F. Russell and Michael C. Grier, however, carried out the contracts, and the present Montgomery building was
completed the same year. It is advantageously situated, at the corner of Mill and Bloom streets, in the center of business operations,
and is still one of the prominent objects of the town. It has a
front of sixty feet on Mill street, extending fifty feet on Bloom
street, and is three stories high.

Journalism.

Generally speaking, journalism in Danville is not in the front
line of local progress. There is an evident want of the comprehensive power and consequent influence of the progressive newspaper. It should lead the way in giving tone and character to its
locality presenting its advantages, inviting the investment of capital, extending the labor market, and thus aid in building up the
town and giving it character abroad. It should reflect in its columns
the material progress, the intellectual, social, moral and religious tone
of the community.

The local journal should be on the front line of progress, and at
the same time the steadfast conservator of established principles.
It should not only disseminate the current news of the day; but its
manifest power should be devoted to the welfare of the community.
On a higher plane than a mere agent of *news,* it should defend the

right and oppose the wrong on all subjects involving human rights, moral ethics or social economy. An intelligent people at the present day will demand something more of a family visitor than a mere dispenser of news. Positive ideas are required, and always pointing in the right direction. The local journal should lead the way in every wholesome enterprise, presenting local advantages, inviting the investment of capital, extending the labor market and thus aid in building up and giving tone and character to its locality. It should reflect in its columns the material progress, the intellectual, moral and social advancement of the community.

When we survey the active and growing trade in our midst, with the noble work of our moral and religious institutions, and then peruse our local journals, we pause and wonder what has become of the boasted power of the press. On the other hand there seems to be a misapprehension in relation to the claims and the importance of the newspaper. I know by experience that the local journalist has many difficulties to encounter, not the least of which is the want of appreciation, especially when he essays to lift the standard above the common level, and fails to charm the prurient desire for that which is akin to gossip. Too often, the journalist who panders to the depraved appetite of the unthinking will thrive and grow rich, where he who aims to elevate society would starve to death. Much of the character of the local journal depends on the community. If the public prefers to pay for trash, petty gossip or party twaddle, then is the community in a measure responsible for the trifling character that too often marks the public journal of the present day. The *American* under the control of its founder, established a reputation throughout the State, not because it carefully noted local occurrences but because it was a reflex of its locality, presenting continually the past, the present, and the future probabilities of Danville. The business enterprises, its vast capabilities and its general sentiment were known and judged by the standard presented in its columns. But a local journal should be a reflex of public sentiment only when that sentiment is right, or negatively, in its efforts to correct that which is erroneous. It should be progressive, leading public sentiment onward and upward, instructing the young and guiding their ambition in a proper direction. It should inform all who read its pages, not only on the current events of the day but on all subjects that lie within the scope of newspaper discussion. It should lead the way in every material interest and in all that can minister to the public welfare. In a word, it should be a household companion, whose cheerful presence adds to the sunshine of life, whilst it also educates, ministering to the pleasure and profit of all who peruse its columns. Such is a model newspaper. And now for a hasty sketch of the Danville newspapers during the last sixty-seven years.

Newspapers.

The history of the pioneer newspapers in Danville is very meager. No files were kept and their very names are almost forgotten. One copy of the *Express*, dated 1818 is all I could find. It is faded with time and contains little about the local situation at that day. The *Columbia Gazette* was published by George Sweeny in 1813 and this was no doubt the first newspaper enterprise in Danville. In 1815 Jonathan Lodge established the *Express*. It was afterwards published by Lodge & Caruthers. Judge Cooper was also among the early editors of this place. The *Watchman* was established in 1820 by Mr. Sweeny, on the corner of Market and Ferry streets, now occupied by the residence of Doctor Simington. All these papers were mainly reprints of foreign and domestic news; except when Judge Cooper and George Sweeny pointed their sharp goose quills at each other. This was the introduction of newspaper war in Danville; and that spirit has marked the course of local journalism ever since. It is a war that is not over yet," though it shakes no "bloody shirt."

"The Danville Intelligencer."

The *Danville Intelligencer* was founded by Valentine Best, in 1828, as the organ of the Democratic party. Valentine Best was a man of strong will, ardent passions and in his dealings scrupulously honest. He stood deservedly high in the respect and confidence of the public generally, though his paper was intensely Democratic and one of the most bitter and unrelenting against a political opponent. The *Intelligencer* from its first issue in 1828, to the present time, has been the local organ of the Democratic party. In the days of Mr. Best it was arrayed against the Whigs, and many a thrust he gave that grand old party. And when the Republican party began to manifest its power, his warfare was directed against it with equal ardor and determined hostility. In 1850 Mr. Best was elected to the Senate of Pennsylvania. The contest however was less a political than a local one. The issue was the question of creating Montour county. Accordingly he received the votes of those who favored the project and was opposed by those who objected to the measure, without respect to party. In order to carry his bill through the Senate, which without his vote was a tie, politically he by his own vote and the sixteen Whig votes became Speaker of the Senate. He was much abused, but he bore it all patiently, believing that the end justified the means. It was the Democratic party especially that denounced him for what was regarded as a betrayal of the party, more especially as in the distribution of the offices in the Senate he by his vote gave one half to the Whigs. But he finally carried his darling project, and he returned home, believing that the sacrifice he had made of his party standing for the benefit of his immediate constituents would be properly estimated. He had almost made himself a political martyr to accomplish the purpose for which he was elected. But he was mistaken. Gratitude is a quality little known in political parties. If a partisan loses *caste*, even in its own service, the pharisees of the organization curse him, simply because others do. Mr. Best had served his purpose. But the majority of his party ignored his claims when he sought a nomination for Congress in 1856. This is a bitter lesson that many earnest politicians have learned. After devoting his energies and the best years of his life to a party, he finds that political parties, like corporations, have no souls. After the death of Valentine Best, which occurred in 1858 the *Intelligencer* was published for some time by Oscar Kepler, in the interest of Mrs. Best. The establishment was then purchased by a number of leading Democrats, dividing the amount into shares, as it still remains. The first editor under the company proprietorship was J. S. Sanders. He took charge on the 10th of September, 1858. Mr. Sanders kept up the paper to its old-time standard, and being a first-class printer he made many improvements in its mechanical department. In 1862 he left Danville and assumed control of a paper in Berwick. In the meantime, Thomas Chalfant had succeeded to the editorship of the *Intelligencer*, in which position he still continues. Mr. Chalfant moved the office from the basement of the Best residence to the second story of Reed's building, by the canal, and afterwards to the room in Assembly building which was formerly occupied by the *Montour American*; where it is now.

The Danville Democrat.

The *Danville Democrat* was established by Charles Cook, of whom a sketch will be found in this book. It was commenced in August, 1840. He called it the *Danville Democrat and Tariff Advocate*, though it always opposed the Democratic party. Mr. Cook continued its publication until 1864, when he sold the office to Joel S. Baily as stated elsewhere. He also published a German paper during the campaign of 1844, which he called *Der Tariff Advokat*. In its editorial ability the *Democrat* was far above the average. While located in the Montgomery building, in 1845 the office was burned with that building. The old hand-press fell through the floor to the cellar but was rigged up and did good service for many years afterwards. During the latter years of its existence the *Democrat* was located on the second story of the building now occupied by W. C. Davis, on Mill street, in the First ward.

The Montour American.

The *Montour American* was founded by the author of this volume. The first number was published on the 11th day of December, 1855, in the Montgomery building. It was at a time when the Whig and Democratic parties each had a local organ—the one conducted by Charles Cook and the other by Valentine Best. The new paper, as might be inferred, had a hard struggle for existence in the beginning. But in the succeeding spring it joined in the support of Fremont, and the paper steadily gained in patronage, and proved a success under the administration of its founder. Indeed, the *American* was a popular favorite, and in its palmy days had a wide circulation among all parties. In 1859 I sold the *American* to George B. Ayers, of Harrisburg. During his ephemeral editorship, he called it *Montour Herald*. After a few months he abandoned it and returned to Harrisburg, having lost the greater portion of its patronage. In October of the same year I repurchased the material, and resumed its publication. The old name was restored and its former patrons returned to its support. It was now located in the second story of Gross' building. The *American* was prosperous and now was firmly reëstablished, enjoying its old-time popularity. But as there were now two Republican papers in Danville, it was deemed best by politicians, that they should be united, as there was naturally always some trouble about a division of the party patronage. Accordingly in January, 1864, I sold the *American* to Joel S. Baily, of Chester county, Pennsylvania. Charles Cook also sold the *Democrat* to the same purchaser, who united the offices and located in the Assembly building. But in the Autumn of the same year, Mr. Baily, tired of the business, sold it, and I once more assumed its control, and once more gathered its scattered patronage. After some time I moved the office into the Montgomery building, entrance on Bloom street. Here I greatly improved the material of the office and enlarged the paper, and here I brought the first power press, as I had previously brought the first jobbing press to Danville, and subsequently I also brought the first steam power to a newspaper office, as well as piloting the way in many other improvements. In 1871 the office was sold to William H. Bradley and Lewis Gordon for $5,000 cash. The *American* office having originally cost $600, it will be seen that my efforts increased its value $4,400. Some few years later Mr. Gordon sold his interest to Joel Bradley, and subsequently William H. Bradley sold his interest to Edward Baldy, who afterwards sold to his brother, and it is now published by Bradley & Baldy, on Mill street, having removed it from Moyer Lyon's building which had been expressly built for the office. There is no vanity or egotism in appending the fact that the *American* to-day has lost popularity but is still supported as the local organ of the Republican party.

The Medium.

After the sale of the *Montour American* to Messrs. Bradley and Gordon, in 1871 I established *The Medium* in a second story of Moyer Lyon's block. This was a semi-weekly and is known as the gem of all the Danville newspapers. Many of its files were bound and are carefully preserved ; and although it was published less than a year, yet as much as twenty dollars has been refused for a bound

copy of its file. To the *Medium* office I brought the second, as I
had also brought the first, newspaper power press to Danville. The
printer boys in the *Medium* office, H. L. Gould, R. W. Eggert, N.
C. Prentiss and Clarke Umstead, well remember that model press
as the most complete and beautiful machine they ever saw in a
country printing office. Richard W. Eggert had charge of the
newspaper department, and took especial pride in making it a thing
of beauty. In fact he is proud of it yet. In the spring of 1872,
very unfortunately, I sold the *Medium* office to a company called the
" Danville Publishing Company." This was done with a view to
establish a large printing house in Danville. They changed the
name to *The Independent* and moved the office to the basement of
Thompson's hall.

"*The Independent.*"

The Danville Publishing Company was organized under a charter
granted by the Legislature. Mr. William J. Reed was chosen president, Mr. William Keiner treasurer an I D. H B. Brower secretary.
I was also employed as editor. The company then bought a new
chromatic jobbing press on credit and also incurred a debt of several
hundred dollars in New York. All this time not a cent of the stock
was paid in, and in less than nine months the establishment was
seized for the debts referred to : it was sold by the sheriff and I
never received a penny for the *Medium* office. My loss was over
$2,000. The loss of the company was nothing as they never paid
anything. By some mystery to me unknown, the office fell into the
hands of S. P. Kase. This loss to me, with the loss met in adjust-
ing the complicated interests involved in the sale of the *American*,
swept away the fruits of all my toil for many years and left me without means to pursue my favorite profession.

The Mentor.

In the autumn of 1873 as the material of *The Independent* was
lying idle, I joined a party consisting of Richard W. Eggert, John
Lesher, William H. McCarty and myself in publishing *The Mentor*.
A printing house was built in the rear of the Mansion House, now
occupied by the *National Record*, and the printing material was
leased from Simon P. Kase. But it was not a success, and it was
abandoned the following year.

The Danville Record.

In the spring of 1876 Mrs. A. P. Fowler purchased the printing material of S. P. Kase and employed me to conduct an independent paper for "The Danville Printing Company, limited," to be styled *The Danville Record.* The first number was issued on the 16th day of March, 1876. It at once received a large circulation and was patronized very liberally by the business men of Danville. And here it is proper for me to say, that of all the devoted friends I ever had, and I have had many, there is none more richly entitled to my grateful remembrance than Mr. A. P. Fowler, of Scranton. He is true as steel to every promise, generous and faithful, a friend in whom there is no guile. Ah! would the world had more like him! In my charge the *Record* flourished for two years when circumstances rendered it necessary that the material should be sold. I was not in condition to buy, and as the hard times gave little encouragement for business in this locality the office was transferred to the new owners in March, 1878.

The National Record.

The *National Record* is a continuance of the *Danville Record*, commencing in the spring of 1878, the material of the *Danville Record* having been purchased by James Foster, Harry Vincent and Victor A. Lotier. After some time Foster and Vincent sold their interest to Victor A. Lotier, by whom the paper is now published. It has been enlarged and is a vigorous Greenback organ. Among the people it is valued mainly for its local department which is under the charge of Richard W. Eggert, who is an excellent compositor as well as a lively localizer. The *Record* is now the largest paper in Danville and has a fair share of patronage. It is published every Saturday.

Sageburg.

Sageburg, sometimes called East Danville, is perhaps the most enterprising as well as the most beautiful section of this borough, and mainly constitutes the Second ward. From the ward line on Market street, it extends for half a mile or more up the river and is covered with various iron manufactories on the left and dotted over with handsome residences on the right, between Market street and the river bank.

Sageburg did not however derive its name from the peculiar wisdom or sage appearance of its inhabitants, for they are as lively and pleasant and seem to be as "gay and happy" as any other community. Indeed they appear to have more taste than common, if we may judge by the elegance of their dwellings, the neatness of their premises and the peculiar charm of their surroundings. The picturesque beauty of a vine-clad residence on the banks of the Susquehanna, almost in the shadow of Blue hill, that lifts its lofty crest for hundreds of feet above the majestic stream, can only be painted by the pencil of the artist or the pen of the poet.

Many years ago, only a single log building occupied the territory now known as Sageburg. In this building an old man by the name of Sage followed the coopering business. Not very poetic indeed, but he was a quaint and curious specimen of the *genus homo*. Being a bachelor and anxious no doubt, like all the race of man, to leave behind him some memorial more substantial than a flour barrel to perpetuate his name, and evidently anticipating a brighter future for the locality, he gave it the name of "Sageburg," by which it is known at the present time, though it then contained only the one building and that a cooper-shop. But the prospective growth of Danville in the distant future no doubt was dimly apparent to the old pioneer. He has long since passed away. His shop is no more and the skillful workmanship of his hands is forgotten. But his name still survives by courtesy, though it has no legal recognition. Other portions of the territory have since been known by different names, originating from different sources, such as Snydertown, Lundy's Lane, Amsterdam and Kulp's Eddy, but all are included in the general name of Sageburg.

Sageburg has become one of the most stirring portions of Danville. The price of property is advancing and in no part of the town can you find so many handsome dwellings, surrounded by shrubbery and all the adornments that make pleasant and happy homes. The business establishments that have sprung up on the line of the railroad, the prospective free bridge, the advantages and beauty of the location, and above all the enterprise of the inhabitants, conspire to immortalize the name of the old cooper, whose highest ambition was to make a good flour barrel and dub the old woolen shop with the name his father gave him.

Sageburg, or East Danville, though partially cut off from direct trade with the surrounding country on either side of the river, has outgrown all other portions of the town. In all its improvements, thrift, enterprise and taste are happily blended. Its manufactories teem with the fruits of industry; its elegant residences and cottages, where fruits, flowers and the clinging vines in their season lend a charm to the scene, make it the favorite ground for summer promenading. It is the care bestowed upon their adornments that give it a rural beauty, combined with the advantages afforded by a town.

Among the public institutions of Sageburg, or East Danville, apart from the religious or educational, is the "Washington Fire Company." They have a handsome building on Market street, and are always prompt at the tap of the bell as well as efficient in action. Their hall is furnished in excellent style and decorated with peculiar taste, rendering it one of the most pleasant places to spend a social hour or to meet for mental improvement. Among the oldest in the fire department is Ex-Chief William C. Walker, but still among the most active, always prompt on time and ready for duty.

The general intelligence, public spirit and social order of Sageburg, like its external beauty, thrift and enterprise, will compare favorably with any other locality of equal population.

Perhaps the handsomest building in that quarter is the "Cottage drug store." This was built by D. C. Hartman about 1860 and is now occupied by Doctor Jordan as a residence and also as an excellent drug store.

St. Paul's Methodist Episcopal Church.

I have consulted the authentic records of the Methodist Episcopal church and also drawn largely on the memory of those who watched its progress with prayerful solicitude; but I am chiefly indebted to Mr. Duncan C. Hartman for the names and dates in the earlier days of the church. How vividly the subject recalls the scenes of my own childhood and all the "fond recollections that cluster around the memory of home." Well do I remember old "Father Gruber," and "Father Hunter" in the missionary days of Methodism, when the devoted preachers of the old school were the bold and fear-

less soldiers of the cross and heroes of God, who sacrificed homes
of ease without regret, and braved a weary life of toil without complaint. They were men whose lives demonstrated the doctrine they
preached, and whose death was the triumph of a living faith. The
humble piety and simplicity of manners that marked the personal
character of Methodists in the olden time, was also exhibited in their
dwellings and in the unpretending "house," where they gathered
to worship. With one accord they ignored the frivolities of society,
enforced the doctrine of humility and labored earnestly for the
world's redemption. The fervent zeal, impassioned eloquence, and
earnest solicitude for the welfare of others, readily explains their
wonderful success.

The precise period when the first Methodist preacher arrived at
this place, is not now known ; but they were the second religious body
organized here. The first regular conference appointment for Danville was in 1791. This place was then included in Northumberland
circuit, which extended from Northumberland up the North Branch
of the Susquehanna to Wyoming Valley, and up the West Branch
to Great Island. The distance traveled by the circuit rider in making
his round was three hundred miles, which was accomplished in six
weeks. When the nature of the country and the roads are considered the hardships of the preachers of that day may be imagined,
and it required something more than the pittance allowed them, to
cheer them onward in their arduous labors. This territory for
many years was supplied by only two or three ministers, and it included present circuits and stations of Williamsport, Newbury,
Muncy, Milton circuit and station, Northumberland, Mifflinburg,
Lewisburg, Catawissa, Bloomsburg, Berwick, Bloomingdale, Orangeville, Sunbury and parts of Bellefonte district. Some thirty or forty
Methodist preachers are now employed on the same territory.

Previous to 1804 Danville and the circuit in which it was located
belonged to the Philadelphia conference. In that year it was transferred to the Baltimore conference. In 1807 it was returned to the
Philadelphia conference. In 1810 it was included in the new Gen-
nessee conference and in 1820 it was re-assigned to the Baltimore
conference, of which it still continues to be an appointment.

The following is a list of the preachers who successively, and we
might add successfully, labored in Danville and vicinity by appointment of conference:

1791, Richard Parrott, Lewis Browning.

1792, James Campbell, William Colbert.

1793, James Campbell, James Paynter.

1794, Robert Manly, John Broadhead.

1795, James Ward, Stephen Timmons.

1796, John Seward, Richard Sneath.

1797, John Lackey, John Higby.

1798, John Lackey, John Lead.

1799, James Moore, Benjamin Bidlack, D. Stephens.

1800, Ephraim Chambers, Edward Larkin, Asa Smith.

1801. Johnston Dunham, Gilbert Carpenter.

1802, Anning Owen, James Aikins.

1803, Daniel Ryan, James Ridgeway.

1804. Thomas Adams, Gideon Draper.

1805, Christopher Frey, James Saunders.

1806. Robert Burch, John Swartzwelder.

1807. Nicholas Willis, Joel Smith.

1808, Thomas Curren, John Rhodes.

1809, Timothy Lee, Loring Grant.

1810, Abraham Dawson, Isaac Puffer.

1811, B. G. Paddock, H. Baker, R. Lanning.

1812, George Thomas, Ebenezer Doolittle.

1813, Joseph Kincaid, Joseph Chamberlayne.

1814, John Haggard, A. Dawson

1815, Reynolds M. Everts, I. B. Cook.

1816, John Thomas, Alpheus Davis.

1817, Benjamin Bidlack, Peter Baker.

1818, Gideon Lanning, Abraham Dawson.

1819. John Rhodes, Darius Williams.

1820, John Rhodes, Israel B. Cook.

1821, Marmaduke Pearce, John Thomas.

1822, John Thomas, Mordecai Barry.

1823. Jacob B. Shephard, M. Barry.

1824, Robert Cadden, F. McCartney.

1825, Robert Cadden, Richard Bond.

1826, John Thomas, George Hildt.

1827, John Thomas, David Shaver.

1828, Charles Kalbfus, William James.

1829. James W. Donahay, Josiah Forrest.

1830, James W. Donahay, A. A. Eskridge.

Berwick circuit was formed in 1831 from that portion of Northumberland circuit, which made the labor of the preachers a little less. Danville was still included in the old circuit of Northumberland and was supplied by the following preachers:

1831, David Shaw.

1832, Marmaduke Pearce, James Forest.

1833, Josiah Forrest, James Reed, Jr.

1834, Henry Tarring, Oliver Ege.

1835, Henry Tarring, John Guyer, R. Beers, Thomas Myers.

Danville circuit was organized in 1836, and also embraced the territory of the present Montour, Bloomsburg, and part of Orangeville circuits. The circuit of Danville has been supplied by the following laborers:

1836, Joseph S. Lee, R. W. H. Brent.

1837, Samuel Ellis, Stephen Hildebrand.

1838, Robert T. Nixon, William Hirst.

1839, Robert T. Nixon, J. W. Houghewent.

1840, George Bergstresser, Joseph A. Ross.

1841, George Bergstresser, G. Guyer.

1812, John Ball, James Guyer.

1843, John Ball, S. G. Hare.

1844, James Ewing, George A. Coffey.

1845, James Ewing, B. F. Brooks.

In the year 1846, Danville was erected into a station. Since that time the following conference appointments have been made for this place :

1846, John Guyer.

1847, Philip B. Reese.

1849, Thomas Mitchell.

1850, Joseph France.

1853, James Brads.

1855, Thomas M. Reese.

1856, J. Wilson.

1857–8, William Harden.

1859–60, B. B. Hamlin.

1861–3, J. H. C. Dosh.

1864-5, A. M. Barnitz.
1866-7, J. McK. Reiley, D. D.
1868-71, F. Hodgson, D. D.
1872 3, S. Creighton.
1874-5, F. B. Riddle, A. M.
1876-8, W. A. Houck.
1879-80. J. Max Lantz.

This brings up the succession to the present date. The present pastor, J. Max Lantz, is an eloquent preacher highly esteemed by his people.

Rev. Wilson was the most unpopular of any preacher stationed here during my time.

Rev. William Harden was a noble worker in the cause, and has gone to his reward.

Rev. Riddle was an enigma. He was a man you could readily imagine would come in with a rush, rattle about four hundred words in a minute, close up suddenly, pop out at the back door, jump over the fence and push for home three laps ahead of every body else. He was a good scholar and said some excellent things; but before you could grip them, he would jam in something else and the result was a muddle.

Rev. Barnitz was a solid thinker and a plain, earnest, effective preacher. He was highly esteemed.

Rev. J. McKendree Reiley, D. D., was perhaps the most popular of all the Methodist preachers, stationed here in recent years. He was in high favor with the community and was the chosen orator on public occasions.

Rev. Dr. Hodgson was a finished scholar and was in the front rank as a controversialist. He wrote several books of great merit. He also has finished his work and gone to his rest.

Rev. Dosh was an earnest and pleasant speaker and served his mission well.

Revs. Creighton, Reese, Hamlin and Brads, all made an honorable record here, and could not fail in accomplishing much good.

Rev. Houck, now in Lock Haven, is a splendid logician, remarkable for the clearness and force of his conclusions. As a pastor he is equally felicitous, kind in his sympathies, but stern and exacting where christian duty is involved.

6

Rev. Lantz the present pastor in charge, is regarded as one of the best speakers with which conference has favored Danville. He is highly esteemed by his people and cannot fail to make a good and lasting impression on his charge.

In looking over the list of preachers away back to the beginning of the century, how many delightful associations and stirring scenes are called to mind, by the octogenarians, as they peruse the names of the laborers who have broken the bread of life to the people of Danville. The introduction of one and the solemn farewell of another—the glowing eloquence of the young—the powerful logic of the learned—the kind persuasion of the compassionate—the fervent appeals of the enthusiastic—and the solemn warning of the aged, are brought from the store house of memory, as the thoughts go back to the time when their living voices were heard in our midst. Many of these marshals in the camp of God, after performing deeds of heroism more glorious than the taking of a strong city, or conquering a world, have long since fought their last battle and gone to their reward ; and other sentinels on the towers are on their last watch, and soon will lay their armor by, "having fought the good fight, kept the faith, and finished their course," one by one will follow the van guard to that bourne from whence no traveler returns, to join the faithful of all ages and wear the starry crown of everlasting life.

The first class in Danville was formed in 1815, and was originally composed of George Lott and wife, Mrs. Donaldson, William Hartman and wife, and Samuel Steele.

Public service, as well as class and prayer meetings were alternately held at private dwellings for a number of years, afterwards in the school-house that formerly stood on Church street, where also the first sabbath-school was organized in 1831. Public worship, on particular occasions, was also frequently held in the court-house. There Bishop Asbury preached on his visit to Danville, as did also the eccentric Lorenzo Dow. A brick church was erected in 1839 for the use of the Methodist congregation, after having liberally contributed to the building of other churches : but in 1848 it was found to be insufficient to accommodate the membership, so they set about building the present church edifice, having sold the former house.

The present Methodist church building is on Mahoning street. The size is fifty by eighty feet and with its galleries will seat eight or nine hundred. The basement is used for class-room, Sunday-school and similar purposes. The material is brick, surmounted by a modest cupola containing one of the finest toned bells in this region of country.

War Record.

Neither Danville nor Montour county need blush to read its military record. For a score of years previous to the close of the last century the territory now included in Montour county, was on the border, and from necessity nearly all the citizens were required to bear arms in defense of their families and their homes. The peace with great Britain was no security against the stealthy and treacherous attacks of the savage foes of the whites. These border troubles kept alive the military spirit of the pioneers until the angry disputes with England about the impressment of our sailors brought us into conflict with that power a second time. Then followed the Black Hawk war, the Florida war, the Mexican war, and more recently the most deplorable of all, the civil war. In all these conflicts the people of Danville and of Montour county did not falter, they did their duty. they bore a fair and chivalrous part in them all. To develop the martial element and render it efficient, a number of military companies were organized at different periods.

THE DANVILLE MILITIA.—This is the first company of which we have any record, and what we have is unsatisfactory. We only know that at the close of the last war with England, it was flourishing and well organized. It then had on its roll one hundred members, rank and file ; and was commanded by Captain Samuel Yorks, who had seen active service as lieutenant in the "Danville Blues." Captain Yorks was the *beau ideal* of a military officer, tall, symmetrical and with a commanding presence. Thomas W. Bell was one of the subordinate officers of the company. Others are forgotten, two thirds of a century having almost obliterated the recollection of those early citizen-soldiers.

THE DANVILLE BLUES.—This was a rifle company commanded by Captain Isaac Blue. The names of its members can only be recalled in part. The imperfection of the roll is a source of regret, as it would be a great satisfaction to all, and especially to their descendants, to know the names of those who so freely responded to the

call of their country. The reader will find some matters of interest
in relation to this company under the title of "Going to Black
Rock." The following is a portion of the roll that can be recalled:

Isaac Blue, captain.	Asa Moore,
Isaiah Blue,	Abner Moore,
Herbert W. Best.	John Mills,
Daniel Cameron,	John McCoy,
Colin Cameron,	David Petrikin, surgeon,
Alexander Campbell,	—— Sanders,
John Dugan,	Samuel Yorks, lieutenant,
Edward Morison,	Jacob Sechler.

This company was in active service on the frontier in 1813, and
was stationed at Black Rock, where it suffered severely from the
malignant fever, then known as the Black Rock fever. Some of the
members died of the fever notwithstanding the skillful efforts of
Doctor Petrikin in their behalf. One of the victims of the epidemic
was Alexander Campbell.

THE DANVILLE LIGHT HORSE—A company of Light Dragoons
commanded by Captain Clarke of Derry. This company of cavalry
was a great favorite of the people in its palmy days, especially was
it in high favor with the juveniles. Many of the most enterprising
young men of Danville, who were the cavaliers of that day, were
members of the "Light Horse." Well armed and equipped, their
spirited and showy horses, their fine military dress and thorough
drill, led by their gallant captain, with Trumpeter Sanders in his
gay, scarlet uniform in the van, sounding his clarion notes to the
great delight of juvenility, they made the day of parade one of the
great gala days, ranking with Christmas and the Fourth of July.
And right fortunate were the boys who were permitted to go to Washingtonville to witness the regimental parades in that ancient village.

The organization of the "Light Horse" dated back to 1810, and
although not mustered into service during the war that followed, they
had promptly volunteered, and were highly indignant when the
government refused to accept their services. The denunciations they
heaped upon *Simon* the *Tanner* for this refusal were neither few nor
far between. They deemed him ignorant of his military duties, because he failed to appreciate such a valiant company.

A sham battle was fought about this time, perhaps in lieu of the reality. During this contest the captain came off *hors de combat*, being seriously injured by the fall of his charger. No official report of the battle was ever made. But the members of this brilliant cavalry company have all passed away. Many of them attained a great age. The last survivor of the gallant chivalry who so gloriously rode their war horses through the streets of Danville has long since departed. He was almost ninety years of age, when he gave to Mr. J. F. the particulars I have noted of the Light Horse company of Danville. The following are all that can be gathered of their muster roll :

Charles Clark, captain,	—— Kipp,
John Blue,	—— King,
Elisha Barton,	William Kitchen,
James Boyd,	Daniel Montgomery,
Lucas Brass,	Lewis Maus,
Isaac Bear,	Joseph Maus,
James Donaldson,	Robert Moore,
John Donaldson,	Thomas Moorhead,
William De Pew,	Peter Pursel,
Charles Evans,	William Sheriff,
Charles M. Frazer,	James Stevenson,
Charles Frazer,	Henry Sanders,
John Gulick,	Daniel Woodside,
John Gaskins,	James Woodside,
James Hamilton,	Thomas Woodside.

COLUMBIA GUARDS.—This company was organized in 1817, and was long the pride of the village. This company was originally and all through the long half century of its existence, composed of the very best *solaier* material of Danville and vicinity. It embraced many of the enterprising and patriotic young men of the community. The muster roll at the organization of the company or very soon thereafter, has been preserved, and is as follows :

Anthony, John,	Montgomery Daniel W.,
Barber, William,	Montgomery, John,
Baum, Samuel,	Marshall, Henry,
Barber, Daniel,	Moore, John,
Best, John,	Moore, Charles,
Boon, Anthony,	Moore, Andrew Y.,

Blackwell, Matthew,
Clark, William,
Clark, Thomas,
Colt, Thomas,
Colt, William,
Colt, James,
Cathcart, William,
Cornelison, Isaac,
Carson, James, captain,
Donaldson, Alexander,
Donaldson, William,
DePew, William,
Frick, Frederick,
Fisher, ——,
Grier, Thomas,
Goodman, Charles,
Hurley, William G.,
Hughes, Ellis,
Hibler, Jacob,
Huntington, Samuel,
Irwin, Jared,
Kent, Adolphus,
Kitchen, Amos E.,
Landy, John,
Lyon, Asher,

Moore, Burrows,
Moore, Samuel,
Moohead, Thomas,
McWilliams, Hugh,
McCallister, Hector,
Maus, William S.,
Mellon, Gideon,
Patterson, Matthew,
Potter, George, captain,
Pervin, John,
Sholes, Orrin,
Sechler, Jacob,
Savage, ——,
Thiel, John M.,
Thiel, Casper,
Underwood, Samuel,
Woodside, David,
Woodside, Robert,
Wieman, Jacob,
Warner, Isaac,
Wiley, Thomas,
Wilson, James,
Wilson, Charles,
Young, John.

The Columbia Guards, together with the Northumberland Artillerists, Capt. Priestly, the Warrior Run Infantry and others, constituted the Northumberland and Columbia battalion of volunteers, commanded by Major R. Coleman Hall. In the summer of 1823 there was a battalion parade in Danville, on the then open ground between Bloom and Center streets. Dr. W. H. Magill, then a young man was surgeon of the battalion. The parade is said to have been the grandest military display ever witnessed in Danville.

The Columbia Guards were first commanded by Capt. Potter, and subsequently by Capts. Carson, Colt, Best, Wilson and Frick, until 1846, stretching over a period of about thirty years. In that year the first call was made upon the citizen-soldiery since the organization of the company. Prompted by a patriotic desire to serve their country in the Mexican war, their services were offered and accepted, and the Columbia Guards, under the command of Capt. Wilson, numbering ninety-four, rank and file, were mustered into the service of the United States on the 28th day of December, 1846. We pause not now to recall the mingled emotions of patriotism and personal affection, of hope and fear, of joy and sorrow, that pervaded this community when this gallant company took up its line of march from the peaceful parade to the stern duties of camp; from the calm sunshine of home to the battle and the storm. But they lingered not, for the flag of their country was unfurled, their brethren were engaged in actual combat. Brown had fallen at Matamoras, like a hero in battle, and the banks of the Rio Grande had drank the blood of a Ringgold, and they hastened to the defense of the "starry banner," many, alas! to return no more.

The first engagement of the Guards was at the storming of Vera Cruz, and there, at the opening of their brilliant campaign, the lamented Capt. Wilson died on the 10th of April, 1847. Capt. Wilson was a model officer. Though naturally kind, yet austere and punctilious on parade, and under his charge the Guards became thoroughly versed in military tactics, and perhaps the best disciplined company in the regiment to which they were attached. His remains were brought home and buried with due honors among his family and kindred. From Very Cruz, the company, under the command of Dr. C. H. Frick, proceeded in the victorious march of Gen. Scott towards the city of Mexico. In the battle of Cerro Gordo they took a prominent part, and lost one of their number, John Smith, who was killed by a musket ball in storming the heights. At the bloody battle of Chepultepec they lost two more of their comrades. William Dietrich and John Snyder fell on that memorable day, when

> "A thousand glorious actions that might claim
> Triumphant Laurels and immortal fame,
> Confused in glorious actions lie,
> And troops of heroes undistinguished die."

On approaching the capital of the enemy, the defense of San Angelos, with all the military stores—a post of distinguishing honor and vast responsibility, and of peculiar danger—was committed to the Columbia Guards, and on the 13th day of September,

1847, they were among the first in Gen. Scott's triumphant march into the city of the Aztecs and the halls of the Montezumas.

After an absence of nearly two years, when Mexico was conquered,

> "When wild war's deadly blast was blown,
> And gentle peace returning,"

they returned to Danville on the 28th day of July, 1849.   And is there one

> "Whose heart has ne'er within him burned,
> As home his footsteps he has turned
> From wandering on a foreign strand?"

It is utterly impossible to describe the mingled emotions of joy and sadness awakened by the solemn march of the Guards into Danville. That day will never be forgotten, for the record is stamped in the hues of living reality.   The whole community joined to welcome and honor the arrival of the Guards.   But, alas! their ranks were thinned : over half their number answered to the " roll call " no more, and there were tears of thanksgiving and shouts of joy for those who came, and there were burning tears and silent anguish, the saddest syllables of nature's woe, for those who came not—for the husband and father whose place was vacant in the ranks.   To the widow and the orphan all the "pomp and circumstances of glorious war," the waving banners, the nodding plumes and the martial music inspired no joyful emotion.   To them it was but the echo of sorrow and the deep notes of a funeral march.

A little time developed the fact that most of those who returned had contracted the diseases of an uncongenial climate, and one by one they have passed away.   Jesse G. Clarke, Ad. Ray and their lamented commander, the noble-hearted Dr. Clarence H. Frick, followed on that returnless march, to the music of the tolling bells, beyond the reach of war's alarms.

> "An army now might thunder past,
> And they heed not its roar."

A little remnant still survives, but they, too, are treading the down-hill of life, and they too, ere long will rally to the last " reveille," and form into line with the platoon already advanced beyond the river of death—but their names and their gallant deeds in the service of their country will be cherished while patriotism or gratitude continue to animate and ennoble the human heart. Honored by the especial confidence of their commander-in-chief, himself the greatest captain of the age, and complimented by Governor Geary, the hero of two wars, Danville may feel an honest pride in her patriotic company, the Columbia Guards.

New members soon took the place of those who went to Mexico to find a lonely grave beneath its chaparal, and the company again assumed its old-time gaiety, under the command of Captain George W. Forrest.

After Captain Forrest removed to Lewisburg, Oscar Ephlin was chosen captain. Under his command they entered the Union army, where the brave recruits who filled the places of the veterans, had a taste of actual service. After serving their time they were honorably discharged and disbanded as a company. The elder members in Mexico, and the younger in the war for the Union, have made for themselves a record that is alike honorable to themselves and to the borough of Danville.

The flag of the old Guards, riddled and torn in the Mexican campaign, is still displayed on public occasions, and always calls forth the warmest feelings of patriotism and local pride, as its tattered fragments proclaim the heroism of the brave men who followed its beacon light through the battle and the storm. On one occasion it caught the eye and was instantly recognized by Governor Geary, while addressing a mass meeting; and none will ever forget his glowing tribute to the " old Guards," which the sight of their well-known flag inspired.

The following is the roll as mustered into the United States service, for the Mexican war :

CAPTAIN,

John S. Wilson.

LIEUTENANTS.

Clarence H. Frick,	First lieutenant.
Edward E. La Clerc,	Second lieutenant.
William Brindle, . .	. Second lieutenant.

SERGEANTS.

| George S. Kline, | First sergeant. |
| James D. Slater, | . . Second sergeant. |

Robert Clark,   Third sergeant.
Charles Evans,   Fourth sergeant.

CORPORALS.

John Adams,   . . First corporal.
James Oliver. . .   Second corporal.
John Smith, ... Third corporal.
Arthur Gearhart,   Fourth corporal.

MUSIC.

Thomas Clark.   Drummer.
Jesse G. Clark,   Fifer.

PRIVATES.

Charles W. Adams,	Jasper Musselman,
Alvin M. Allen,	Edward McGonnell,
Jacob App,	George Miller,
George W. Armstrong,	William Moser,
Frederick Brandt,	Archibald Mooney,
Samuel Burns,	Mahlon K. Manly,
Elam B. Bonham.	John G. Mallon,
William Banghart,	Alexander McDonald,
John Birkenbine.	Daniel Martial,
Samuel D. Baker,	Richard H. McKean,
Francis Bower,	Charles Moynthan,
Francis R. Best.	Robert McAlmont,
William Brunner.	Hugh McFadden,
William H. Birchfield.	James McClelland,
Randolph Ball,	Norman B. Mack,
Peter Brobst,	William McDonald,
Abram B. Carley,	Casper Oatenwelder,
Michael Corrigan,	Daniel Poorman,
William Dieterech,	Peter S. Reed.
William Erle,	Philip Rake,
Daniel S. Follmer.	James A. Stewart,
Charles W. Fortner,	Peter M. Space,
Robert H. Forster,	Jonathan R. Sanders,
Sewell Gibbs,	Oliver C. Stevens,
Edward Grove,	Daniel Snyder,

George Garner,
Thomas Graham,
Shepherd W. Girton,
Samuel Huntingdon,
Adam Heisler,
Henry Herncastle,
Oliver Helme,
William S. Kertz,
William King,
Jerome Konkle,
Charles Lytle,
Ira Lownsberry,
Robert Lyon,
John A. Lowery,
Benjamin Laform,
Benjamin J. Martin,

Edward Seler,
Peter Seigfried,
John C. Snyder,
John N. Scofield,
William Swartz,
Joseph H. Stratton,
William H. Swaney,
John A. Sarvey.
Benjamin Tumbleton.
Adam Wray,
William White,
George Wagner,
Jacob Willet,
Jerome Walker,
George Wingar,
Peter W. Yarnell.

The Columbia Guards, as an organization, are no more. But the history of their deeds will remain and will long be gratefully cherished by their fellow-citizens. Their names are recorded in the history of their country, and their fame is our own.

In the war with Mexico, the Guards were company C, in the Second regiment, Pennsylvania Volunteers, commanded by Colonel, afterwards Governor John W. Geary.

MONTOUR RIFLES.—This company was organized in Danville, on the 13th of July, 1855, under the command of Capt. J. J. Zuber. August Fogel was first lieutenant and M. Rosenstein was second lieutenant. In 1859 Capt. Zuber was promoted to a majorship and some adverse influences caused the dissolution of the company. Most of its members entered the United States service ; the greater portion enlisted in company E, Sixth regiment Reserves. The company was commanded by M. K. Manly. John Horn was one of the lieutenants of company E.

THE FIRST IN WAR.—The first military company that left Danville for the war, was recruited and commanded by Capt. William M. McClure. This company included one hundred of our boldest and bravest young men. I only regret that I can find no muster-roll of this gallant company. They enlisted for three months and honorably served their time. They were in the battle of Falling

Waters and had one member killed, whose name was Amos Zuppinger, the first soldier killed in battle ; his was the first blood shed for the Union in the civil war. Capt. McClure afterwards commanded company F, in the One Hundred and Twelfth artillery, and for brave conduct was subsequently promoted to the position of colonel of the regiment.

THE BALDY GUARDS.—This company was organized in Danville and mustered into the service of the United States on the 25th of September, 1861, under the command of Capt. Joseph F. Ramsey. The best elements of young and vigorous manhood in Danville were embodied in this company, nor did it disappoint the ardent hopes of the friends it left behind. The company was named for P. Baldy, Sr., a millionaire and an old citizen of Danville. He recognized the honor by giving *two dollars* to each member on the eve of their departure. They were attached to the Ninety-third regiment, Pennsylvania Volunteers, and were designated as company H of that regiment. Their first battle was on the Peninsula, at Williamsburg, and they subsequently were in all the sieges and battles of the army of the Potomac, until the closing scene at Appomatox. On the resignation of Capt. Ramsey in 1862, Charles W. Eckman became captain of the Baldy Guards, on the 21st of October in that year. The company, in passing through the ordeal of the war lost many of its members and when the work was done the remnant of the gallant company was honorably discharged and returned to the peaceful duties of private citizenship. The following is the roll of the Baldy Guards as the company was mustered into the service on the 25th of September, 1861 :

CAPTAIN.

Joseph F. Ramsey.

LIEUTENANTS.

| Leffred H. Kase, | First lieutenant. |
| Charles W. Eckman, | Second lieutenant. |

SERGEANTS.

M. B. Goodrich,	. . . First sergeant.
A. B. Patton,	. Second sergeant.
J. T. Howe,	. . Third sergeant.

William Young,	Fourth sergeant.
Seth C. Freeze,	. . . Fifth sergeant.

CORPORALS.

Joseph Fenstermacher,	. First corporal.
Jared Runyan, ...	Second corporal.
Joseph H. Johnston,	. . Third corporal.
Charles W. Weaver, . .	. Fourth corporal.
Orville D. Harder, ...	Fifth corporal.
Oscar Sharpless, ...	Sixth corporal.
Frederick Laubach, ...	Seventh corporal.
Silas Hartman, ...	Eighth corporal.

MUSICIANS.

L. D. Houghawout,	Joseph L. Hale.

CLERK.

Shelden T. Gibbs.

QUARTER-MASTER.

James Aubl.

TEAMSTER.

John C. Snyder.

PRIVATES.

John Ammerman,	T. H. Mench,
Joseph Bear,	J. B. Mutchler,
J. Byerly,	J. Miller,
H. C. Barnhart,	J. C. Miller,
L. S. Brocious,	J. R. Mowrer,
George Boyer,	P. McClure,
J. D. Cannady,	T. Morrall,
B. A. Cleaver.	P. Miller,
P. H. Eckman,	P. P. Osmun,
D. R. Eckman,	R. Perrin,
B. N. Gearhart,	Eli Pennsyl,
P. Everett,	J. W. Philips,
T. J. Foley,	S. Quinn.
W. Frymire,	A. Reynolds,
W. Flanigan,	C. R. Rishel,

H. F. Freese,
Charles E. Foley,
H. Fortmer,
Clark Guinn,
C. V. Gulick,
A. Goss,
William Henrie,
J. Hower,
J. Houser,
J. B. Johnson,
J. R. Johnson,
R. Jenkins,
J. Keim,
Charles Kneibeller,
G. D. Kreigh,
William Kneer,
Samuel Kurtz,
J. Lawrence,
John Levers,
Hiram Layland,
H. H. Leisenring,
J. B. Moore,
William Miller,
M. Murry,

R. Ramsey,
W. R. Rouch,
Charles L. Sholes,
Charles Stephens,
E. Shissler,
W. Slay,
J. M. Shannon,
William M. Snyder,
Charles W. Sholes,
H. F. Snyder,
William Smith,
W. Stephens,
W. W. Sechler,
J. H. Sperring,
J. Stewart,
Oscar Tittle,
W. Turner,
J. Wertz,
G. S. Walker,
A. B. Warntz,
C. Woods,
C. Wagner,
L. Yoder,
William Davis.

On the promotion of Capt. Eckman, Joseph H. Johnson was made captain, and served in command of the Baldy Guards to the close of the war.

SECOND ARTILLERY.—Company F, One Hundred and Twelfth regiment, Pennsylvania Volunteers, or Second Pennsylvania artillery, was organized in Danville, by Capt. William M. McClure. A large portion of its members were of Danville and vicinity. This regiment served with much distinction and did much hard service during the war. Among the Danville boys connected with this company were:

Samuel Strawbridge, lieutenant,   Elias Kulp,
J. Moore Wilson, lieutenant,   John McMullen,
Edward Thatcher, corporal,   Phillip Manning,
Charles Mowrer, corporal,   Martin Mazael,

John Laciscus, corporal,	Charles Mattees,
D. H. McCarty, corporal,	John Marshall,
Jonathan Bare, corporal,	Clarence Price,
Thomas Reichelderfer, bugler,	George Robison,
Robert Curry,	I. S. Smith,
Peter Cooper,	Daniel Smith,
John Farrell,	James Weidel,
J. Hendrickson,	Richard W. Eggert,
William R. Johnson,	A. J. Grantz.

DANVILLE FENCIBLES.—This company was organized in Danville, in 1862, under command of Capt. Joseph E. Shreeve. This company was in the bloody battle of Antietam and there it lost seven in killed, namely: J. M. Hassanping, D. Van Ronk, Jacob Long, Daniel Klase, Samuel Hilner, Hiram Hummel and John Gibson. Eighteen were wounded. Among the latter were James Foster, John Leighow, George Lovett, Charles Flick and D. R. Shutt. The company roll as mustered into service was as follows, and it was attached to the One Hundred and Thirty-second regiment, Pennsylvania Volunteers:

OFFICERS.

Joseph E. Shreeve, ... Captain.
George W. Vangilder. . . . . First lieutenant.
Charles N. Norris, ... Second lieutenant.

PRIVATES.

Henry B. Adams,	Jacob Long,
Sylvester W. Arnwine,	George Lovett,
Conrad L. Aten,	Samuel Langer,
Arthur W. Beaver,	Thomas Maxwell,
J. J. Bookmiller,	Leonard Mayer,
W. H. Carrell,	John McCoy,
Isaac D. Crewit,	William C. McCormick,
John M. Crist,	Jacob H. Miller,
S. E. Cooper,	Levi Miller,
Franklin Divine,	Watkin Morgan,
Samuel V. Dye,	Cornelius C. Moyer,
William Earp, junior.	Jacob W. Moyer,
James S. Easton,	James McKee,

Hiram S. Eggert,
John Ephlin,
Joseph Feidell,
Charles W. Fitzsimmons,
J. B. A. Foin,
James Foster,
Charles Flick,
Patrick Fleming.
Samuel Flickinger,
George Francis,
John Gibson,
Thomas Goodall,
A. Jerome Harder,
John M. Hassenplug,
G. K. Hassenplug,
John Harig,
Joseph Hale,
Samuel Hilner,
Alexander Huntingdon.
Hiram Hummel,
George Hunt,
William Irvin,
Thomas James,
John R. Jenkins,
James W. Jones,
Evan Jordan,
Michael Kessler,
Wellington Klase,
Michael Lanigan,
William Lawrence.
Conrad Lechthaler,
John Leighow,
N. Ferree Lightner,

William B. Neese,
Joseph H. Nevius,
James M. Philips,
David H. Rank,
Isaac Rantz,
John P. Reaser,
Simon Reedy,
Jonathan Rice,
William A. Ringler.
Edward W. Roderick,
August Schreiber,
Aaron Sechler,
Henry Schick,
David Shutt,
Edwin L. Smith,
E. Dallas Smith,
George Snyder,
John Stine.
Samuel Stall,
William Stewart,
William Sunday,
Oliver W. Switzer.
Daniel Vanronk,
Archibald Vandling,
John H. Wallace,
Samuel M. Wate,
Angus Wright.
Matthew R. Wright,
Andrew Waugh,
James D. Wray,
James Williams,
John S. Ware,

After the battle of Antietam Capt. Shreeve was promoted to major of the One Hundred and Thirty-second regiment and Charles N. Norris was made captain of the company. The company was received with great honor on its return to Danville.

COMPANY E.—Company E, Sixth Pennsylvania Reserves, was organized in Danville under command of Capt. M. K. Manly, one of the survivors of the Mexican campaign. Charles Richart and John Horn were the lieutenants. Charles Richart subsequently became captain of the company. This company passed through an ordeal of fire and shared alike the dangers and the glory of the Reserves. Among the privates in this company were William Keiner, who lost his leg ; Nicholas Freeze. killed at Harrison's Landing ; Jacob Miller, lost a foot ; Ernest Aderhold, lost a leg. There are a few others whose names can be recalled. but no trace can be found of the roll among the survivors. These are William Bottles, Gotlieb Kerchner, Raub, Ord and Snyder. The most of this company was either killed or wounded.

Our Soldiers.

The following are the soldiers who enlisted in the Federal army in the war for the Union, from 1861 to 1865. This list includes Montour county, but does not include the drafted men from either the town or the county. There may be errors in the list, but it is as correct as much patient labor could make it :

Of the number here reported, fifty-two were in the regular army and four hundred and fifty-six in the volunteer service.

ANTHONY TOWNSHIP.

John Watts, artillery.

Samuel Gray. artillery.

James Koons, One Hundred and Thirty-first Pennsylvania volunteers.

Thomas Mohr, private.

Jacob Binder, private.

William R. Johnson, company F, One Hundred and Twelfth Pennsylvania volunteers.

Jacob Robinalt, Eleventh Pennsylvania volunteers.

Samuel Robinalt, D, Seventh Pennsylvania volunteers.

Perry Watts, C, Ninety-sixth Pennsylvania volunteers.

James Candy. H, Ninety-third Pennsylvania volunteers.

Jacob Candy, H, Ninety-third Pennsylvania volunteers.

Adam Bidler, F. One Hundred and Sixth Pennsylvania volunteers.

7

COOPER TOWNSHIP.

John Kime, company H, Ninety-third Pennsylvania volunteers.

Daniel Kime, H, Ninety-third Pennsylvania volunteers.

William Miller, H, Ninety-third Pennsylvania volunteers.

Michael Breckbill, D, Seventh Pennsylvania volunteers.

Samuel Sprout, D, Seventh Pennsylvania volunteers.

Isaac Wertman, E, Twelfth Pennsylvania volunteers.

John McMullin, F, One Hundred and Twelfth Pennsylvania volunteers.

Simon Reedy, A, One Hundred and Thirty-second Pennsylvania volunteers.

A. Crossley, F, One Hundred and Twelfth Pennsylvania volunteers.

DERRY TOWNSHIP.

Thomas H. Switzer, company A, One Hundred and Thirty-first Pennsylvania volunteers.

O. B. Switzer, A, One Hundred and Thirty-first Pennsylvania volunteers.

John Gibson, A, One Hundred and Thirty-first Pennsylvania volunteers.

Peter Cooper, F, One Hundred and Twelfth Pennsylvania volunteers.

Sergeant Samuel E. Cooper, A, One Hundred and Thirty-second Pennsylvania volunteers.

Jeremiah Black, A, One Hundred and Thirty-second Pennsylvania volunteers.

James T. Powers, G, Eighth Pennsylvania volunteers.

Newson L. Sagess, D, Seventh Pennsylvania volunteers.

John Dugan, D, Seventh Pennsylvania volunteers.

Frank G. Blee, A, One Hundred and Thirty-second Pennsylvania volunteers.

W. W. Switzer, G, Fourth Pennsylvania volunteers.

David Gibson, One Hundred and Sixteenth Pennsylvania volunteers.

Philip Springer, E, Sixth Pennsylvania reserves.

William C. McCay, D, Seventh Pennsylvania volunteers.

Samuel Fleckinger, A, One Hundred and Thirty-second Pennsylvania volunteers.

Joel Metz, E, Sixth Pennsylvania reserves.

Corporal George Snyder, A, One Hundred and Thirty-second Pennsylvania volunteers.

J. P. Bearer. A. One Hundred and Thirty-second Pennsylvania volunteers.

DANVILLE, NORTH WARD.

Franklin Lewis, Eighty-fourth Pennsylvania volunteers.

Samuel M. Wate, company A, One Hundred and Thirty-second Pennsylvania volunteers.

Gomer Jones, K, Fifth Pennsylvania volunteers.

Joseph R. Patton, band, One Hundred and Sixth Pennsylvania volunteers.

Charles M. Zuber, band, One Hundred and Sixth Pennsylvania volunteers.

J. C. Millhouse, band, Fifty-first Pennsylvania volunteers.

Fred Laubach, H. Ninety-third Pennsylvania volunteers.

Captain J. F. Ramsey, H, Ninety-third Pennsylvania volunteers.

Thomas Wenck, H, Seventh Pennsylvania volunteers.

Augustus Shriver, A, One Hundred and Thirty-second Pennsylvania volunteers.

Nathaniel Everhart, H, Ninety-third Pennsylvania volunteers.

Martin Taylor, Twelfth United States.

William H. Rouch, H, Ninety-third Pennsylvania volunteers.

Clarence Price, F, One Hundred and Twelfth Pennsylvania volunteers.

Alfred B. Patton, H, Ninety-third Pennsylvania volunteers.

George Francis, A, One Hundred and Thirty-second Pennsylvania volunteers.

Jared Runyan, H, Ninety-third Pennsylvania volunteers.

John L. Miller, H, Ninety-third Pennsylvania volunteers.

William M. Miller, Twelfth United States.

Stephen Johnson, E, Fourth New York volunteers.

William Turner, H, Ninety-third Pennsylvania volunteers.

Israel Wertz, H, Ninety-third Pennsylvania volunteers.

William Horff, E, Sixth Pennsylvania reserves.

Reuben Ramsey, H, Ninety-second Pennsylvania volunteers.

John Miller, E, Sixth Pennsylvania volunteers.

James Bailor, Twelfth United States.

Harman Bailor, Twelfth United States.

Peter Bailor, Twelfth United States.

Samuel S. Gulick, A, One hundred and Thirty-second Pennsylvania volunteers.

Jacob Bookmiller, A, One Hundred and Thirty-second Pennsylvania volunteers.

Andrew Waugh, A, One Hundred and Thirty-second Pennsylvania volunteers.

George Focht, E, Ninth Pennsylvania reserves.

Captain M. K. Manly, E, Ninth Pennsylvania reserves.

John Byerly, H, Ninety-third Pennsylvania volunteers.

Isaac Barto, F, Forty-eighth Pennsylvania volunteers.

James R. Johnson, H, Ninety-third Pennsylvania volunteers.

David H. McCarty, F, One Hundred and Twelfth Pennsylvania volunteers.

William H. Miller, E, Fifty-fourth Pennsylvania volunteers.

Levi M. Miller, A, One Hundred and Thirty-second Pennsylvania volunteers.

S. E. Ridgway, F, Mathew's battery.

Charles Kneibler, H, Ninety-third Pennsylvania volunteers.

David R. Shutt, A, One Hundred and Thirty-second Pennsylvania volunteers.

Thomas James, A, One Hundred and Thirty-second Pennsylvania volunteers.

Francis Trees, Sixty ninth Pennsylvania volunteers.

James Burns, Pennsylvania volunteers.

John Nester, Pennsylvania volunteers.

Patrick Tenenty, Pennsylvania volunteers.

Charles Eckhart, band, One Hundred and Sixth Pennsylvania volunteers.

J. B. A. Foin, A, One Hundred and Thirty-second Pennsylvania volunteers.

Nicholas Freeze, E, Sixth Pennsylvania volunteers.

Daniel Klase, A, One Hundred and Thirty-second Pennsylvania volunteers.

James Moore, H, Ninety-third Pennsylvania volunteers.

Joseph Heffer, D, Seventeenth Pennsylvania volunteers.

William C. Heffler, E, One Hundred and Twelfth Pennsylvania
volunteers.

William F. Deshay, Twelfth United States.

John L. Deshay, Twelfth United States.

John Wood, Sixty-ninth Pennsylvania volunteers.

Evan Jordan. Fifteenth United States.

Elijah Fields, C, Twelfth United States.

Robert Fields. C, Twelfth United States.

Aaron Gibson, E, Sixth Pennsylvania reserves.

John F. Mullen, E. Twelfth United States.

Richard Jenkins, A, Third Maryland volunteers.

Josiah Robinson, G, Third Maryland volunteers.

James Auld, H. Ninety-third Pennsylvania volunteers.

William Davis, H, Ninety-third Pennsylvania volunteers.

Reese Davis, A. Fifty-fourth Pennsylvania volunteers.

William Price, H, Ninety-third Pennsylvania volunteers.

Angus Wright, A, One Hundred and Thirty-second Pennsylvania
volunteers.

Mathew R. Wright, A, One Hundred and Thirty-second Pennsylvania volunteers.

James Stewart, D, Sixty-ninth Pennsylvania volunteers.

Charles L. Sholes, H. Ninety-third Pennsylvania volunteers.

Thomas Goodall, A. One Hundred and Thirty-second Pennsylvania
volunteers.

William Davis, A. One Hundred and Thirty-second Pennsylvania
volunteers.

John Morris, A, One Hundred and Thirty-second Pennsylvania
volunteers.

Peter Green. D. Sixty-ninth Pennsylvania volunteers.

F. Finnegan. D, Sixty-ninth Pennsylvania volunteers.

Thomas McManus, D, Sixty-ninth Pennsylvania volunteers.

Patrick Hardy, United States regulars.

William Finnegan, United States regulars.

George Lovett. A, One Hundred and Thirty-second Pennsylvania
volunteers.

Samuel Ricketts, G, Third Maryland volunteers.

George Hacker, A, One Hundred and Thirty-second Pennsylvania
volunteers.

George Bingham, E. Sixth Pennsylvania reserves.

Thomas W. Levers, E. Sixth Pennsylvania reserves.

William Ringham, Thirteenth Pennsylvania volunteers.

Adam Hernberger, A. One hundred and Thirty-second Pennsylvania volunteers.

John Levers, H. Ninety-third Pennsylvania volunteers.

John Boyer, I. Fifty-second Pennsylvania volunteers.

Jonathan Davis, I. Fifty-second Pennsylvania volunteers.

Samuel Bryant, I, Fifty-second Pennsylvania volunteers.

Michael Hurley, I. Fifty-second Pennsylvania volunteers.

Daniel Van Ronk, A, One Hundred and Thirty-second Pennsylvania volunteers.

Seth C. Freeze, H, Ninety-third Pennsylvania volunteers.

Sheldon T. Gibbs, H, Ninety-third Pennsylvania volunteers.

Franklin Devine, A. One Hundred and Thirty-second Pennsylvania volunteers.

Robert Wood, F, Forty-eighth Pennsylvania volunteers.

Richard Hopkins, F, Forty-Eighth Pennsylvania volunteers.

John Stine, A, One Hundred and Thirty-second Pennsylvania volunteers.

John Sheldon, H. Sixth Pennsylvania volunteers.

Frank Kneidt, F. Matthew's battery.

Jacob Haag, F, Matthew's battery.

James Henegan, D. Sixty-ninth Pennsylvania volunteers.

John McDonald, D. Sixty ninth Pennsylvania volunteers.

Patrick Conners, D. Sixty-ninth Pennsylvania volunteers.

James Williams, A, One Hundred and Thirty-second Pennsylvania volunteers.

Richard Grogan, K. One Hundred and Sixth Pennsylvania volunteers.

William Paugh, D. Sixty-ninth Pennsylvania volunteers.

Michael Kessler, A. One Hundred and Thirty-second Pennsylvania volunteers.

Thomas Kennedy, D. Fifth Pennsylvania volunteers.

James Kennedy, D, Sixty-ninth Pennsylvania volunteers.

John Ephlin, Twenty-eighth Pennsylvania volunteers.

Thomas Lafferty, D. Sixty-ninth Pennsylvania volunteers.

John Burns, D. Sixty-ninth Pennsylvania volunteers.

Patrick Burns, D, Sixty-ninth Pennsylvania volunteers.

Terrence O'Niel, D, Sixty-ninth Pennsylvania volunteers.

Thomas Smith, Pennsylvania volunteers.

Charles Rogers, Pennsylvania volunteers.

John Reed, Pennsylvania volunteers.

James Moran, Pennsylvania volunteers.

Patrick Kelley, Pennsylvania volunteers.

John Greeny, Pennsylvania volunteers.

James McCarty, Pennsylvania volunteers.

Hugh Biadly, Pennsylvania volunteers.

Frank Burns, Pennsylvania volunteers.

James Ellitt, Pennsylvania volunteers.

Thomas Coughlin, Pennsylvania volunteers.

John Paugh, Fifth United States.

Philip Renn, Twelfth United States.

James Eastin, A, One Hundred and Thirty-second Pennsylvania volunteers.

Thomas Davis, H, Seventh Pennsylvania volunteers.

Evan Edwards, E, Fifty-fourth Pennsylvania volunteers.

John Jordon, E, Fifty-fourth Pennsylvania volunteers.

George Morris, E, Fifty-fourth Pennsylvania.

Patrick O'Connor, D, Sixty-ninth Pennsylvania volunteers.

William Weidall, B, One Hundred and Sixth Pennsylvania volunteers.

Watkin Morgan, A, One Hundred and Thirty second Pennsylvania volunteers.

Charles McMullen, C, Sixty-ninth Pennsylvania volunteers.

Isaac Kear, E, Fifth United States.

Abram Price, E, Sixth Pennsylvania reserves.

Isaac Rantz, A, One Hundred and Thirty-second Pennsylvania volunteers.

Peter Connell, E, One Hundred and First Pennsylvania volunteers.

Mathias Veraskoski, Forty-sixth Pennsylvania volunteers.

John Price, Sixty-third Pennsylvania volunteers.

John Huntingdon, C, Fourteenth Pennsylvania volunteers.

Philip Effinger, K, Fifty-second New York volunteers.

Martin Mazella, F, One Hundred and Twelfth Pennsylvania volunteers.

Henry Agga, D, First Pennsylvania volunteers.

Jonathan Rice, A, One Hundred and Thirty-second Pennsylvania volunteers.

Conrad Lichthaler, A, One Hundred and Thirty-second Pennsylvania volunteers.

Joseph Hale, A, One Hundred and Thirty-second Pennsylvania volunteers.

Philip McClure, H, Ninety-third Pennsylvania volunteers.

Francis Hafey, One Hundred and Ninth Pennsylvania volunteers.

William McClean, D, One Hundred and Ninth Pennsylvania volunteers.

Philip Evert, H, Ninety-third Pennsylvania volunteers.

H. F. Freeze, H, Ninety-third Pennsylvania volunteers.

Charles V. Gulick, H, Ninety-third Pennsylvania volunteers.

Mathias Fish, Fifth Pennsylvania volunteers.

John Doyle, D, Sixty-ninth Pennsylvania volunteers.

Robert McCoy, A, One Hundred and Thirty-second Pennsylvania volunteers.

Arthur W. Beaver, A, One Hundred and Thirty-second Pennsylvania volunteers.

Joseph Bryant, K, Fifty-fourth Pennsylvania volunteers.

Isaac D. Crewit, A, One Hundred and Thirty-second Pennsylvania volunteers.

Dennis Leary, D, Sixty-ninth Pennsylvania volunteers.

Owen Burns, D, Sixty-ninth Pennsylvania volunteers.

William Smith, D, Sixty-ninth Pennsylvania volunteers.

Stephen Sullivan, D, Sixty-ninth Pennsylvania volunteers.

John McWilliams, D, Sixty-ninth Pennsylvania volunteers.

John Marshall, E, One Hundred and Twelfth Pennsylvania volunteers.

Martin Murray, H, Ninety-third Pennsylvania volunteers.

Samuel Quinn, H, Ninety-third Pennsylvania volunteers.

Richard Lanigan, A, Fifth Pennsylvania volunteers.

James Quinn, A, Fifth Pennsylvania volunteers.

William Thomas, E, Fifty-fourth Pennsylvania volunteers.

Richard Jenkins, H, Ninety-third Pennsylvania volunteers.

James Foster, A, One Hundred and Thirty-second Pennsylvania volunteers.

William Stewart, A. One Hundred and Thirty-second Pennsylvania volunteers.

Patrick Riddles, D, Sixty-ninth Pennsylvania volunteers.

Henry Bogart, E, Twelfth United States.

William Markle, E, Twelfth United States.

John Mintzer, E, Twelfth United States.

George Kear, E, Fifth United States.

Isaac Melon, Twelfth United States.

John Bubb, E, Twelfth United States.

Michael O'Gorman, B, Fifth United States.

Caleb Roberts, E, Twelfth United States.

Lieutenant John Horn, E, Sixth Pennsylvania reserves.

William Keiner, E, Sixth Pennsylvania reserves.

Joseph Walton, E, Sixth Pennsylvania reserves.

John McKone, G, Fifty-seventh New York volunteers.

John Roberts, G, Third Maryland volunteers.

Richard W. Eggert, F, One Hundred and Twelfth Pennsylvania volunteers.

Adam J. Grantz, F, One Hundred and Twelfth Pennsylvania volunteers.

DANVILLE, SOUTH WARD.

Captain Joseph E. Shreve, company A, One Hundred and Thirty-second Pennsylvania volunteers.

George W. Hoffman, band, One Hundred and Sixth Pennsylvania volunteers.

R. S. Simington, surgeon, Ninety-third Pennsylvania volunteers.

William Young, H. Ninety-third Pennsylvania volunteers.

William W. Sechler, H, Ninety-third Pennsylvania volunteers.

Joseph Johnson, H, Ninety-third Pennsylvania volunteers.

Charles Mummey, D, Eighty-fourth Pennsylvania volunteers.

Oscar G. Mellin, band, Fourth Pennsylvania reserves.

Charles Gross, band, One Hundred and Sixth Pennsylvania reserves.

Harman Leiby, H, Ninety-third Pennsylvania reserves.

William A, Mellin, E, Twelfth Pennsylvania reserves.

Joseph Hale, H, Ninety-third Pennsylvania reserves.

Charles Smith, A, One Hundred and Thirty-second Pennsylvania reserves.

Archie Vandling, A, One Hundred and Thirty-second Pennsylvania reserves.

John McCoy, A, One Hundred and Thirty-second Pennsylvania reserves.

David Keffer, Thirteenth Pennsylvania reserves.

Henry Adams, A, One Hundred and Thirty-second Pennsylvania reserves.

W. Forest, D, Seventh Pennsylvania reserves.

Samuel Lunger, A, One Hundred and Thirty-second Pennsylvania reserves.

Thomas E. Frame, E, First Pennsylvania reserves.

James Corcoran, D, Seventy-sixth Pennsylvania reserves.

Arthur F. Henrie, band, Sixth Pennsylvania reserves.

Thomas Adams, Sixth Pennsylvania reserves.

Lieutenant Charles C. Norris, A, One Hundred and Thirty-second Pennsylvania volunteers.

Lieutenant M. B. Goodrich, H, Ninety-third Pennsylvania volunteers.

Andrew Derry, artillery, Ninety-third Pennsylvania volunteers.

James Shepherd, H, Seventh Pennsylvania volunteers.

William Nago, D, Eleventh Pennsylvania volunteers.

John Wallace, A, One Hundred and Thirty-second Pennsylvania volunteers.

William Earp, A, One Hundred and Thirty-second Pennsylvania volunteers.

William L. Snyder.

Conrad S. Aten, A, One Hundred and Thirty-second Pennsylvania volunteers.

Henry J. Aten, band, One Hundred and Sixth Pennsylvania volunteers.

George Dean, band, Sixth Pennsylvania volunteers.

Wellington Klase, A, One Hundred and Thirty-second Pennsylvania volunteers.

Daniel Klase, A, One Hundred and Thirty-second Pennsylvania volunteers.

William Kelly.

Jacob Moyer, A, One Hundred and Thirty-second Pennsylvania volunteers.

Samuel A. Mills, band, Sixth Pennsylvania reserves.

William Mitting, Seventh Pennsylvania volunteers.

Thomas Morrall, H, Ninety-third Pennsylvania volunteers.

Sharps M. Snyder, A, One Hundred and Thirty-second Pennsylvania volunteers.

James D. Ray, A, One Hundred and Thirty-second Pennsylvania volunteers.

Benjamin F. Hagenbach, band, Sixth Pennsylvania reserves.

David Ross, L, Twelfth Pennsylvania volunteers.

John Ware, A, One Hundred and Thirty-second Pennsylvania volunteers.

Joseph L. Frame, band, Ninety-third Pennsylvania volunteers.

Hiram Eggert, A, One Hundred and Thirty Second Pennsylvania volunteers.

Edward Milward, G, Seventy-seventh Pennsylvania volunteers.

George C. Williams, E, Sixth Pennsylvania reserves.

Henry Laland, H, Ninety-third Pennsylvania volunteers.

D. A. Laland.

Lieutenant William Roberts, G, One Hundred and Ninth Pennsylvania volunteers.

Lieutenant Abraham Lang, I, One Hundred and Ninth Pennsylvania volunteers.

James Jones, A, One Hundred and Thirty-second Pennsylvania volunteers.

William Williams, I, Twelfth Pennsylvania volunteers.

William Watts, I, Twelfth Pennsylvania volunteers.

Joseph Fenstermacher, H, Ninety-third Pennsylvania volunteers.

Frederick Brodt, H, Ninety-third Pennsylvania volunteers.

J. Houpt, Forty-ninth Pennsylvania volunteers.

E. D. Smith, A, One Hundred and Thirty-second Pennsylvania volunteers.

Corporal N. Ferree Lightner, A, One Hundred and Thirty-second Pennsylvania volunteers.

S. P. Harder, F, Mathew's battery.

O. D. Harder, H, Ninety-third Pennsylvania volunteers.

John T. Howe, H, Ninety-third Pennsylvania volunteers.

Charles W. Sholes, H, Ninety-third Pennsylvania volunteers.

George E. Hunt, A, Ninety-third Pennsylvania volunteers.

Charles Savage, Jr., F, Mathew's battery.

Joseph D. Miller, H, Ninety-third Pennsylvania volunteers.

Samuel Hibler, H, Seventh Pennsylvania volunteers.

John W. Hibler, Fifty-fourth Pennsylvania volunteers.

Edwin Lockart, E, Sixth Pennsylvania reserves.

George Yeomans, surgeon, Twenty-third Pennsylvania reserves.

Herber Painter, I, Fifty-eighth Pennsylvania reserves.

Gutlep Kercher, E, Sixth Pennsylvania reserves.

James Hilt, Pennsylvania volunteers.

George Archer, E, Seventy-fourth Pennsylvania volunteers.

Henry H. Leisenring, H, Ninety-third Pennsylvania volunteers.

Alexander Culp, Artillery, Ninety-third Pennsylvania volunteers.

James G. Moore, D, Eighty-fourth Pennsylvania volunteers.

Lieutenant G. W. Vangilder, A, One Hundred and Thirty-second
    Pennsylvania volunteers.

John Stewart, H, Ninety-third Pennsylvania volunteers.

Samuel Kerst, H, Ninety-third Pennsylvania volunteers.

William Stephnagle, H, Ninety-third Pennsylvania volunteers.

Charles Stephnagle, H, Ninety-third Pennsylvania volunteers.

J. W. Flannagan, H, Ninety-third Pennsylvania volunteers.

Joseph Gross, E, First Pennsylvania volunteers.

Marks Wise, I, Twelfth Pennsylvania volunteers.

Jacob Sperring, H, Ninety-third Pennsylvania volunteers.

Alfred Reynolds, H, Ninety-third Pennsylvania volunteers.

Captain Alexander J. Frick, D, Eighty-fourth Pennsylvania volun-
    teers.

Captain William M. McClure, F, One Hundred and Twelfth Penn-
    sylvania volunteers.

Lieutenant S. D. Strawbridge, F, One Hundred and Twelfth Penn-
    sylvania volunteers.

Pursival Miller, H, Ninety-third Pennsylvania volunteers.

Thomas Maxwell, A, One Hundred and Thirty-second Pennsylva-
    nia volunteers.

Robert D. Magill, steward.

John G. Moore, band, Fifth Pennsylvania reserves.

Christopher Woods, band, Sixth Pennsylvania reserves.

Simon Derlacher, H, Sixth Pennsylvania reserves.

Joseph Rose, E, Sixth Pennsylvania reserves.

Abner H. Brown, band, Sixth Pennsylvania reserves.

William Ackey, E, Sixth Pennsylvania reserves.
George Deen, E, Sixth Pennsylvania reserves.
M. B. Johnson, E, Sixth Pennsylvania reserves.
George Hughes.
Samuel May.

LIMESTONE TOWNSHIP.

John T. Newcomer, company D, Seventh Pennsylvania volunteers.
F. J. Newcomer, D, Seventh Pennsylvania volunteers.
Martin Keifer, D, Seventh Pennsylvania volunteers.
William Dinkle, C, Third Pennsylvania volunteers.
William Fink.
David Werlty, One Hundred and Thirty-first Pennsylvania volunteers.
Charles F. Bennett, United States regulars.
Luke S. Brass, K, Ninty-fifth Pennsylvania volunteers.
Charles E. Wagner, D, Seventh Pennsylvania volunteers.
Hiram Wertman, D, Seventh Pennsylvania volunteers.
Jacob Smith, One Hundred and Thirty-first Pennsylvania volunteers.
William Keifer, D, Seventh Pennsylvania volunteers.
Thomas Kersteller.
Daniel G. Dildine, D, Seventh Pennsylvania volunteers.
Jacob O. Caldwell, H, Fifth Pennsylvania volunteers.
Conrad Springer, E, Six Pennsylvania reserves.
Daniel F. Wagoner, D, Seventh Pennsylvania volunteers.
Samuel V. Dye, A, One Hundred and Thirty-second Pennsylvania volunteers.
Charles Balliet, D, Seventh Pennsylvania volunteers.
Daniel Rank, D, Seventh Pennsylvania volunteers.
James Bryson, Captain, D, Seventh Pennsylvania volunteers.
W. Caldwell, D, Seventh Pennsylvania volunteers.
Jacob Balliet, D, Seventh Pennsylvania volunteers.
Joseph D. Fulton, D, Seventh Pennsylvania volunteers.
—— Carnthan, D, Seventh Pennsylvania volunteers.
C. W. Fitszimmons, A, One Hundred and Thirty-second Pennsylvania volunteers.

LIBERTY TOWNSHIP.

Charles F. Bennett, company E, Twelfth regulars.

Reuben Bennett, E, Twelfth regulars.

William C. Best, H, Fifty-third Pennsylvana volunteers.

J. P. Bare, F, One Hundred and Twelfth Pennsylvania volunteers.

Martin Bower, K, Fifty-first Pennsylvania volunteers.

John McElrath, F, One Hundred and Twelfth Pennsylvania volunteers.

Robert Curry, One Hundred and Thirty-second, Pennsylvania volunteers.

William Clark, F, One Hundred and Twelfth Pennsylvania volunteers.

Jacob Hendrickson, One Hundred and Twenty-first Pennsylvania volunteers.

Emanuel Kertz,

Jacob Johnston, E, Sixth Pennsylyania volunteers.

Jacob Long, A, One Hundred and Thirty-second Pennsylvania volunteers.

John Marshal, F, One Hundred and Twelfth Pennsylvania volunteers.

James L. Miller, H, Fifty-third Pennsylvania volunteers.

C. Marshal, E, Sixth Pennsylvania reserves.

R. F. Nesbit, H, Twelfth regulars.

John Perry, E, Twelfth Pennsylvania volunteers.

Richard Rozel, K, Eleventh Pennsylvania volunteers.

Z. Robinalt, H, Fifty-third Pennsylvania volunteers.

Simon Springer, H, Fifty-third Pennsylvania volunteers.

J. S. Smith, F, One Hundred and Twelfth Pennsylvania volunteers.

Levi B. Schock, One Hundred and Thirty-first Pennsylvania volunteers.

Michael Thornton, H, Fifty-third Pennsylvania volunteers.

MAHONING TOWNSHIP.

John Stineman, Fourth New York volunteers.

Peter McAfee, company E, Sixth Pennsylvania reserves.

Joshua McAfee, Fifty-second Pennsylvania volunteers.

Charles Flick, E, One Hundred and Thirty-second Pennsylvania volunteers.

Charles Waters, 1, Fifty-second Pennsylvania volunteers.

Samuel Gray, F, Mathew's Battery.

John Watts, F, Mathew's Battery.

Charles Rishel, H, Ninty-third Pennsylvania volunteers.

Christian Wager, E, Sixth Pensylvania reserves.

Abram Voris, E, Sixth Pennsylvania reserves.

John Campbell, F, Mathew's Battery.

Henry Bogar.

William Turvey, E, Fifty-third Pennsylvania volunteers.

Daniel Turvey, E, Fifty-third Pennsylvania volunteers.

Henry Vincent, A, One Hundred and Thirty-second Pennsylvania volunteers.

Thomas Jones, A, One Hundred and Thirty-second Pennsylvania volunteers.

Michael Rouch, D, Sixty-ninth Pennsylvania volunteers.

Philip Cassiday, A.

William Edmunds, A, Sixty ninth Pennsylvania volunteers

William Smith, H, Ninety-third Pennsylvania volunteers.

John R. Mowerer, H, Ninety-third Pennsylvania volunteers.

Aaron Sechler, A, One Hundred and Thirty-second Pennsylvania volunteers.

John Leighow, H, One Hundred and Thirty-second Pennsylvania volunteers.

Jacob Sanders, D, Sixty-first Pennsylvania volunteers.

Charles Mowerer, F, One Hundred and Twelfth Pennsylvania volunteers.

Henry S. Neuss, F, Mathew's Battery.

George W. Mowerer, F, Mathew's Battery.

Henry Wireman, F, Mathew's Battery.

John H. Christian, F, Mathew's Battery.

Charles Shipman, F, Mathew's Battery.

J. W. Houser, E, Twelfth Pennsylvania volunteers.

John Houser, H, Ninty-third Pennsylvania volunteers.

Joseph Robey, E, Twelfth Pennsylvania volunteers.

James M. Philips, A, One Hundred and Thirty-second Pennsylvania volunteers.

H. Kostenhacker, E, Sixth Pennsylvania reserves.

David D. Moser, E, Twelfth Pennsylvania volunteers.

Alfred Roberts, D, Seventh Pennsylvania volunteers.

Thomas H. Sanders, D, Seventh Pennsylvania volunteers.

William A. Fetter, D, Seventh Pennsylvania volunteers.

G. W. Robinson, F, One Hundred and Twelfth Pennsylvania volunteers.

John Bubb, E, Twelfth Pennsylvania volunteers.

Benjamin Rudy, teamster.

MAYBERRY TOWNSHIP.

Joseph R. Mutchler, company H, Ninty-third Pennsylvania volunteers.

Samuel Hilner, A, One Hundred and Thirty-second Pennsylvania volunteers.

William Miller, H, Ninety-third Pennsylvania volunteers.

P. P. Osburn, H, Ninety-third Pennsylvania volunteers.

Joseph Long, A, Ninety-third Pennsylvania volunteers.

William Hanly, Forty-sixth Pennsylvania volunteers.

Joseph Simmeason, Forty-sixth Pennsylvania volunteers.

M. Ely, One Hundred and Thirty-first Pennsylvania volunteers.

VALLEY TOWNSHIP.

Dennis Bright, Lieutenant.

Joseph Rowes, E, Sixth Pennsylvania reserves.

Hiram Humel, A, One Hundred and Thirty-second Pennsylvania volunteers.

Henry F. Snyder, H, Ninety-second Pennsylvania volunteers.

Alpheus D. Ott, E, Sixth Pensylvania reserves.

W. B. Neese, A, One Hundred and Thirty-Second Pennsylvania volunteers.

William Sunday, A, One Hundred and Thirty-second Pennsylvania volunteers.

Philip Evart, H, Ninety-third Pennsylvania volunteers.

Charles H. Rishel, H, Ninety-third Pennsylvania volunteers.

Stephen L. Rush, F, Fifty-fourth Pennsylvania volunteers.

Lieutenant J. Moore Wilson, F, One Hundred and Twelfth Pennsylvania volunteers.

P. Maning, Jr., F, One Hundred and Twelfth Pennsylvania volunteers.

Jonas Roup, E, Sixth Pennsylvania reserves.

George S. Walker, H, Ninety-third Pennsylvania volunteers.

Edwin Thatcher, F, One Hundred and Twelfth Pennsylvania volunteers.

Daniel Miles, D, Sixty-ninth Pennsylvania volunteers.

Richard Riddle, E, Twelfth Pennsylvania volunteers.

Joseph Fagles, A, One Hundred and Thirty-Second Pennsylvania volunteers.

John Wood, D, Sixty-Ninth Pennsylvania volunteers.

James Thomas, D, Sixty-Ninth Pennsylvania volunteers.

C. West, F, Fifty-fourth Pennsylvania volunteers.

John Boyer, F, Fifty-fourth Pennsylvania volunteers.

William M. Snyder, teamster.

David Henrickson, A, One Hundred and Thirty-second Pennsylvania volunteers.

Amos Appleman, A, One Hundred and Thirty-second Pennsylvania volunteers.

Thomas Welliver, E, Sixth Pennsylvania reserves.

Evan Jordan, E, Twelfth Pennsylvania volunteers.

William Stephens, E, Fifty-third Pennsylvania volunteers.

WEST HEMLOCK TOWNSHIP.

Joseph Weidel, company F, One Hundred and Twelfth Pennsylvania volunteers.

Oscar Tittle, H, Ninety-third Pennsylvania volunteers.

Martin Tarner, G, Eleventh Michigan volunteers.

George W. Crossly, H, One Hundred and Fifth Pennsylvania volunteers.

Sylvester W. Arnwine, A, One Hundred and Thirty-second Pennsylvania volunteers.

William H. Correll, A, One Hundred and Thirty-second Pennsylvania volunteers.

B. F. Heilman, E, Sixth Pennsylvania reserves.

Thomas Welliver, E, Sixth Pennsylvania reserves.

8

RECAPITULATION.

Townships.	Enrolled.	In Service.
Anthony, ...	157	13
Cooper, ...	79	10
Derry, ...	141	19
Danville, North ward, ...	868	197
Danville, South ward, ...	623	127
Limestone, ...	158	26
Liberty, ...	191	25
Mahoning, ...	170	45
Mayberry, ...	46	9
Valley, ...	162	29
West Hemlock, ...	60	8
	2,264	508

ADDITIONS.

Surgeon J. D. Strawbridge, Army of the Cumberland.

William L. Jones, company H, Ninety-third Pennsylvania volunteers.

J. C. Sylvis, I, Twelfth Pennsylvania cavalry.

Isaac Mellin, United States army.

E. K. Hale, band, One Hundred and Twelfth Pennsylvania volunteers.

Charles Ely, Third Maryland volunteers.

Samuel Roberts, Third Maryland volunteers.

J. S. Hale, H, Third Maryland volunteers.

Captain G. W. Reay, Third Maryland volunteers.

Ed. Watkins, Third Maryland volunteers.

George Danks, Third Maryland volunteers.

Moses Gibbons, Third Maryland volunteers.

William Gibbons, Third Maryland volunteers.

William Roberts, Third Maryland volunteers.

Andrew H. Brown, Twelfth Pennsylvania cavalry.

William O. Butler.

I. T. Patton, C, One Hundred and Eighty-seventh Pennsylvania volunteers.

Lieutenant David Ware.

Charles Ware.

William Ware.

J. D. Ware, One Hundred and Eighty-seventh Pennsylvania volunteers.

Benton B. Brown, C, One Hundred and Eighty-seventh Pennsylvania volunteers.

George Tillson, Two Hundred and Tenth Pennsylvania volunteers.

Frank Finegan.

John McGuire.

James M. Irland, E, Ninth Pennsylvania cavalry.

Reese H. Flanegan, One Hundred and Eighty-seventh Pennsylvania volunteers.

Thomas McManus.

Lieutenant M. Rosenstein, Sixth Pennsylvania reserves.

Isaiah Devers, H, Eleventh Pennsylvania volunteers.

John Clave, H, Eleventh Pennsylvania volunteers.

Patrick Rollan, H, Eleventh Pennsylvania volunteers.

Peter Yerrick, H, Eleventh Pennsylvania volunteers.

Ad. Ray, H, Eleventh Pennsylvania volunteers.

Jonathan Waters, H, Eleventh Pennsylvania volunteers.

John Clark, H, Eleventh Pennsylvania volunteers.

Matthias Murray, H, Eleventh Pennsylvania volunteers.

John Lee, H, Eleventh Pennsylvania volunteers.

Moses Gibbons, H, Eleventh Pennsylvania volunteers.

Edward Cuthbert, H, Eleventh Pennsylvania volunteers.

Thomas Stoddart, H, Eleventh Pennsylvania volunteers.

John Robinson, H, Eleventh Pennsylvania volunteers.

Frederick Harris, H, Eleventh Pennsylvania volunteers.

William Millner, H, Eleventh Pennsylvania volunteers.

Isaac Devers, H, Eleventh Pennsylvania volunteers.

E. O. Ridgway, H, Eleventh Pennsylvania volunteers.

Warren M. Ridgway, C, One Hundred and Eighty-seventh Pennsylvania volunteers.

Amos Suppinger, H, Eleventh Pennsylvania reserves.

[The last named was the first Danville soldier killed in the war.]

Thirteenth Regiment, Pennsylvania Volunteer Militia.

Among the gallant soldiers who volunteered for the common defense, the Thirteenth regiment must not be forgotten. I belonged

to that regiment and I am proud of it.   We had a fighting colonel,
and "our captain was as brave a man as e'er commission bore."
When a portion of the rebel army crossed Mason and Dixon's line, we
joined our friends and neighbors to repel the invasion.   The excite-
ment was great on the occasion.   The whole town of Danville was
in commotion.   All day on Sunday, squads were hurrying to and
fro, the yeomanry were rallying on every side.   The fife and drum
broke strangely on the usual stillness of the Sabbath, and the national flag proudly floated in the autumn breeze.   Soon two companies were organized, one under Captain John A. Winner, and the
other under Captain William Young.   Both had seen active service,
and the latter had been wounded in the side at one of the battles on
the Penisula.   On Monday, the 16th of September, 1862, while the
battle of Antietam was raging near the border, we were crowded
into freight cars, and, amid the wild huzzas of our neighbors and
the hurried good bye of our families, we departed for the scene of
deadly strife.   At Georgetown we had a little unpleasantness with
some lunatics full of benzine, and there the first blood was shed
from the nasal organ of a home guard.   At Harrisburg we camped
on the capitol ground and slept quite cosily under the trees, between the capitol building and the executive department.   Some of
the boys wandered through the city until the regulation hour had
passed, but before daylight all were under the blankets.   Being
fully armed and equipped and with forty rounds, and rations for
an indefinite time, we took the train on the Cumberland Valley
railroad and sped toward "My Maryland."   At Carlisle we halted
about twenty minutes, and the good people there, in their gratitude
towards us in so promptly coming to their defense, served us with
a lunch, including hot coffee and various delicacies.   It then occurred to some one that the ladies should be thanked for the kindness they manifested towards us.   To this duty I was unanimously
called, upon which William T. Ramsey and John H. Hunt placed
a board across a mortar box some two feet high, and urged me on
the frail platform.   I began, "Ladies of Carlisle—" at that in-
stant the board broke, and down I went into the mortar !   That
ended the speech, and I hastily crawled out of the artistic mud and
made for the cars.   It was a short speech, but it was greeted with
a perfect "storm" of applause, not so much on account of the senti-

ment expressed, but on account of the gestures—they were so natural, and that is one of the highest points in oratory. The speech was also remarkable for its brevity, and I have often thought it were well if a plank would break more frequently and cut off some other speeches as briefly. I am aware that there is a counterfeit version of this episode in circulation, but don't you believe a word of it.

At daylight we reached Hagerstown, and it is worthy of note, that ours was the first regiment of minute men that reached the line of defense. The following is the roster of the gallant Thirteenth:

Regimental Officers.

Colonel—James Johnson.
Lieutenant Colonel—J. F. Means.
Major—S. H. Newman.
Adjutant—J. W. Chamberlin.
Sergeant Major—B. S. Powers.
Quartermaster—J. W. McKelvy.
Surgeon—Dr. Reiber.
Assistant Surgeon—Dr. Vandersloot.
Drum Major—B. W. Mussleman.
Hospital Steward—Dr. I. Pursell.
Ward Master—William W. Hays.
Chaplain—Benjamin G. Welch.
—*Postmaster*—Wilbur G. Brower.
Colonel's Clerk—Alex. M. Russel.

Muster Roll, Company A, 13th Regiment P. V. M.

Captain—John A. Winner.
Lieutenants—First, W. A. M. Grier; second, John C. Perrin.
Sergeants—First, John G. Hammer; second, Simon Lyon; third, Elias Knerr; fourth, T. C. Hullihen; fifth, William R. Pursel.
Corporals—First, Robert Adams, junior; second, William T. Ramsey; third, John W. Thatcher; fourth, Benjamin K. Vastine; fifth, George Irwin; sixth, Samuel Earp; seventh, John Werkheiser; eighth, Samuel Haman.
Drummer—John H. Hunt.
Quartermaster Sergeant—Reuben Riehl.

PRIVATES.

John Adams,
Charles S. Baker,
Peter Baldy, junior,
A. Russel Best,
P. F. Bourgenot,
D. H. B. Brower,
Wilbur G. Brower,
S. L. Butterwick,
William Bryant,
Nelson Carr,
Robert M. Cathcart,
Charles W. Childs,
W. H. Cool,
William Cummings,
Stephen Cuthbert,
J. M. Criswell,
William Deen,
William Dent,
Wesley Deshay,
Joseph A. Doran,
Christian Ernest,
Edward Evans,
Josiah Frantz,
S. B. Flick,
Evan Fisher, junior,
Herbert Gaskins,
A. Mont. Gearhart,
Edmund Gearhart,
W. H. Gearhart,
Charles H. Gibbs,
Frank Gibbs,
Samuel F. Griffin,
Isaac X. Grier,
Michael Haupt,
Lamar Hahn,
D. C. Hartman,
William W. Hays,

William H. Jenkins,
J. Hervey Kase,
Charles Kaufman,
Alfred Kneass.
Frederick Kreps,
Henry Kocher,
Charles Limberger,
William C. Lyon,
Saul Lyon,
John V. Martin,
Franklin Miller,
William McLain.
Moses Netter,
George B. O'Connor,
Samuel J. Pardoe,
Theodore Palmer,
Isaac Pursell,
West Perry,
A. D. Rockafeller,
Alexander M. Russel,
Warren Ridgway,
J. C. Shaver,
Cyrus F. Styers,
Joseph Sechler, junior,
Henry C. Snyder,
S. Y. Thompson,
Lewis Tittle,
John L. Vastine,
T. J. Vastine.
S. C. Vansant,
Josiah Wolf,
Samuel Werkheiser,
Reuben Werkheiser,
Peter Werkheiser,
Benjamin G. Welch.
William Wands,
Robert Wilson,

Hezekiah Holbert,
Richard Jenkins,

Samuel Welliver,
Samuel Ware, junior.

MUSTER ROLL, COMPANY K, THIRTEENTH REGIMENT P. V. M.

Captain—William Young.

Lieutenants—First, Alfred Mellon ; second, Alfred B. Patton.

Sergeants—First, M. B. Munson ; second, A. Jerome Harder ; third, George W. Ramsey ; fourth, Alexander Hoffner.

Corporals—First, Alfred Yerrick ; second, Hugh P. Libhart ; third, Lewis Byerly ; fourth, William Miller.

Quartermaster—Samuel Moore.

Drummer—B. W. Mussleman.

Fifer—John Geist.

PRIVATES.

Oakly V. Ammerman,
James M. Ammerman,
Samuel Ammerman,
John C. Alexander,
James Best,
W. H. Byerly,
Sylvester Blocksage,
John Bedow,
Charles W. Boudine,
Joseph H. Campbell,
Martin Cornelison,
John Deen,
Joseph E. Dougherty,
Leonard Dimmick,
William D. Everhart,
Cornelison C. Herr,
Duncan W. Hefler,
John Hale,
Jeremiah S. Hall,

William F. Horner,
David James,
John W. Kress,
Samuel Kelley,
George Lunger,
William A. Leighow,
Victor A. Lotier,
David W. Moore,
D. Clinton Millard,
Franklin Myers,
William P. Pursell,
Irvin T. Patton,
L. Rhodenheffer,
William Riffles,
F. W. Rockafeller,
D. M. Springer,
George S. Sanders,
William Trease,
George W. Watts.

The regiment was composed of the above two companies from Montour county, two from Columbia, two from Luzerne, and four from Bradford county, and in the ranks were some of the most prominent professional and business men of the several counties. At Hagerstown we learned that during the battle of Antietam, that

closed about the time we arrived, seven of our friends of the One
Hundred and Thirty-second regiment were killed.   They were J.
M. Hassenplug, D. Van Ronk, Jacob Long, Daniel Klase, Samuel
Hilner, Hiram Hummel, and John Gibson.

Eighteen were wounded, viz : Harry Adams, Jacob H. Miller,
E. D. Smith, John Leighow, S. W. Arnwine, James Foster, William
Ringler, George Lovett, John Morris, William B. Neese, D. R.
Hendrickson, David R. Shutt, E. W. Roderick, Charles Flick, S.
V. Dye, Archie Vandling, C. C. Moyer, and John S. Ware.

From Hagerstown we were hurried towards the field of battle a
few miles below, but the enemy "skedaddled" across the Potomac,
no doubt because they heard we were coming.   This is not intended
as a joke, for the moral effect of the report that *all* Pennsylvania
would be hurled upon them, struck terror to the hearts of the inva-
ders and hastened their retreat.   We were next encamped in the
woods near one of the most magnificent springs of water we ever
saw.   Here we were startled by an alarm that four thousand cavalry
were close at hand, and would in a few moments attack our lines.
Every man was soon in his place in the ranks, except a few who
started for Danville on "double quick," and never halted until they
got home.   From this place we returned to Hagerstown, and from
thence, one hot Sunday, we marched through the sun and dense
clouds of dust ten miles, to Greencastle, where we remained about a
week.   There the boys, between the routine duties of mounting
guard and dress parade, did some foraging, and amused themselves
in various ways.   Some few, of course, did not join in mischievous
pranks.   John V. Martin was too conscientious even to steal a rail
from the fence of a rebel to cook his dinner, but others less particular not only took the fence, but scooped up the poultry to cook.
One day nearly the whole battalion was firing at a squirrel that was
promenading over the tall oak trees.   But either the sharp shooters
were not there or the rifles were defective, for the squirrel escaped,
but it was a comfort to reflect that rebels are bigger than squirrels,
and consequently not so hard to hit.

Many episodes occurred that we promised not to mention.   Of
course these promises were made under some coercion, as the parties making the demand for silence always seemed to take a tighter
grip of their fire-locks, and we noticed a peculiar expression in their

eyes. So we promised not to tell who got a new cap for nothing at Carlisle—to say nothing about Mose Netter's canteen that was so popular on account of its contents—about the soldier boy who borrowed the slippers of one who was sound asleep—about the military disadvantages of the doctor's army shoes—about the squad that stole the eggs from a setting hen. How " Mont.," by pure strategy, outflanked the commissary department. How Charley Kaufman mustered as a private soldier, without ever dreaming that one day he would be burgess of Danville.

All these, and many other pranks unknown in time of peace and contrary to the rules of war, we promised to suppress. Finally, after a campaign of two weeks, we were mustered out and sent home, where we arrived without the loss of a single man! We marched into Danville in open order as proudly as if we had taken Richmond, knowing that we had killed as many of the enemy as they had of us.

But, seriously, many of our comrades in that wild and stirring crusade have since departed to the land of eternal rest. We recall them to-day as we glance over the roll, and we honor them, for we know that every man who rose from his shelter tent that dark night, in the woods of Maryland, and hastened to his place in the ranks at the whispered alarm of the coming foe, was ready to defend his country with his life.

There were several other military companies organized in Danville and had an ephemeral existence. There was the " Danville Troop," commanded by Captain H. P. Baldy. This company disbanded about the beginning of the civil war, and many of its members enlisted in other organizations and gallantly fought through the war.

After the war there was a company of " Fire Zouaves " organized under Captain John A. Winner. But for some reason it soon dissolved, and now there are only those belonging to the National , Guard.

COMPANY F, NATIONAL GUARD.—This company was organized in Danville in 1878, and was at first commanded by Captain P. E. Maus, and was mustered as Company F of the Twelfth regiment, National Guard of Pennsylvania. Captain Maus resigned in 1880, and J. Sweisfort was elected and commissioned captain of the company.

John W. Hibler recruited a company that was for a time encamped on the capitol ground at Harrisburg. The company was afterwards sent to the South, where John W. Hibler died.

Samuel Hibler, his brother, was also an officer in the Union army. These were the sons of Jacob Hibler, who resided on Market street.

Joseph F. Ramsey was the first captain of the Baldy Guards, and with his company was mustered into the service of the United States on the 25th of September, 1861. He served in that capacity until the fall of 1862, when he resigned. He was wounded at the battle of Williamsburg; and the siege in the Chickahominy swamp with the terrible fight of seven days, broke down his health and necessitated his resignation. After regaining his health he again joined the army and was made lieutenant colonel of the One Hundred and Eighty seventh regiment Pennsylvania volunteers. Since the war he has been connected with the oil trade.

First Sunday School.

For the following sketch of the first Sunday School in Danville, and the brief but interesting biographical notes of its founders, I am indebted to John Frazer, Esq., of Cincinnati.

Robert Raikes is known as the originator of Sunday schools. He was an editor, and published the *Gloucester Journal.* At first he employed and paid teachers to give instruction to the children that had no other means of either religious or secular education. This was in 1781. Reverend Robert Stork soon joined him in the pious work, and success crowned their earnest efforts. In five years from the first Sunday school, organized under the superintendence of Robert Raikes, there were two hundred and fifty thousand Sunday school scholars receiving regular instruction in the various cities and towns of England. At first the instruction given was mainly in the ordinary branches, and extended but little more to the moral or religious training of the children than the common schools of the present day.

In Scotland, the first Sunday schools, mainly devoted to religious training, were first instituted. The Sunday schools in Scotland were more like those of the present day than were those of England, and yet they were far behind the standard of excellence now attained. In 1786, Bishop Asbury, of the M. E. Church, established the first Sunday school in America. It was in Virginia. Shortly after that date the Society of Friends planted the Sunday school in Philadelphia, and in 1791 Bishop White, of the Episcopal Church, was president of a Sunday school in that city.

There is also another claimant for the first Sunday school in America. Dr. Hildreth says that a kind old lady at the Fort, now Marietta, Ohio, gathered the children of the garrison together on Sundays and gave them religious instruction on the general plan of the Sunday school. Parson Story gave her efficient aid in the pious work, and she continued the Sunday school after the good parson was called away. This was in 1792, and about one year after the establishment of the institution in Virginia by Bishop Asbury.

In 1809, a Sunday school was organized in Pittsburgh, which was the first in this State outside of Philadelphia. In 1816, the New York Sunday School Union was established, and the American Sunday School Union was organized in 1824, and now the Sunday school system became a power and found its way into every village and hamlet throughout the country. It has steadily grown in numbers and in influence, and now the number of Sunday school libraries in the United States is nearly five thousand, and the regular scholarship is not less than three millions.

The first Sunday school in Danville was established in 1817, mainly through the efforts and influence of Judge William Montgomery. In July of that year he induced a few others to join him in the good work, among whom were Evans, Russel, Barret, and Daniels. About twenty boys were gathered together on Sunday, the 2nd day of August, 1817, and the first Sunday school of Danville was opened. It was in a private room on Market street. Judge Montgomery and Jeremiah Evans were the superintendents. John Russel was treasurer, and Josiah McClure was secretary. But they had no books, no tickets, no maps, nor any of the thousand advantages enjoyed by the Sunday schools of the present day. Soon they procured red and blue tickets containing a text of scripture. For every six verses in the Bible or Testament repeated from memory, the scholar received a blue ticket. A red ticket was worth six in blue, and were good for the purchase of books. This was the pioneer school of all the flourishing Sunday schools now in this place. The constitution of the first Sunday school in Danville was written by Judge Montgomery, and was long in the possession of Honorable Paul Leidy, and a copy, with the signatures of the original signers, is now among the records of the Grove Church. The following is a correct copy of the document :

CONSTITUTION OF THE MALE SUNDAY SCHOOL OF DANVILLE.

Article 1. The object of this society shall be to teach children to read and commit portions of scripture, catechism, hymns, &c., to memory.

2. The society shall consist of fourteen members.

3. The officers shall consist of two superintendents, a treasurer. and secretary.

4. It shall be the duty of the superintendents to attend every Sunday, or at least one of them, at the place of meeting, and remain there until school is dismissed, also to preside at all meetings of the society, to keep order, take the vote on all questions of debate, appoint committees, sign all orders for the payment of moneys, &c.

5. It shall be the duty of the secretary to keep all papers delivered to him, to collect fines and keep correct minutes of the society ; also an account of the books distributed, and to whom.

6. It shall be the duty of the treasurer to keep all moneys, to pay all orders when properly signed, and when required by the society, to give a statement of his accounts.

7. An election of officers shall take place quarterly, on the first Mondays of August, November, February and May.

8. Six members shall form a quorum to transact business.

9. The members shall be divided into committees, two of whom shall attend every Sabbath at the appointed hours, and remain until school is dismissed, under a penalty of twelve and a half cents for neglect, for the use of the school.

10. The school shall be opened by reading a chapter, by singing a hymn, or by prayer.

11. Each member shall have the names of his class enrolled, see that they attend punctually, perform all their duties with propriety, and reward them accordingly.

12. Tickets shall be issued for the encouragement of the pupils.

13. It shall be the duty of the teachers to report to the superintendents such children as shall merit rewards, and the superintendents to give such premiums to the children as in their opinion will incite them to further improvement.

14. No member shall leave the school during the hours of tuition, without leave of absence from one of the superintendents.

15. All unnecessary talking, as well as light, trifling behavior, shall be avoided by the teachers during school hours, and it shall be the duty of each teacher, as far as ability has been given, to be careful to instruct the scholars in the knowledge of Divine things.

16. When a scholar has been absent from school two Sabbaths, he shall be visited by the teacher of the class to which he belongs, who is to report the cause of such absence to the superintendents. This rule should be strictly adhered to, as it may prevent the scholars from breaking the Sabbath.

17. Alterations or amendments of the constitution cannot be made without the concurrence of three fourths of the members.

18. The society, two thirds of all the members concurring, shall have power to raise money for the use of the school.

19. It shall be the duty of each and every member to attend the quarterly meetings, and all other meetings that may be deemed necessary by the superintendents, under a penalty of twelve and a half cents each for neglect, for the use of the school.

IRA DANIELS,	JEREMIAH EVANS,
JAMES HUMPHREYS,	WILLIAM WOODS,
JAMES MONTGOMERY,	JOSEPH PRUTZMAN,
WILLIAM WILSON,	D. C. BARRETT,
JOSIAH McCLURE,	W. MONTGOMERY,
JOHN IRWIN,	JOHN RUSSEL.
WILLIAM WHITAKER,	CHARLES M. FRAZER.

DANVILLE, *June*, 1817.

From this document, it appears that there were no female Sunday school scholars in that day, and consequently there was still much to learn and an open field for great improvements.

This first Sunday school, in Danville, was organized as above stated, on the 2d day of August, 1817, in a private dwelling on Market

street, east of Pine.   A brief, biographical note of each of the old
founders of the first Sunday school in Danville is appended.

Doctor Ira Daniels was a native of Connecticut.   He and Doctor Petrikin were the village physicians of that day.   They succeeded Doctor Barrett, who was the successor of Doctor Forest, the
first physician of the place.   Doctor Daniels was editor of the *Express*, the second newspaper of the county, which succeeded the
Columbia Gazette, the first journal in this place, and which was published only a year or two.   The Doctor rendered effective aid in
drawing up the constitution and in obtaining the coöperation of
others in establishing the school.   He was a member of the committee, of which Hon. William Montgomery was the chairman, and
drew the last two articles of that instrument.

James Humphreys, a worthy citizen, who cheerfully joined in the
good work of establishing the school.

James Montgomery was a member of the large and influential family of that name, who did so much to establish and aid the village
in its early days to obtain a position for usefulness and to give it a
reputation for sound morality.   His brother, Rev. John Montgomery, was a teacher in the school, and subsequently became superintendent, and continued in that capacity until he removed to
western Illinois where he labored long and faithfully as pastor of a
church.   They and Rev. William B. Montgomery, were sons of
Col. John Montgomery, one of the earliest pioneers who reclaimed
Mahoning to civilization and religion.   He (James) died in 1826,
at the early age of thirty-five years.

William Wilson, the village justice, who most respectably filled
that office for an age.   After a long and useful course here, rearing
a large family, and when well advanced in years, he removed to Illinois, near the Mississippi river, where he died in 1848, at the good
old age of eighty-three years.   His decendants still reside in Knox,
Rock Island, and Mercer counties, and in Chicago.

Josiah McClure, one of the prominent and popular citizens at
that period, held the office of register and recorder of Columbia
county, being the first incumbent : he was also the first secretary of
the school, and faithfully discharged his official duties.

John Irwin was one of the early residents, and a hotel keeper,
who united with the others in promoting the good work, and he lived

to see the institution permanently established. He was one of the thirty-four subscribers to an agreement to contibute to the support of the preaching of the Gospel in 1785, before the erection of the old Grove church.

William Whitaker was a Hibernian who emigrated from Europe to Philadelphia, and soon afterwards to Danville, whilst it was yet a small village. He was an assiduous promoter of the school. About this period the Methodist church was formed and he was one of its zealous members. The father of a large family, he lived to see them arrive at years of maturity. His daughter and grand children still reside in Danville. His son, Doctor William H. Whitaker, resided in New Orleans, and afterwards in Mobile, where he died in 1870, leaving a large family who reside there and in the vicinity.

Jeremiah Evans was a merchant then residing here, and who subsequently removed to Mercersburg. He was one of the most efficient members of the society, and one of the superintendents elected at the organization of the school in 1817.

William Woods was well known as a leading Methodist, who aided in the organization of that sect when they possessed but slender means for such an enterprise ; he was one of the class leaders. His piety and energy commanded the confidence of his colaborers and coreligionists, as well as the respect of the entire community. Thus it will be seen that the school was established by pious and enterprising men, irrespective of religious creeds, though a majority of them were Presbyterians. Owing to the paucity of its friends at its inception it was found expedient for all to unite, who could assist in promoting its objects. Some of Mr. Woods' family still reside in Danville, actively engaged in business pursuits.

Joseph Proutzman was a prominent and popular citizen. He came to Danville after having been elected sheriff of the county to succeed Henry Alward, the first one, about a year anterior to the organization of the school. After the expiry of his sheriffalty he resumed his former profession, that of surveyor, for which his mathematical attainments and skill well fitted him. Subsequently, and until his decease, he was a justice of the peace.

Don Carlos Barrett was a native of Norwich, Vermont. His birth dated back to 1788. He was a most accomplished and successful teacher. His academy at Cincinnati in 1808, 1809, and

1810, was a grand success. His school in Danville at the time the Sunday school was formed was a most prosperous one, being patronized by the principal citizens of the place, and by those of the vicinity and neighboring villages. Whilst busily engaged in his school by day he studied law by night. Upon his admission to the bar he removed to North Carolina, and subsequently to Erie, from thence to Texas just prior to the revolution, and during that eventful period, together with Austin and Houston, constituted the "Consultation," the triumvirate which exercised supreme control during that sanguinary conflict. After the new nation had secured its independence he resumed his law practice and resided at Bastrop. Here, after a life of great activity and usefulness he died in 1838, at the age of fifty years.

Hon. William Montgomery was born in Philadelphia in 1776, and was taken by his parents, when in his infancy, to Northumberland, and from thence to Danville. From Danville the family had to flee several times from prowling parties of war-like savages. They sought refuge at Northumberland, or Fort Augusta. In early manhood he was appointed one of the associate judges of Northumberland county, for which position his intelligence and sterling integrity well fitted him. When the new county of Columbia was formed, he continued to hold his office in the new county to the close of his long and spotless life, in January, 1846. It may truly be said of him, " he felt that a christian is the highest style of man." The only surviving members of his family are Rev. Samuel Montgomery, residing at Oberlin, and his grand-children and great-grand children in Pennsylvania, Ohio, Illinois, Michigan, and Nebraska.

John Russel, one of the pioneers, was a man much respected. He was a merchant, and one of the first in this place. Always ready to join in every enterprise for the moral as well as the material advancement of the community he warmly advocated the establishment of the Sunday school, and was a co-laborer with Judge Montgomery in the organization of the first Sunday school in Danville. He was chosen treasurer, and ever manifested a deep interest in the success of the school. John Russel was a man of merit, modest, loving the quiet of his family and his home, but was called to public life in 1824, when he was appointed prothonotary of the county by

Governor John Andrew Shultz. He served six years with great credit to himself and satisfaction to the public.

Charles M. Frazer, the last survivor of the society, was born in Philadelphia, in February 1788. In his infancy, during the summer of that year, his parents brought him to Mahoning where his childhood, youth, and early manhood were passed, in the old homestead farm, now in part included in the corporate limits of Danville. He was educated in the old log school-house, which stood about thirty paces east of the first Grove church, under the tuition of Master Gibson and other teachers of the olden time. which was about the close of the last century. He cordially aided in founding the school and in its support, during his residence here. He resided for half a century in this vicinity with the exception of two years in California, in 1855–56. Having survived all the other members of the society many years, he died in Peoria, in October, 1876, in his eighty-ninth year. His children, grand-children, and great grandchildren reside in Ohio, Illinois, Missouri, Kansas, and Peru, South America.

The Old Log House.

Green in the memory of many is the old log cabin where first they hailed the dawn of life, or which perchance is associated with well remembered scenes in the long past. Among pioneers the old log cabin is a sacred institution, one that never fails to call back the hallowed memories of childhood's home. Danville is not without these monuments of the past generation ; and these quaint old structures, in the eyes of those who are now treading the down hill of life, are no less sacred as cherished memorials of the past, than are the remembrances of those whose lives began in the grand old mansion or the lordly palace.

Among the ruins of the fire in Reed's block, was an old house. It had been disguised for years in a coat of weather-boards, and, by the rise of Mill street, it was left far below the pavement. It was lost to sight. Its original garb gave place to another, and that too was crumbling away with age. But the fire stripped off the shell, and brought out the old log house, only to disappear again, and this time, forever. The ancient beams that left the primitive forest a century ago were exposed in the glare of the flames in the rude

9

dressing of the pioneer, and the style of the olden time. There
were the windows and doorways far below Mill street as it is now,
but all right as it was then. This was one of the oldest buildings
in Danville. It was cemented with mud between the logs and covered with clap-boards in its early days. The chimney, we pre-
sume, was on the outside, like the smoke stack of a furnace. But
that old building is not without its legends of ghosts and its tales of
horror, as well as more pleasant scenes connected with those who
trod its threshold in *auld lang syne.* One frail mortal, tired of life,
committed suicide within its walls, and there too, others first saw
the light of day. How much of joy and of sorrow, in that old
house, was felt by those who have long slept in the grave uncon
scious to pleasure and pain, as the old building itself. Years ago it
was used as a school-house and the scenes enacted there "could a
tale unfold" that would raise each individual hair, like the quills on
the fretful porcupine. I only know that a friend of mine, then a
school boy, was the subject of a terrible wallopping in that rude
temple of literature. He has not forgotten it yet. As he watched
the scene, that wallopping came back to his memory, bright as the
flames that played around the old familiar logs, and the image of
the stern old school master seemed to rise from the burning floor,
and assume a grotesque form, as it vanished in the dense volumes of
smoke that filled its chambers. The school master of that day was
an autocrat, and played the tyrant in his little kingdom of the school-
room, and to-day the advancement in the science of teaching is no
less remarkable than the improvement in architecture.

Well, the old log house is gone. Another monument of the past
has vanished in smoke.

Old School Days.

The school houses in the olden time were rude and unpretending
structures. Some had no glass in the windows—oiled paper answered
the purpose. Great logs were piled in the wide hearths, for stoves
were scarce. The seats and desks were in keeping with the structure, so arranged that the larger scholars occupied positions behind
long desks which ran with either side of the wall, and faced the
"master," while the younger ones occupied the more uncomfortable
benches immediately in front, where their feet scarcely ever touched

the floor. So much for the house, and now for the school. The
" master " was estimated according to his sternness, and the scepter
of his power was the symbol of brute force. They didn't think of
teaching more than spelling, reading, and "cyphering." There
were no free schools, but the poor could attend the school, and the
county paid the teacher three cents a day for each scholar on the
poor list.

The "master's standing in the community was not alone meas-
ured by the dexterity with which he could "point a quill," but the
respect entertained for him was somewhat akin to that of the revered "circuit rider," who was generally consulted on such matters
as related to civil progress, local government, etc., and whose opinions thereon were highly esteemed and duly regarded. The "master " generally " boarded 'round " in turn among the parents of the
scholars, and his " week at our house " was looked forward to with
mingled feelings of pride and regret by the younger folks, but with
satisfaction by the parents, especially the good housewife, as she
would take an inventory of her crocks of preserved fruits, or re-
arrange the "spare room " to give it an extra air of cozy comfort
and welcome.

Don't you remember the time when you were wont to be startled
with the stern command of " mind your books?" How it made
the little chaps jump and hold up their books before their faces,
whilst they made furtive side glances towards the frowning tyrant
who wielded the birch ! Don't you remember how the " big boys "
would sometimes cram their caps in their pockets, and, meek as innocent lambs, say, " Master, please let me go out," and then ske-
daddle? But one at a time was allowed to go out, and to keep
things right a small paddle or shingle was hung near the door. On
one side, in large black letters, was the word *In*, and on the other
Out. This was to be turned on passing out and in. Sometimes a
mischievous fellow would watch his chance, when one was out, and
turn the " pass " to " in," and then ask to go out, because he wanted
to join the one already out. The " master," peering over his specs,
would examine the shingle, and satisfied that all were " in," would
grant permission. How many of our readers remember the old
" pass " that hung beside the door ? They had no bells, but called
the scholars by rapping smartly on the door-frame with a wooden

rule, accompanied with the word of command, "Books! books!" when every urchin scampered for his seat, took up his book and pretended to study with wonderful earnestness, but all the time peeping around to see what was going on. Next, you would hear, " Master, Sam's a'pinchin' me !" or, " Joe's *a'scrougin'* me !" The mischievous boy, by way of punishment, was compelled to pass across the room and take a seat with the girls—a doubtful kind of punishment. Some blushed like lobsters, and others seemed to enjoy it.

There was one day in the year when the "master's" anger was braved, and that was in the time-honored custom of "barring out the master" on Christmas. On that great occasion, the plot being previously laid, the scholars assembled long before school time, and piled up the seats to barricade the door. All preparations made, they waited the coming of the "master." At last he came, and with threats alarmed the more timid, but the "big boys," no less determined, withstood the onset. An agreement to give free pardon and a general treat to the school was slipped out under the door, with the offer of opening the door if the "master" would sign and return the paper. Sometimes he returned it with his signature at once, and other times he kept them imprisoned for the day and punished them besides. "Barring out the master" was a common custom all over the country, but it has long since been abandoned, though many who read these lines will remember the exciting scenes connected with this old time custom.

In the winter time the "singing school" was also held in the school house. These, as well as the "spelling matches," were the great excitements of the season. For miles around the young folks joined in making the required number, at fifty cents each for the quarter. At the appointed time they assembled, bringing each a singing or "tune book," a tallow candle, and generally a sweetheart. They were soon arranged on the rude seats, holding the stump of a tallow candle, wrapped in paper, in one hand, and the book in the other. Those who were fortunate enough to own a singing book were regarded with something like envy, yet they commanded a considerable amount of respect. The "singing master" was usually a tall Yankee, wearing a "churn on his head and a "swallow-tailed" coat on his back. His pantaloons were a world to short, and his twang was of the nasal persuasion. They had no blackboard, but with a short stick the "master" sawed the air as he sang out *fa, sol, la, me. sol.* When he came to the end of the space, he made a sudden turn as the tails of his coat described a semi-circle. "Old Hundred" was then a favorite. When "singing school" was out the grand occasion was manifest in the scramble for partners, and many a long walk home resulted in a match.

Once on a very dark night, when singing school was out and some had gone quite a distance, an unpretending young man called out, "Hello! Becka! Becka!" as loud as he could bawl. "Hello! Jerry!" came back on the night breeze and resounded through the near woodland. It was Jerry's "lady love," who had gone some distance on the dark way homeward. "May I go home with ye, Becka?" was Jerry's next. Again she responded, "Oh, well, Jerry, I reckon!" He did go home with her, and in due course of time they were married and lived in a little frame house on the outskirts of town. He was a shoemaker, and fond of tobacco, and was in the habit of taking very large quids, about the size of a duck-egg, and when exhausted would dry them in a bag that hung in the chimney-corner. When perfectly dry, Becky would smoke them in her short clay pipe. One morning, as a neighbor called to have some cobbling done, he heard the following conversation: "Jerry, any more old chaws?" "Wall, I dunno, Becky, looky in th' ba i-g!" Thus, they lived long and happy together, and some of their descendants may perchance be living in Danville to-day.

There were no church choirs then. All who could sing in the congregation joined in the hymn, two lines of which were "given out" at a time. And when melodeons were first introduced, they were refused admission into many of the churches. Choirs were another innovation that are no improvement, and the time may come again when true worshippers will return to the old-time congregational singing.

Incidents.

In 1824, the "Codorus," a small steamboat of about one hundred tons, arrived at Danville, on an experimental trip up the Susquehanna, and was received with great demonstrations of joy by the citizens. A public banquet was given to the officers of the boat, at the old Cross Keys tavern that stood on the river bank. The banquet was numerously attended, and high hopes were entertained of the speedy and successful navigation of the Susquehanna river by steam. But, alas, these bright visions were of short duration. The boat proceeded on her voyage, and when near Berwick exploded her boiler, killing or fatally injuring a number of her crew. This terrible disaster dispelled all hope of successfully navigating the river by steam. More than half a century has passed away and no attempt has been made since the fatal voyage of the "Codorus," of York.

James Hamilton the junior member of the firm of King & Hamilton, merchants, in 1813, was a suitor for the hand of Miss Lydia Evans, but his ardent love was not reciprocated. He was rejected by the fair Lydia. This rejection made him desperate, and he committed suicide, by shooting himself with a pistol. This was the first suicide that occurred in the town of Danville, and it was long remembered with horror. These sad occurances have not been frequent in this place. Perhaps young folks do not love as desperately as they did in the olden time, or the fair maidens of to-day are less cruel than they were in early times. We have no record of any subsequent suicide in Danville, for a similar cause : as those who are rejected, instead of blowing out their brains, gracefully retreat and then seek a more congenial spirit.

In 1778, one evening at dusk, Gen. Daniel Montgomery noticed what seemed an empty canoe floating down the river. Taking a small boat he rowed out to inspect the strange craft. Approaching the canoe he saw an Indian lying in the bottom apparently armed with bow and arrows. On second thought he resolved to pull up to the canoe. On coming along side he found that the Indian was dead. A dead rooster was fixed to the bow of the canoe, a bow and arrows were in his hands and a card was on the Indian's breast, bearing the words, "Let the bearer go to his master King George or the devil." Montgomory drew the canoe ashore, where many citizens inspected its curious freight. It was then sent adrift and has never been heard of since. It proved to be the corpse of a noted chief among the Indians, named "Anthony Turkey." He was killed on the Kingston Flats, while on a murderous invasion among the settlers in Wyoming valley, and his dead body was sent afloat in an old canoe, as it was found by Montgomery.

My grandfather and grandmother Goodman were among the old residents of Danville. They are buried side by side in the old Lutheran grave-yard. Grandfather Goodman was a coverlet weaver, and made bed coverings according to the fashion of that day. They were woven of bright colors in fanciful patterns. Some were ornamented with birds, flowers, stars, or trailing vines. An old record speaks of him as a "man of culture." He had a good library, chiefly German books, many of them in large quarto, Leipsic editions. He devoted much time to study. Grandmother survived him a number of years, and was killed by being thrown from a wagon by a runaway horse. My uncle Philip Goodman's daughter, Eliza Ann, was married to Doctor Samuel G. Maus. He was a man of considerable prominence in his profession, and was for a number of years in partnership with Doctor Logan, father of Senator Logan of Illinois. Doctor Maus died at Pekin, Illinois, in February, 1872. This union between Doctor Maus and Ann Eliza Goodman, brings the writer of this volume into outside relationship with the Maus and the Frazer families.

The first dancing school in Danville was opened by Philip Graham of Milton, in the Pennsylvania hotel then kept by Philip Goodman and now by J. V. Gillaspy. This dancing school was attended by the young folks of the town, and also by many from the surrounding country. Among the latter was Philip F. Maus, then quite a youth. His father, Joseph Maus, had been persuaded to send him in order that he might keep pace with the times. Mr. Philip F. Maus did not take kindly to the exercise and soon abandoned it. He now laughs heartily at the idea of his scholarship, and does not regret that his tastes and habits, in early life, were of a more substantial character.

Philip Goodman, uncle to the writer, for a long time kept the old "Pennsylvania," now the Revere House, near the bridge. He also kept a store in the same building, where he carried on an extensive trade with surrounding farmers, especially in exchanging goods for wheat. Mr. Maus, at the Mausdale mill, ground the wheat and sent the flour in barrels down the river on boats. Immense quantities of flour by this mode of transportation, were sent to Philadelphia and Baltimore. These boats had only to be guided on their downward voyage; but returning up stream was a tedious and la-

borious process. They were pushed up with long poles set on the
bottom of the river, braced against the shoulder of the boatmen,
when a tramp, from bow to stern, would send them up the length
of the boat. And yet, in this tiresome way a crew often pushed a
boat twenty miles a day.

Going to Black Rock.

During the war of 1812, the company commanded by Captain
Isaac Blue, (father of Samuel Blue, now a resident of Danville,) was
under marching orders, and when on the eve of departure the company was halted in front of the stone mansion to give a parting salute to the veteran General William Montgomery. As the old General came to the door the company " presented arms," whilst they
listened to a brief address. General Montgomery told them to be
good soldiers and at the same time take good care of themselves,
"and be ever as now, ready to defend and support the Government." On the conclusion of his patriotic address the volunteer
company fired a salute, wheeled and marched away with cheers for
General Montgomery, the flag and the Union. On this occasion
General Montgomery was dressed as usual, in Continental costume—
knee breeches and silver buckles. But alas; many of those brave
and patriotic volunteers of Danville never returned. They were
not slain by the British or Indians ; but by a fatal malady known as
Black Rock fever—a fever of a typhoid character, and by local circumstances rendered peculiarly malignant. Samuel Yorks, Sr., was
a lieutenant in this company and survived the campaign. It is not
many years since the good old man calmly fell asleep, and now, after the turmoils of a long and active life, he rests in an honored
grave.

Doctor Petrikin was also connected with this company.

Evangelical Lutheran Church.

The first Lutheran church in this region was in Mahoning township as it is now. In that day it was called Ridgeville. Some time
prior to 1800 a man named Shelhart visited this place, whether he
was a regularly ordained minister or not, cannot now be told. The
first record of a church organization, is dated 1803 and the first regular pastor was Johann Paul Ferdinand Kramer. From 1805 to 1808

there is no record, except that which was kept by M. C. F. S. Who he was or whether he was pastor, we are not informed. Then there is a blank until 1810, when Rev. J. F. Engel took charge and remained until April 1816. Here again there is a blank until 1820. From this date until 1828 the congregation was ministered to by Rev. Peter Kesler. Rev. Peter Kesler seems to have been the only Lutheran preacher then in this region of the State, as he served all the congregations in this and adjoining counties. After Rev. Kesler left the field the Lutherans aided in building a church under the impression that they would have the privilege of worshipping in the church when completed. But they were disappointed. Rev. Jeremiah Shindel came from Bloomsburg about that time and preached regularly in the old court-house and organized a congregation of those who adhered to the Lutheran church. This was in 1830 after he had preached a year or two in the church, now the Episcopalian. The removal to the court-house was in consequence of some disagreement in relation to the occupancy of the church. Rev. Shindel remained five or six years, then the congregation was left without a pastor for some time. During this period some became discouraged and united with other churches. After some time those who adhered were united with the Catawissa charge and had preaching once a month by Rev. William Eyer. This continued for a year and a half when a call was given to Rev. Meyer. He labored among the people with much acceptance; but the congregation was neither large nor rich and Rev. Meyer resigned for want of adequate support. They were then without a pastor until 1843 when Rev. Elias Swartz, sustained in part by the Home Missionary Society and under the guidance of the Great Head of the Church, ministered to this long neglected people. On his arrival he found only twenty members left. Some had been called to their last account; others had become discouraged and found a home in other congregations, where they are now among the most exemplary and influential citizens of this place, exerting a salutary influence in the cause of the Redeemer; but wholly estranged from the peculiar Church of their fathers, and while their former brethren bless them for what they are doing in behalf of the kingdom of Christ, yet many of them regret the necessity that drove them from their home into the bosom of strangers. Many of them sigh to think that so many of the sons and daughters of the Church of the Reformation, and bearing the name of the great Reformer, were compelled for the want of the bread of life to abandon the household of their fathers.

Danville had now become a considerable town, numbering between two and three thousand inhabitants. The various denominations who had been better supplied with pastors, had become firmly established; when Rev. Swartz, with the little remnant of the former flock, (and these were mostly poor in this world's goods,) held a series of meetings which were abundantly blessed by the visitations of divine favor and the outporing of the spirit. As the result of this meeting he received into the communion of the church by the rites of Baptism and Confirmation between forty and fifty members. After laboring successfully for about a year they formed the design of building a suitable church edifice for their accommodation. A meeting was called and the following persons were duly appointed to superintend the erection of the House, viz: William G. Miller, Thomas Ellis, Samuel Gulick and William Sechler. The church was built and dedicated to the service of God, with the title of the Evangelical Lutheran Church of Danville, Pennsylvania. This occurred during the first week of June, 1845. The officiating ministers present on the occasion were Revs. Elias Swartz, William Eyer and Jacob Smith. On the following March, Rev. Swartz having become somewhat discouraged on account of straitened circumstances, a heavy church debt resting on the congregation, and the consequent meager support he received, he finally resigned his pastoral relation and accepted the call of a Lutheran congregation in Maryland. The Danville congregation was then connected with the Milton charge, and served by Rev. Ruthrauff, once in two weeks for the space of nine months. At the end of that period, a call was given to Rev M. J. Alleman, who accepted the call and entered on his labors, and served the congregation with great acceptance until 1848, when he resigned and went to Sunbury, and took charge of one of the churches in that place. The congregation was then without a pastor for nearly two years, when Rev. P. Willard, agent of the Theological Seminary at Gettysburg, was called. He commenced his pastoral labors in this place in 1850. He found the members scattered and disheartened, some debt still remaining, and the trustees without a deed for the ground on which

the church was built. But a new zeal seemed to be infused into
the remnant of the flock. Past troubles were for a time forgotten,
and they once more in the faith and work of the Gospel emulated the
spirit of their fathers and came up rejoicing to "the help of the Lord
against the mighty." The number of communicants in February,
1850, had already reached to the number of 142. A series of meetings were held in February and March of this year, which resulted in
the accession of about one hundred. In oneness of spirit and purpose the pastor and people harmoniously labored together. The
church lot was enclosed, a legal deed obtained for the lot, and in
every respect the church seemed to rise above all her difficulties. A
lot was also purchased about this time for a cemetery, and in 1853
a parsonage was purchased. Union and brotherly love prevailed,
and walking in the light of life and the comforts of the Holy Ghost,
many were added to the church and the work of the Lord pros-
pered in their hands.

In 1854 the church became too small to accommodate the congregation, and with this subject the elements of discord entered the
membership, as the same question had operated in a thousand other
instances. Seven sites for the new church were reported, and on
the first vote a majority voted for the old location. The German
portion of the congregation now refused to give their consent, and
threatened the trustees with a prosecution if they persisted in building an exclusive English Lutheran church. Another meeting was
therefore called in January, 1855, to ascertain fully the sense of the
congregation in regard to the project, as well as the locality.
Seventy-three votes were cast for a site in the North ward and
seventy for the old location in the South ward. Much dissatisfac-
tion prevailed; unkind feeling arose during the protracted contro-
versy, some of which was even directed against the pastor. A division of the congregation was then contemplated, and an amicable
proposition was made to join in the erection of another church in
the North ward and secure the services of a separate pastor, but was
again withdrawn. A lot was, however, purchased in the North
ward; and the Church Council resolved to grant Rev. P. Willard
permission to leave as soon as he could secure another place. This
was, doubtless, the part of wisdom under the circumstances, as Rev.
Willard had freely given expression to his views on the subjects of

dispute, and of course rendered himself personally obnoxious to a portion of the congregation. He soon received a call from Perry county, Pennsylvania. which he accepted, and preached his farewell sermon on the 11th of May, 1856, after serving this charge for more than six years.

We had the pleasure of an acquaintance with Reverend Willard, and with many others regretted the separation, although it seemed necessary in order to restore harmony to the church. His is a man of considerable ability, possessing much energy of character, and had it not been for the unfortunate circumstances adverted to he would no doubt have realized the hopes and expectations of the people of God who rejoiced in the success that attended the first years of his ministry in this place. In July of the same year, the congregation extended a call to the Reverend M. J. Stover, of Waterloo, New York. He accepted and entered on his charge on the first of September, 1856, and was duly installed on the 21st of October, in the same year. The sermon was preached by Reverend George Parsons, President East Pennsylvania Synod. The charge to the pastor on his installation was delivered by Reverend E. A. Sharrats, of Bloomsburg, and the charge to the people by Reverend A. Fink, of Lewisburg. Reverend Stover entered upon the responsible duties of his high calling with an earnest desire to harmonize the discordant elements and establish his people in the unity of the spirit. His labors thus far had been crowned with success. He held a series of meetings during the winter which resulted in the upbuilding of the membership in the faith and hope of the Gospel, and bringing many new converts into the church. His ministration had calmed the troubled waters and restored the confidence and brotherly love that characterized the church through long years of toil and trouble.

This is known as the *Pine street Evangelical Lutheran Church.* It is a large and handsome brick building, and a fine parsonage now adjoins it. The congregation worshipping there is large. It occupies an influential position in the community, and as far as human judgment extends is "abounding in the work of the Lord."

After Reverend Stover came Reverend E. Huber, but he remained only six months. He was followed by Reverend P. P. Lane who remained two years. During his pastorate the church was completed and dedicated. The next pastor was Reverend E. A. Sharratts, who served the congregation two years and six months. Then came Reverend George M. Rhoads and labored with great acceptance and marked success for four years. He was followed by Reverend U. Graves, who remained two years; and February, 1874, the present pastor, Reverend M. L. Shindel, was called and took charge of the congregation. Reverend Shindel is now in the seventh year of his pastorate, and every year the bonds of Christian confidence between the pastor and his people seem to grow stronger and stronger. His labors have been greatly blessed in building up the church in the faith and hope of the Gospel.

Trinity Lutheran Church.

This handsome church, on the corner of Market and Church streets was built in 1861, though the congregation, which was a branch diverging from the old Lutheran congregation, was organized in 1859. It is proper to say that increasing numbers and a division on the locating of a new church were the chief causes of separation. The building is in the Norman Gothic style and is seventy-five by forty-five feet. It was originally surmounted by a neat and elegant spire, one hundred and twenty feet high; but during a great storm that passed over Danville the spire was blown down and was never re-built. The basement contains a lecture room, Sabbath school room, and a study. The auditorium is a model of beauty harmonizing in all its parts. The ceiling is adorned with the richest fresco, and the pulpit and surroundings are oak. The windows are of stained glass, representing all the hues of the rainbow, filling the chamber with a soft and mellow light. There are some three hundred communicants and the Sunday school is attended by about two hundred scholars. The first pastor of this church was Rev. D. M. Henkel. He was succeeded by Rev. Cornman. Rev. Anspach was the next pastor, and he was followed by Rev. M. C. Horine, the present pastor. Rev. Horine is devoting his life to usefulness in the cause of education, as well as the exercise of his ministerial duties. He is, the superintendent of common schools of Montour county, and never were the duties of the office more faithfully discharged than now. We have had A. B. Putnam, William Butler, a conscientious and an excellent man. Then we had Mr. Henry who died a few years ago; but good as they were, they did not excel Rev. Horine, and this is the voice of the public.

St. John's Lutheran Church.

The German speaking portion of the Lutheran church, organized a separate congregation, and were chartered as St. John's German Evalgelical Lutheran Church. They purchased the old church on Market street, built in 1843. This was in 1858. Rev. Eyer was called to the pastorate and served until his death in 1874. In 1875 Rev. J. W. Early became the pastor in connection with Mahoning and Lazarus. Rev. Early has been much blessed in his labors and is still in this charge, and bids fair to minister to this people for many years to come. And although the congregation felt the depressing effects of the late hard times; yet their church is without debt and improvements of the building are in contemplation.

J. B. Moore.

J. B. Moore, a former resident of Danville, kept a drug store in the building now occupied by Mr. Askins. Mr. Moore also contributed to the improvement of the town by building several snug houses in the Second ward. He afterwards sold his drug store to Samuel Hays and removed to Philadelphia in 1861. Subsequently he purchased a lot on the corner of Thirteenth and Lombard streets in that city, where he erected a large and elegant building in which he keeps a first class retail drug store. I have heard some of our leading physicians say, that without exception, Mr. J. B. Moore is the most complete chemist and druggist that ever located in Danville. The scientific papers he has contributed to the leading pharmaceutical journals of the United States have elicited the highest commendation of the profession, and his new discoveries in chemistry and pharmacy have been as highly approved. The honorable position Mr. Moore has attained in his profession, reflects credit on Danville, that was long the place of his residence. With his professional attainments, his liberal spirit and generous nature, it needs only time and good health to secure a niche in the temple that never decays.

Doctor Joseph Parry.

Doctor Joseph Parry came to Danville from Wales, his native place, when he was but a child. When nine or ten years of age he began on light work about the Rough and Ready rolling-mill. He soon began to develop musical talents of the highest order, and at the age of nineteen years he became a composer and competed successfully for the prizes offered by the Eisteddvodan committee. Soon his remarkable talents attracted the attention of the lovers of music on both sides of the Atlantic, and he was generously aided in procuring a year's instruction in the Royal Academy of Music in London ; subsequently by his own efforts he was enabled to remain two years longer, and finally won the highest prize at the Academy. Cambridge conferred on him the degree of Bachelor of Music, and subsequently Doctor of Music. He then returned to Danville and taught in an institute here, between 1871 and 1874. In 1874 he accepted the professorship of music in the university at Aberystuith, Wales. His compositions are now widely known, and in both hemispheres his reputation is established as one of the most eminent composers of the nineteenth century. Danville may well feel an honest pride in the world-wide reputation of Doctor Joseph Parry.

The Academy.

The Danville Academy was established at an early day by General William Montgomery. He granted a number of lots for that purpose, lying west of Mill street, between the river and Mahoning creek ; stipulating it should be under the control of the Presbyterian church, and that one of his decendants should always be on the board of trustees. The building is a neat, two-story brick on the corner of Market and Chestnut streets. It is surrounded by pleasant grounds and shaded by a number of large maple trees. During the long years since its institution, there have been a number of teachers engaged in dispensing its blessings to successive generations. Those within my own recollection were Bradley, Weston, Wynn, Pratt and Kelso. Among these, J. M. Kelso, is no doubt the most thorough and successful educator. For some years he taught in the Danville Institute. This was founded by himself in the Montgomery building and of which he was principal. Some of our most intelligent and active men in the various professions and pursuits of life, were educated or prepared for college in the Danville Institute, under the tutilage of J. M. Kelso. In fact the college authorities declared that no young men came better prepared than those who had been under the training of Mr. Kelso. His method is thorough and substantial. His present assistant is Miss Flora E. Dorey, also an excellent teacher.

Among the Dead.

John Yerrick, an uncle by marriage to the author of this book, was a quiet, inoffensive man, who strictly attended to the duties of his position in life. Kind hearted, honest and true, he lived a peaceful life, enjoying the good wishes of all around him. He was the ever-faithful sexton of the Protestant Episcopal church without intermission from the building of the church in 1828 until his death which occurred in 1862 in the seventy-ninth year of his age.

William Kitchen, familiarly known as "Squire Kitchen," was one of the old residents of Danville, and for a number of years acted as a justice of the peace. He was also an auctioneer and many a curious joke he cracked on such occasions. Many will remember his mock solemnity, when scolding his turbulent audience for permitting "their minds to run on worldly things, and forgetting the sale." At the merry makings of the young folks, the "Squire" and his violin were always in demand, and well they knew the squeak of his old brown fiddle. No wonder he became a popular favorite. His genial nature and goodness of heart were proverbial. He always possessed a buoyant, playful disposition up to the very last. Many who read this note will pause and call to mind some droll remark of " old Squire Kitchen." whose heart was always kind, and whose jokes, though sharp, never injured any one. He died at an advanced age regretted by all who knew him.

William Hancock came from England and was for a time employed at the Montour iron works. In 1847 he joined with John Foley in establishing the Rough and Ready rolling-mill. He afterwards became sole proprietor of the works. Finally when it became the National iron works he was chosen president of the company. William Hancock was an upright, enterprising citizen, and added much to the business life and prosperity of the town. He built a splendid mansion on Market street and another in Riverside. He was always popular with the workingmen, honorable in all his business transactions, and will long be kindly remembered by those who have shared his favors or enjoyed his friendship.

John G. Montgomery was a prominent lawyer of Danville. After serving with much credit in the State Legislature he was elected to Congress in 1856 ; but died before the commencement of his term. He fell a victim to the mysterious poisoning at the National hotel, in Washington city, in the month of March, 1857, during the inauguration of James Buchanan. He returned home and after lingering a little while, died in the prime of life. He was born in Paradise, then Northumberland county, Pennsylvania, in 1805, and died on the 24th of April, 1857.

Paul Leidy was one of the leading lawyers of Danville and held a high position in the respect and confidence of the community. He represented this district in the Thirty-fifth Congress of the United States. He had also served as prosecuting attorney of Montour, held many positions of trust, and died respected by his fellow citizens.

John Foley was William Hancock's partner in the Rough and Ready rolling-mill. He was also a local preacher in the Methodist church. He left the firm at one time and took a trip to Europe to revisit the scenes and friends of his youth. Previous to his departure the workingmen presented him with a gold headed cane. The presentation address was made by the writer of this volume in the court-house. The ceremony was followed by a banquet at the Montour House. Mr. Foley returned to Danville and after some time he removed to Baltimore, where he died a few years ago.

John T. Heath was a brass founder and plumber, and also kept a small grocery on the corner of Pine and Walnut streets. He was something of a curiosity, and was noted alike for his honesty and fair dealing and for the marvelous tough stories he could tell. He could tell a fish story with the most profound solemnity ; such as having seen a man at Philadelphia ride across the Delaware to Camden, on the back of a sturgeon. He could also tell snake stories with an air of seriousness that challenged the confidence of his wayside audience. And yet John T. Heath was a good man, did no harm to his neighbor and was highly respected in his day and generation. He left Danville years ago and has since died.

John Patton was a wheelright and one of the early mechanics that gave character to Danville. By the kindness of his children,

10

the later years of his life were spent in comfort and with little of worldly care. Many a pleasant hour I spent with him under the tall elms that stood on the banks of Mahoning; and well I knew that I lost a friend when John Patton died. Indeed, if "good" can be justly applied to mortal man—one who contributed a share to the business current and the moral sentiment of Danville, that man was John Patton. An earnest christian, an example of steadfast, practical piety, and yet always cheerful as a summer morning. He has gone to meet the reward of the christian soldier who has fought the good fight, kept the faith and finished his course.

Mannassa Young was a prominent member of the African Methodist Episcopal church of Mount Zion, and was also superintendent of the Sabbath school. He was a portly man, weighing nearly four hundred pounds. For twenty years he served as watchman at the company store and was always faithful. He died in February, 1870. His death was peaceful. He died as the Christian dies.

William Thompson was a barber and a man of more than ordinary intelligence. He was well posted on public affairs, and although he did not live to see the day, he confidently predicted the freedom of his race in the near future. He died in the prime of life.

Sydney S. Easton died in October 1862, in the fifty-eighth year of his age. He was a contractor in connection with the public works in various portions of the State, and for some time had been engaged at the Pennsylvania iron works. He built a fine residence on Market street, now occupied by William T. Ramsay, who married a daughter of Sydney S. Easton. He (Sydney S. Easton) was highly esteemed, kind in his disposition and charitable to all, he never turned away from the needy. He was a member of the Protestant Episcopal church, and in his life adorned the doctrines he professed. Rev. E. N. Lightner delivered a beautiful and appopriate address over his remains in the church. The Masonic fraternity escorted him to the grave.

Isaac Gulick, an upright citizen, held a number of local positions of responsibility and died some twenty years ago.

A. P. Alward, long a justice of the peace, died as old age was approaching.

John Moore, one of the enterprising business men of Danville, died at a good old age. He built the Mansion House.

Jacob Cornelison, proprietor of the "White Swan," contracted disease in the army and died in 1865, comparatively young.

Cornelius Garretson, a man of considerable prominence died at a good old age. He was at one time proprietor of the Montour House.

John Harmon, was a quiet and industrious citizen, working as book-binder, barber, watchmaker and saloon keeper. He was in the forty-fourth year of his age and died on the 4th of June, 1870.

Robert Winter, was among the honest, industrious and pious citizens of Danville. He was a baker and made good, honest loaves. He fell asleep some years ago.

John Cooper.—Judge Cooper was a lawyer of more than ordinary ability, and was also considered good authority on literary subjects of a general character. Perhaps the deference paid by the public, the homage paid to his learning and ripened judgment, made him somewhat arrogant in the latter years of his life. He was very quick and restive on the slightest opposition ; and many anecdotes are told of his sudden ebullitions and emphatic expressions when provoked. He was much respected as the most learned though the most eccentric lawyer of Danville. He died on the 22d day of June, 1863, in the seventy-ninth year of his age. He was the father-in-law of Hon. John G. Montgomery, the victim of the hotel poisoning at Washington.

Peter Hughes was a marble worker and was proprietor of the yard now owned by H. F. Hawke & Co. He was also honored by being elected associate judge. He died about 1872.

B. W. Musselman was a good citizen and served as drum major in the war for the Union. He died in 1875.

Jacob Hibler was one of the substantial business men of Danville. He carried on the tanning business on Front street, and sold to Mr. Houpt. He died a number of years ago, much regretted.

Thomas Jemison was a contractor and aided in many public improvements. He had many warm friends. Died in 1863 or 1864.

Jacob Reed was a Danville merchant, somewhat peculiar ; but really a good man. He died a few years ago.

Samuel York, Jr., was the first president of the First National

Bank of Danville. He was always a man of high standing in the community and died much regretted a few years ago.

James Cousart, long a confidential clerk at the Rough and Ready iron works, died a year or two ago, when scarcely past the meridian line.

Daniel Reynolds, the Danville hatter and an honest man died some three years ago.

James G. Maxwell, a member of the Legislature in 1849, died some years ago, and his brother Thomas Maxwell died in 1875.

Thomas Clark was a machinist, a quiet good man, familiarly called "Uncle Tom." He died some years ago.

A. J. Ammerman was the merchant of East Danville. An active enterprising business man. He died in his prime.

B. W. Waples was superintendent of the Grove's limestones quarries. He was a man of much executive power, strong in his friendships and generous to all.

James Voris was one of the old substantial citizens and held a high place in the respect and confidence of the people. He died on the 24th of May, 1866, aged 78 years and 7 months. He sleeps in the Presbyterian grave-yard where a marble tombstone tells the brief and pointed history of man, namely that he was born; lived his day, died, has gone to his reward.

Joseph D. Hahn was an active man and held a number of local offices. He died in middle life.

William Buckley built and kept the "Hudson River House." He died in 1875.

Charles C. Baldy built a fine, iron-front block on Mill street and kept a hardware store for a number of years. He died six or seven years ago.

Isaac R. Freeze, a young merchant and a man of promise, died in 1870 just as he had crossed the threshold of manhood.

Eli Trego came from Chester county and was connected with the Montour iron works at their commencement. He was also a justice of the peace, his office and residence adjoined the Montgomery building. He died on the 14th of February, 1856, and was buried with Masonic honors. His remains were first taken to the Episcopal church where Rev. E. N. Lightner, the rector delivered the most eloquent and impressive funeral discourse I ever heard.

Samuel Alexander was a worthy and respectable citizen. Long an earnest and devoted Christian in communion with the Methodist church, he saw his approaching end with calmness, and met the last great foe like a good soldier of the cross. He was also an ardent patriot during the war, and died triumphantly in the fifty-ninth year of his age.

M. C. Grier was a brother of Judge Robert C. Grier, late of the Supreme Court of the United States. He was one of the substantial citizens of Danville, and occupied many positions of public trust. Long a ruling elder in the Presbyterian church, he adorned the position by the practice of every Christian virtue that lends nobility to the office-bearer in the house of God. Generous to a fault; for like Goldsmith's " village preacher," his very " failings leaned to virtue's side." He was ever ready to deny himself in ministering to the happiness of others. Every good work for the general or the special benefit of his fellow men always found a warm and earnest friend in M. C. Grier. And many there are who will gratefully remember his kindly aid and cherish his memory with a devotion pure as earth affords and lasting as their lives. In a word, M. C. Grier was emphatically a *good* man, and if the world had more like him the sunshine of joy would dispel the darkness of sorrow from many a household. He has gone to his reward, leaving a record untarnished and a name that none need ever blush to own. He died December 25th, 1878.

William Smith. familiarly known as " Billy Smith," for more than thirty years drove stage and omnibus in this place. He was one of the most careful and obliging men to be found in the country, and was favorably known far and wide. His omnibus was always on time and he always had a pleasant answer to a civil inquiry. He died a few years ago much lamented.

J. P., M. J., and John J. Grove, the proprietors of the Columbia furnaces. Large-minded and energetic business men; honest and reliable they were highly respected, and all died in the prime of manhood.

Major Thomas Brandon, one of the *live* men of Danville, with a military turn of mind, died a few years ago.

George A. Frick, prothonotary of the county, and first cashier of the Bank of Danville ; was a lawyer of ability, with a mind well stored with general knowledge. He died suddenly at a ripe old age.

Major J. V. L. De Witt, at one time proprietor of Chulasky furnace, died a few years ago.

Major William G. Scott, of Northumberland county, settled in Danville, to spend the evening of his days, and died at a good old age.

John Rhodes, came to Danville in 1824. He bought the "Pennsylvania House" in 1829. It was originally called the "Farmers' Hotel," and for many years was the chosen hostelrie of the farmers and others while attending court or on other occasions. John Rhodes enjoyed the respect and confidence of a large circle of friends and patrons. He died in 1852 and the property still belongs to his heirs. Two of his sons are still in town, B. K. Rhodes a lawyer and J. Clark Rhodes a merchant whose store adjoins the hotel.

Horace Curtis, a highly-respected teacher of the Second Ward grammar school. He died on April 21st, 1863, aged 52 years.

There is no pretension to a complete list of the dead of twenty-five years, as that would itself fill a volume. The names of a few are added below :

Dr. Isaac Hughes, Dr. E. H. Snyder, George Kipp, S. C. Vansant, I. S. Thornton, J. M. Woods, Samuel Wolf, W. W. Hughes, William Morgan, William Earp, Samuel Ware, William Travel, Rev. J. B. Cook, Charles and Barney Dougherty, John Arms, Mark Myers, George and Lewis Kaufman, Frank Rouch, Samuel Roush, D. N. Kownover, George Basset, Charles H. Waters, Samuel Stroh, Henry Harris, Robert Winter.

Water Works.

The question of supplying Danville with water was long and earnestly debated, and various plans or systems were proposed. Some favored a reservoir on York's Hill and forcing the water from the river by a powerful, stationary engine. Others favored a reservoir, but insisted on bringing the water from Roaring creek in pipes passing under the river bed ; others again were inclined to a connection with the water works at the asylum. Some ten years ago, a company was chartered, as the "Danville Water Company;" but it never got beyond a formal organization. In 1871 some pamphlets were sent to this place, explaining the character and success of the

" Holly system," recently introduced by the Holly firm at Lockport, New York. The town council took up the subject, and whilst all urged a water supply the council was about equally divided between the Holly system and a reservoir. Finally a committee, consisting of George W. Reay, J. W. Sweisfort, William Buckley, and M. D. L. Sechler, was appointed to investigate the subject.

In the later part of April, 1872, the committee went to Elmira, Buffalo, Binghampton, Rochester, Auburn, and other cities where the various plans are in operation. It is worthy of note that a majority of the committee was opposed to the Holly system, but after a full investigation they unanimously reported in favor of the Holly works. Previous to this an election was held at the court house to ascertain the popular sentiment. There was a large majority in favor of water, but owing to some informality the result was not satisfactory. After a warm contest the Holly system was adopted by the casting vote of Burgess, Oscar Ephlin, and a contract was accordingly made with the Holly Company at Lockport, New York. The final vote on adopting the Holly system was as follows: For the Holly works, George W. Reay, William Buckley, Jacob Schuster, George W. Miles, J. W. Sweisfort, M. D. L. Sechler, and Oscar Ephlin, Burgess. Against the Holly works; George Lovett, Samuel Lewis, James L. Riehl, Henry M. Schoch, and Hickman Frame.

The water works are located on the river bank in the First ward. The engines and pumps are a model of beauty and of power. A filterer was constructed some distance out in the river, and the water from thence forced through metal pipes through every portion of the town, not only supplying the citizens but proving a great safety in case of fire. These works have a capacity of two millions of gallons in twenty-four hours, but can be procured of any desired capacity. In the works here, there are two engines of each one hundred and fifty horse-power, two powerful rotary pumps and a gang of twelve piston pumps. There are ten miles of pipe laid and there are about one hundred fire hydrants. The pipe was laid by S. Krebs & Co., under a contract for $87,500. The contract for the engines and pumps, with the Holly Manufacturing Company, at Lockport, New York, was for $36,000. In 1880 the council had a well sunk on the river bank, fifty feet in length, five feet wide, and ten feet deep. The works are now perfectly satisfactory; the wretched filterer in the river having been a source of constant trouble. It is proper to say that the wells as now constructed, belong to the Holly system. The people of Danville, notwithstanding the consequent debt, fully appreciate the great value of the Holly system of water supply, and would on no consideration exchange their magnificent works for any mud-hole of a reservoir that ever sent its doubtful essence through a city, burdened, and yet deprived of pure, wholesome water. We now have an abundance, and the safety these works afford in case of fire as well as the economy in supporting a fire department is alone worth more to Danville than their cost. In point of convenience, purity, cleanliness, health, and safety from fire, the Holly system of water works, so far as our experience with the testimony of other cities extends is superior to all others.

The water works are managed by a board of three commissioners, appointed by the town council. A superintendent, secretary, and other employees are appointed by the commissioners.

The present board of water commissioners consist of John H. Grove, James Cruikshanks, and Doctor R. S. Simington.

Superintendent, James Foster.

Clerk, Charles M. Zuber.

Music.

Music has long been liberally patronized in Danville. I pass over the good old times of the village "singing school," and this is a necessity as but scanty record is left of those primary institutions; when the "master" with his "pitch-fork," nasal twang and swallow tailed coat ruled the hour. Ah! those were delightful days and more delightful nights, when the young folks met at stated periods in the quaint and rugged school-house of the village, each with the latest edition of *fa-sol-la* in one hand and a tallow-dip in the other, wrapped in a paper socket. *Do ra me* had not been invented, gas was unknown and coal oil slept in darkness far down in the earth. Yet the people were contented and happy with the square notes and the light the tallow afforded. It was in the days when *caste*, founded on wealth or accidental circumstances was unknown, and when these humble enjoyments yielded a rich harvest of delight. How the grand notes of "Old Hundred," "Coventry" and "Coronation" awoke the slumbering echoes among the rough-hewn rafters; and how the tender glances of rustic swain, or blushing maiden, mingled in the fitful glare of the tallow-dip and perchance gave a richer zest to the heart-felt music. And what fun and frolic they had at "intermission," and how the joyous hearts of earnest lovers bounded and fluttered when "singing school was out," and going home was in order? Many happy marriages that still bless their decendants, resulted from those happy reunions, and many scenes of wild romance, or rarest humor, enlivened the long remembered hours of joy, in those far off days. Though with many they may be almost forgotten in the rushing, jostling race for wealth and distinction, or only recalled at long intervals as memory for a moment sweeps away the dust of finished years Age or misfortune will bring back the past, that was forgotten in the sunshine of prosperity.

Quaint and curious is the ancient legend, in relation to the origin of instrumental music: namely that Tubal Cain or some antediluvian caught the first idea from the vibration in the wind of a broken branch of the bamboo tree. Equally poetic and perhaps more truthful is the story of its origin in Danville. Do you remember the ragged but happy descendant of Africa, so lustily blowing a horn on the old bridge, near where the iron footway now spans the canal, on Mill street? He manifested a high conception of the sublime science and remarkable skill in execution. In the calm twilight of summer evenings many paused to listen to the stirring music of the enraptured amateur. Among them was Abraham Sechler. His quick ear caught the inspiring notes that soon developed a wondrous power in himself, urging him onward and upward in the scale of musical excellence. The cultivation of that branch of music has ever been his delight and his success has been complete. From childhood a lover of music and catching fresh inspiration from the thrilling notes of the wandering minstrel, as he poured the soul of song through the rude instrument of his choice, on the old bridge; Abraham Sechler resolved to excel. Soon his four brothers joined him in an amateur band. For some time these five brothers practiced together and won a high reputation for proficiency in rendering music of a higher order than the good people of Danville were wont to hear.

The first regular cornet band was organized early in 1838. It was called, "The Danville Independent Band." Abraham Sechler was chosen president and leader on the 25th of April, 1838. Jesse F. Sholes was made secretary and treasurer. He resigned on the 28th day of January, 1839, and Oscar Moore was chosen in his stead. At the organization the members were Abraham Sechler, Jesse F. Sholes, George S. Sanders, Oscar Moore, Jacob R. Sechler, Michael Rissel, George W. Hall, Joseph Hiles, Charles Sechler and Jesse Clark. The uniform was blue cloth. The coats were trimmed with yellow lace and brass buttons. The by-laws also required them to wear "stand-up collars." The constitution and by-laws adopted, were drawn up with much care and contain some excellent rules : among them is one imposing a fine of two dollars in case of intoxication during the hours of duty. In searching the minutes I can find no instance of the fine being exacted, from which it is evident that this law never was violated. But then it was before the days of lager beer or poisoned whisky. For the old records, I am indebted to Mr. George S. Sanders who was one of the members of the pioneer band and who is still among our prominent musicians.

In the course of time the name of the band was changed to " The Danville Cornet Band." In 1855 Charles H. Stoes became its leader, and in 1857 through the aid of the citizens a complete set of new instruments were procured. They were of German silver and that presented to Charles H. Stoes of solid silver, and the band has since been known as " Stoes' Silver Cornet Band." The members were Charles H. Stoes, leader, Moyer Lyon, George S. Sanders, John F. Gulick, B. W. Musselman, A. F. Henrie, E. K. Hale, George W. Hoffman, Charles Sechler, Jacob Weitzel, Joseph R. Patton, O. G. Mellon, H. L. Shick, Joseph Clark and Hugh Pursel.

For years this band was one of the most distinguished in the State, bearing away the honors on many public occasions in various portions of the country. The present members of this band, now " Stoes' Twelfth Regiment Band," are Charles H. Stoes, leader, William McCloud, Abraham Sechler, A. Flanagan, Benjamin A. Gaskins, George S. Sanders, William McCloud, Jr., J. T. Oberdorf, Charles Gross, James Irland, Clark Coder, George W. Hoffman, E. K. Hale, Joseph L. Frame, Peter Keller, Frank Lewis, John N. Hommer, Thomas Hall and H. L. Shick, drum major. In 1856 a new cornet band was organized in Danville, under the leadership and instruction of Abraham Sechler. Its membership embraced a number who had been trained in the original band together with some new material. It met in the Assembly building and was known as " Sechler's Cornet Band," and it soon attained a high degree of proficiency. To this band, J. B. Cox, a photographer, presented a large portrait of each member, in a massive frame. I had the honor of participating in the imposing ceremonies. For some time " Sechler's Cornet Band" bade fair to rival the old organization. But its members volunteered in the army of the United States and served through long years of war and after its dissolution, Mr. Sechler played with Stoes' band. In 1872 a number of musicians joined together in the organization of a new band, which was known as the "Independent Band of Danville." Mr. Gibbons was chosen leader and Abraham Sechler instructor. Its place of meeting was in Frank's building by the canal. For some time it made extraordinary progress, but is now dissolved. Some of its members are playing in Stoes' band. St. Joseph's cornet band was organized some years ago, and also made rapid strides under the instruction of Abraham Sechler, but also disbanded and a portion are in the old and only cornet band now in Danville.

While we acknowledge and admire the rare talents and wonderful execution of Charles H. Stoes, justice demands a recognition of Abraham Sechler, as the Nestor of musical science in Danville, the pioneer of the earliest organized effort in its cultivation, and as such he is worthy of a high place in the musical synagogue. He bore the burden and piloted the way, in the "day of small things." He bared his shoulders to unremitting toil in training the old band and preparing the way to the proud eminence it now occupies. He labored faithfully to sow the good seed, though others might reap the golden harvest in a wider field. In a word let us give to each and all, the honor that is due to all who have devoted their talents and their energies to the cultivation of music, and in giving to Danville the preëminence so generally acknowledged by those best qualified to judge.

Vocal and Instrumental Music.

Vocal and instrumental music on the organ and piano have been very generally cultivated in Danville. A great number of profes-

sors and teachers have sojourned here, during the last quarter of a
century, under whose guidance the standard has been well advanced.
Some of these are remembered and others are forgotten. It is a curious
fact that so many traveling professors, though blessed with musical
ability, are shallow minded in other respects, vain and foppish.
But there are many noble exceptions. Mr. Bachman was a thorough
teacher and possessed a mind well stored with general information.
Many of the Danville ladies in middle life, who excel in music to-
day, were started on the high road by the substantial and skillful
training of Mr. Bachman. He has long since gone to his rest in
the grave ; but the fruit of his work remains, and in musical numbers his memory lives in the evening hymns of many a household
band. There was also Mr. Hess, the two Walkers, Baron Von
Rachow and others who were proficients in music. but seemed to
lack ballast in other departments of their mental organization.
Among the lady teachers, Miss Damon has no rival. She was eminently successful and won a high reputation in this place. She,
like a number of others, was a noble exception to the general criti-
cism of our musical professors. William H. Bourne was a very
successful teacher and a man of general information, but he abandoned the profession for other pursuits. Professor Mason conducted
an institute in Reynold's building for some time with good success.

Harry Earp's Sextant Cornet Band was organized under the leadership of Harry Earp, some three years ago. The members at organization were Harry Earp, leader ; Bergan Gaskins, John F.
Kime, Conrad Aten, William Earp. David Aten. This band is
greatly admired for its high character and splendid execution. David
Aten has since died and his place is vacant.

The First Bank.

The Danville bank was chartered by the State, in 1848. The
first election was held on the 9th of November 1849, at the Montour House. The directors then elected were. Peter Baldy, Sr.,
Dr. William H. Magill, George A. Frick, William Jennison, William Donaldson, Lewis Vastine and M. C. Grier, of Danville ;
Thomas Hayes of Lewisburg ; Jacob Cooke of Muncy ; W. C. Law-
son of Milton ; Jacob W. Smith of Selinsgrove ; John Sharpless of
Catawissa ; and John Grotz, of Bloomsburg. On the 26th of No-

vember 1849, the directors held a meeting at the Montour House and elected Peter Baldy, Sr., president, and on the 18th of December following, George A. Frick was elected cashier. David Clark was elected clerk and B. P. Alward was appointed messenger and watchman. The salaries were for the president $300 ; the cashier $800 ; the clerk $500 and for the messenger $163.

On the 13th of February, 1850, George A. Frick resigned his directorship and J. P. Hackenburg was chosen in his stead.

On the 19th of February, 1850, the bank was opened for business and the first deposit was made by David Clark. In February the capital stock paid in was $200,000.

Peter Baldy, Sr., resigned the presidency of the bank on the 13th of October, 1856, and Edward H. Baldy was elected to that position. George A. Frick, the cashier, resigned that office on the 22d of April, 1862, and David Clark was elected cashier on the same day. A well-deserved vote of thanks was tendered to George A. Frick for his long and faithful services, and his salary was continued until the following July.

According to previous notice a meeting of the stockholders was held on the 15th of April 1865, to decide upon becoming a National Bank, under the laws of the United States. The decision was unanimous in favor of the proposed change. At the same meeting P. Baldy, E. H. Baldy, George A. Frick, William H. Magill, J. C. Rhodes, G. M. Shoop and John Sharpless were elected directors. Since that time the institution has continued to prosper, under its judicious management. The officers at present are, president, E. H. Baldy ; cashier, David Clark ; clerk, George M. Gearheart. It is now the Danville National Bank.

Editorial Association.

The first Editorial Association in the State was organized in Danville in 1857, at least I have no knowledge of any prior organization. In the spring of 1857, through the paper I then published in this place I proposed a convention of Pennsylvania editors at Danville for mutual benefit. The project was opposed on the part of some, on the ground that the diversity of local interests would prevent us from fixing a scale of prices or harmonizing on many subjects. Many, however, seconded this movement and agreed to come to Danville out of deference to the place where it originated.   The 4th of August, 1857, was fixed upon as the time and on that day the following editors met in the Montgomery building, where my office was then located, viz : J. Henry Puleston, *Pittston Gazette ;* W. P. Miner. *Record of the Times*, Wilkes-Barre ; E. H. Rauch, *Mauch Chunk Gazette ;* E. A. Baker, *Jersey Shore Republican ;* O. N. Worden, *Lewisburg Chronical ;* Thomas G. Price, *Working Men's Advocate*, Minersville ; R. W. Weaver, *Star of the North*, Bloomsburg ; Palemon John, *Columbia County Republican*, Bloomsburg ; L. H. Davis, *Montgomery Ledger*, Pottstown ; James Jones. *Jersey Shore Vidette ;* H. B. Mosser, *Sunbury American ;* John Youngman, *Sunbury Gazette ;* Levi L. Tate, *Democrat*, Bloomesburg ; L. F. Irvin, *Berwick Gazette ;* G. L. I. Painter. *Muncy Luminary ;* Jacob Frick, *Miltonian ;* Richard Edwards, *Western Star*, Pottsville ; C. E. Chichester, *Philadelphia Enquirer ;* Valentine Best, *Danville Intenigencer ;* Charles Cook, *Danville Democrat ;* D. H. B. Brower, *Montour American*, Danville.

On motion W. P. Miner was called to the chair. and L. H. Davis was chosen temporary secretary.

The following were appointed a committee on organization : E. H. Rauch, Thomas G. Price, and D. H. B. Brower.

R. W. Weaver. J. H. Puleston. Valentine Best, O. N. Worden, F. A. Baker, were appointed a committee on " business."

The convention then adjourned until two o'clock, P. M.

At the afternoon session the committee on organization reported as permanent officers :

President—Levi L. Tate.

Vice Presidents—V. Best, G. L. I. Painter, O. N. Worden, L. H. Davis.

Secretaries—J. H. Puleston, John Youngman.'

Regrets for unavoidable non-attendance were received from the *Carbon Democrat, Wellsboro' Agitator. Lycoming Gazette*, and *Weekly Phœnix.*

The first movement was as follows :

Resolved, That this association shall be known as the "Keystone Editorial Union," and shall meet annually, at such time and place as may be agreed upon.

Resolved, That we earnestly recommend that from the first of January next, all subscriptions shall be required in advance.

Various subjects of importance were discussed. The chair appointed Rauch, Cook and Jones a committee on resolutions.

At the evening session, the following resolutions were reported :

First. That members of this association will have no dealings with any advertising agent who will not promptly settle his account at the end of every quarter for all advertisements sent within that time ; and any advertising agent failing to do so, shall be published as being no longer our agent.

Second. That we deem it impracticable for editors, in different localities distant, from each other to fix a uniform scale of prices, and that we therefore recommend that it be made a matter of local arrangement, and in no case deviating from the terms set forth in their respective journals.

Third. That believing mutual confidence and coöperation necessary to secure any practical benefit to our profession, we pledge ourselves to use our best efforts, both individually and collectively, to cultivate that spirit.

Fourth. That the publication of personalities reflecting upon the private character of a brother editor, or any other individual, is derogatory to the profession, and should not be countenanced.

Fifth. That it is a violation of that courtesy which should ever characterize the editorial fraternity to employ apprentices who have not served out their full term with their employer, unless by mutual agreement. and we pledge ourselves to discourage it.

Sixth. That we will not take apprentices hereafter for a shorter period than four years.

Seventh. That we pledge ourselves to exclude all advertising of an indelicate nature.

Eighth. That all general laws by the Legislature should, in the opinion of this association, be published and laid before the people as fully as possible, immediately after the close of the session during which they were enacted, and that the cheapest and only successful mode of accomplishing this would be by the passage of an act providing for such publication in every newspaper of the State, at a cost of one half the regular advertising rates.

Ninth. That a copy of these resolutions be forwarded to every newspaper office in the interior of Pennsylvania.

O. N. Worden delivered an amusing address on "The Oldest Printer on Record."

Pottsville was selected as the place, and the first Tuesday in May, 1858, for the next meeting.

The venerable Col. Valentine Best, was unable to take an active part in the proceedings, but to manifest his interest in the movement, he hoisted the American flag at his office, and cordially invited all the members of the association to call at his residence and partake of a collation prepared for the occasion. About eight o'clock in the evening the association enjoyed his hospitality, where Stoes' Silver Cornet Band gave them a grand serenade.

During the ensuing winter the editors of Philadelphia organized an editorial association, and invited the "Keystone Editorial Union," instituted at Danville, to meet them in Philadelphia on the 12th of April, 1858. The invitation was accepted, and there being an evident disposition on the part of the city editors, with the exception of J. W. Forney, and a few others, to swallow the original association, there sprang up a lively discussion between Morton McMichael, William M. Allen, George Raymond, and R. Lyle White on the one side, and J. W. Forney, Dr. John, L. L. Tate, and D. H. B. Brower on the other.

Finally D. H. B. Brower offered the following as a compromise : "That we are willing to go into a general State organization at once, if the association of city editors will agree to a formal union and a new, joint organization, each abandoning the old.

On motion of J. W. Forney, this proposition was agreed to.

The following officers were then elected for the State Editorial Association of Pennsylvania:

President—Morton McMichael.

Vice Presidents—Col. Tate, J. J. Patterson, R. Lyle White, O. N. Worden, Edward Shull, P. R. Freas, H. S. Evans.

Secretaries—L. H. Davis, G. Raymond, J. H. Puleston.

Treasurer—L. A. Godley.

Executive Committee—D. H. B. Brower, J. W. Forney, J. Heron Foster, J. M. Keuster.

Corresponding Secretary—Charles J. Peterson.

The association adjourned to meet at Harrisburg in 1859, but it soon became evident at Harrisburg that the purposes of the association were ignored, and that it was rapidly degenerating into a mere season of carousal. After one or two meetings at the capital, the leading journalists of the State withdrew, and so far as the original design was concerned, it was a failure. The organization was dissolved. Mr. Godey the treasurer, still having some seventy dollars in his hands.

After some years it was resurrected and still retains its organization, meeting annually for a pleasure trip, which seems to be the main object of its existence.

Now and Then.

On taking a survey of Danville, there is nothing more clearly apparent to the careful observer than the growing taste of our people, as well as their enterprise, manifested in the air of neatness that surrounds their dwellings and the improvements and adornments that beautify their homes, notwithstanding the grievous depression under which they are struggling. Nor is it limited alone to private residences, but is seen in the places of public resort. Almost every house, in some portions of the town, can boast some new attraction, if nothing but a tree, a shrub or a flower. It seems as if the scales had fallen from our eyes, and our people, with a common impulse, a new-born zeal and a more refined taste, begin to see the beauty and the utility of pleasant surroundings. Under the influence of this spirit pervading the community old homes are putting on a new garb, and the new are reared with scrupulous care, not only as " a place to eat and sleep," but as a place to enjoy the sweetest hours of life—the pleasures of HOME. Volumes have been written on the duty of making home attractive, and a stroll, especially through East Danville or " York's Hill " will convince you that the lesson is carried out in practice, at least as far as the exterior is concerned. A glance at other portions of the town will also show a general progress in the same direction, and teach us to anticipate the time when the rough places will be redeemed, and teem with the evidences of taste and culture, so pleasant to the eye, and when the very cinder-tips will bloom with the blossoms of the rose. The time is coming

11

when fruitful gardens, trees and flowers will adorn every home, where, as yet, the bare and cinder-coated earth awaits their coming—when Bald-Top will no longer lift its barren heights to the sun, but when picturesque mansions will deck its crown, when fertile gardens, vines and vineyards will adorn its slopes, when shrubbery, roadways and all the improvements of cultivated taste and enterprise shall combine with its native grandeur to make it what it is destined to be. And, surely, Bald-Top has yielded enough of its solid treasures of ore to claim in return its general improvement.

The time was when it was too common to rear a structure in haste, to board it up roughly, and guiltless of paint or ornament to make it a place to stay. Now, where those in similar circumstances build a home it is neat, modestly and tastefully adorned. It is next provided with proper surroundings, and is made pleasant to the eye and cheering to the heart. And there is no doubt that children reared amid the charms of such a home, will unconsciously catch the spirit of the scenes around them, and grow up with a life-long impression of that gentle influence on their hearts and on their minds.

We have said that this progressive spirit of improvement, with the growing taste of our people, is not limited to private residences alone. Our public buildings and places of popular resort of all kinds, bear the same impress, both as regards elegance and convenience.

Perhaps there is no more convincing or enduring evidence of the real character of a people, than that afforded by their public buildings. By that standard, historians judge the nations and peoples that rose and fell in the long past. By that standard, character is given to the people of Thebes, Palmyra, to Pompeii and Herculaneum. Nor these alone, but many others known to have existed, and who left no architectural monuments to guide the antiquarian, are set down as having occupied the lowest grade of intelligence, or as being uncivilized.

But let us come back to Danville. We have no apprehension that Bald-Top or Blue Hill will become volcanic and cover us up with ashes and lava, so that the curious delvers in after times, when they dig down to the cobble-stones on Mill street, or haply discover the

ornate and durable masonry of the court-house, the opera-house, the
asylum, or Groves' Mount Lebanon, will judge our progress as a
people in the arts and sciences and define our exact position in
the scale of civilization, by the style of chisseled granite ; nay more,
fix our moral standard by the sculptured stones they may find among
the ruins of our churches. We are not guarding against such a con-
tingency, still it is no less desirable to leave these substantial memorials to those who come after us. It is, therefore, pleasant to
witness their creation—pleasant to remember, on this centennial
year, that all the stately churches, public edifices and splendid mansions that greet the eye were redeemed from the wild and barren
waste that marked the landscape in the days of the pioneers. The
lessons drawn from the beauties of art or nature are humanizing and
eminently wholesome, as well as lasting. We do not mean to gaze
for an hour with feelings of awe, on the wonders of the world, but
daily intercourse with the one or the other. We mean the impression made upon us by living in their midst and catching the sublime
spirit of their harmony, until their teachings become a part of our
very selves, interwoven with our own nature and lasting as our lives.
The mighty cataract, the grandeur of the mountain among the
clouds, the solid masonry of the Almighty or his Majesty mirrored
in the ocean, may excite our wonder and awe. It may stir the
emotions of our hearts to their very depths, under a sense of the
grand and the sublime, but will have less bearing on our every day
life, than the quiet beauties around us. These calm yet potent
agencies daily inspire our lives by the lessons they daily repeat.

Brick Making.

The first brick made in Danville, were made by Mr. Burkenbine,
near the ground on which the company store now stands. After
him came Charles White, S. Gibbs, and John Turner, who each had
their day in the manufacture, in various localities within the town
limits. Good clay is formed in all portions of the narrrow valley in
which Danville is located. Nearly a score of years ago B. W. Wate
bought out John Turner, and for many successive seasons manufactured brick on an extensive scale, turning out over seven hundred
thousand in a single season. Mr. Wate is an energetic, upright business man, and bids fair to bake oceans of mud into first class brick,

as he is still in the prime of life. In the summer of 1880 he operated at Milton, where the great fire created a pressing demand for
brick. Some years ago Joseph Flanegan commenced the brick ma-
ing in Danville, and continues to make and sell hundreds of thousands every season. His make always find a ready sale. He un-
derstands the business well, and his reputation as a reliable business
man extends far and wide. Reed, Diebert, and others also embarked in the business, but, not being practical men they soon
abandoned the field. Brick have sold from $4 50 to $8 00 per
thousand in this market.

Kiem has also been operating a yard for Wilson M. Gearhart.

Hospital for the Insane at Danville.

This great public institution is located on what had been known
as the " Pinneo Farm," about one mile southeast of Danville. On
the 13th of April, 1868, the Legislature passed an act for the establishment of the hospital and appointed a locating commission, composed of J. A. Reed, Traill Green and John Curwen. After visiting various localities in the district, for which the proposed hospital
was intended, it was finally decided that Danville was the most suitable in all respects. The Pinneo farm of some two hundred and fifty
acres was accordingly purchased, the citizens of Danville con-
tributing a *bonus* of sixteen thousand dollars. On the 23d of April
the commissioners had appointed John McArthur, Jr., architect,
and soon after they chose Doctor S. S. Schultz superintendent, a
a position he has filled ever since May, 1868 with great credit to
himself and to the complete satisfaction of the public. The corner
stone of the hospital was laid by Governor John W. Geary on the
26th day of August, 1869. The building proper is eleven hundred
and forty-three feet long. The center building is two hundred and
two feet deep. They range from three to five stories in height.
The wings contain three hundred and fifty rooms each. Altogether
there are about eight hundred rooms. The chapel is a large
and beautiful chamber and will seat six hundred. It is also the
lecture-room and is furnished with a piano and an organ. The
wing connections are enclosed with iron doors, and the building
contains every department necessary to an institution where so
many unfortunates find a home ; offices, bath-rooms, dining-rooms,

laundries, kitchen. store room and many others. Iron and slate are extensively used in the construction of the building, in order to strengthen it as well as to guard against the danger of fire. The stone in the exterior walls are from the well-known quarry on the premises. The door and window sills and lintels as also the carriage porch are of the Goldsboro' brown stone from York county. The brick in the partition walls were furnished by numerous makers of the neighborhood and were laid by Ammerman and Books. The roof is of the best Peach Bottom slate, furnished by Parry, Gravel & Williams. The kitchen floors and other apartments are also laid with slate. The water tables and quoins are a beautiful white stone from Luzerne county and contrast pleasantly with the darker material of the main wall. It is not the design of this volume to enter into details beyond that which will give the reader a general idea of the complete and substantial character of the building, and its manifold appointments, necessary to serve the purpose for which it was erected. A visit to the institution alone can give a proper, intelligent idea of its excellence. I can only hurriedly refer to its water and gas supply, its heating and ventilating apparatus, its sewerage and all similar improvements essential to the health and comfort of the inmates. Governed by a complete system of laws and regulations, this institution stands on the front line of modern improvements, dispensing in an eminent degree the blessings for which it was designed. In connection with the various appliances of convenience, comfort and economy the visitor will also note the beautiful buildings, fitted for their several purposes, that have sprung up around the main edifice, solid, artistic and presenting a miniature city of surpassing beauty and taste. The order or style of architecture is the Romanesque. The hospital was opened for the reception of patients by public announcement of Doctor Shultz, the superintendent, in October 1872. The first patient was admitted on the 6th day of November, following. From that period to the present time hundreds have been admitted and shared its benefits. Many have been discharged cured, many others have been improved and others still continue to receive its scientific and humane ministrations. Doctor S. S. Shultz, who has managed the institution since its organization in 1868, still remains in his responsible position. He has manifested not only the skill to treat suc-

cessfully all possible cases in the various forms of insanity arising
from physical or mental causes; but in addition to the qualities of
the physician he has also manifested executive ability of the highest
order in the management of the institution. The order and exact-
ness required in each department and in the most minute details at-
est his fitness no less than the higher qualities demanded by his position. Governed by the lessons of experience and the nobility that
religion lends to science, our hospital must reach the highest degree
of usefulness not only in its financial administration; but in ministering to unfortunate humanity. Doctor Shultz is assisted by Doctors Seip and Hugh Meredith. The corps of aids, Mr. Eyer, the
steward; the clerk, Mr. Orth; the supervisors, Miss Dressler and
Mr. Dillon; the engineer, Mr. Kearns; the matron, Mrs. Eyer; the
farmer, Mr. Rote, and the gardener, Mr. Carey are all highly spoken
of in their respective *roles*.

Simon P. Kase.

Simon P. Kase, one of the most remarkable men of the day, was
born in Rush, on the opposite side of the river, on the 27th of August, 1814. His father was long a justice of the peace. He was
the owner of several good farms and was in comfortable circumstances. He had the confidence of those around him and was consulted
in relation to all public questions as well as in private affairs. He
was an elder in the church at Rushtown for many years. His mother
is said to have been a noble woman who endeared herself to all
around her. His brothers and sisters were John, William, Elizabeth, Katy, Charity, Sarah, Susan and Amy. Simon, the subject
of this sketch was the youngest of the family. At twenty years of
age he left his home to enter alone the battle of life. His first
enterprise was building threshing machines, and he carried the first
machine over the mountains to Lebanon county—the first that was
carried on wheels. This first portable machine was hailed by the
agricultural fraternity as a great improvement, and he was very successful. He had the agency of John C. Boyd to sell the patent in
Schuylkill, Berks, Bucks, Montgomery and Lancaster counties. In
six weeks he sold "rights" to the amount of $2,200. In 1835 he
established an agricultural and machine shop in Lebanon county
and carried it on for two years when he sold it and returned home.

In 1837 he built the second iron foundry in Danville. Here he manufactured threshing machines, stoves and mill-gearing, boat-loads of which he sent to various parts of the State. In 1840 he married Elizabeth McReynolds, previous to which he had built the house on Market street now occupied by his daughter. In 1844 Mr. Kase built the first mill for the manufacture of merchant iron, which he conducted for two years in connection with the foundry. In 1846 he completed his rolling-mill, which was an important event in the history of Danville. Mr. Kase also made the first "three high" train of rolls in this place. It worked to perfection and was a great feat, as he had never learned turning or pattern making. But the ad. valorem tariff, adopted by the casting vote of George M. Dallas, completely silenced forges, rolling-mills and manufacto-ries of all kinds. In 1848 he leased his mill to David P. Davis, who finally failed, and he had the mill on hand again, while England was supplying the market of the United States with iron. In 1852 he sold the rolling-mill and it was moved to Knoxville, Tennessee. From 1848 to 1855 he manufactured and sold what is known as Kase's celebrated force pump, supplying them in quantities to par-ties that purchased the patent-right. In this enterprise Mr. Kase realized a sufficiency to retire from business. And he did so, only loaning money to parties that could not be accommodated without paying more than legal interest. Mr. Kase retired with the inten-tion of now enjoying a life of ease, for which his means were am ple ; but how oft our calculations fail and how little we know of the destiny the future has in store for us. In 1857 his brother William induced him to purchase his furnace at Roaring Creek. An in-ventory was made of stock amounting to $25,000. But it seems the stock was not there and S. P. Kase realized only $6,000 out of the whole concern. There were $19,000 gone at one swoop. Out of his real estate he saved only some farms he owned in Iowa. All the rest went for an unjust debt as he regards it to the present day. The money a considerable amount which he still had in hand and his Iowa lands he retained. He then saw the necessity for another struggle with fortune, and accordingly went to New York and hung out his "shingle" to sell railroad iron. Very soon the Flint and Parmaquett Railroad Company applied to him for iron for their road, from Flint to Parmaquett in Michigan. The rails were furnished but the pay not being satisfactory Mr. Kase was finally solicited to take charge of the construction. It was at that time graded only from Flint to Saginaw. The length of the road is one hundred and eighty miles. Mr. Kase assumed the sole management and by the exchange of old for new bonds and in various movements requiring executive ability of the highest order, in two years he completed the enterprise. It was a grand success and its bonds sold at ninety-five per cent.

In 1862, William G. Kase, a nephew, then president of the Reading and Columbia Railroad Company, together with the board of directors, sent for S. P. Kase and solicited him to take sole management as financial agent to build their road, as all their efforts had completely failed. After surveying the route and ascertaining the want of means and the refusal of subscribers to pay their stock, on account of former mismanagement, Mr. Kase at once proceeded to Washington city, where he presented the matter to the Congressional Committee on Railroads, together with a bill appropriating $450,000 in United States bonds for an equal amount of the bonds of the Columbia and Reading railroad. Here he was met and opposed by all the power of the Pennsylvania, and the Baltimore and Ohio railroads and every rival interest. For four weeks the contest was carried on. Mr. Kase made the fact of an inland route between New York and Washington his main point. Of this, the road he represented was an important link, and as there was a possibility of England going with the South, the value of a route remote from the sea board was duly estimated and he gained the point. His next struggle was to complete the road, which he accomplished. But such is the perversity of human nature, that no sooner had Mr. Kase lifted them out of trouble and gave value to their late worthless investment, than they deliberately set about robbing him of his promised reward by the most treacherous procedure. Mr. Kase concluded that it is only safe to confide in those who believe in personal accountability for every act in life.

In 1864 Mr. Kase started improvements in coal mining in McCauley mountain and established the Beaver Creek Coal Company; but after the works were erected the Catawissa Railroad Company refused to furnish cars for its transportation. This induced him to build the Danville, Hazleton and Wilkes-Barre railroad. This road extends from Sunbury to Tomhicken and is fifty-four miles in length. It not only opens the market to the coal; but forms an important link in the direct line between the East and the West. The opposition Mr. Kase encountered from conflicting interests in the prosecution of this great enterprise was enough to discourage any man but himself. But he persevered and finally triumphed, completing and equipping the road; and it was a proud day for him when the first train, laden with excursionists, passed over the road. His judgment was confirmed, his name was vindicated and his great ability was manifested in his wonderful success. Then he was honored and banqueted like a lord by those who never raised a finger to aid him when he struggled alone to secure this great improvement. A brief sketch of this road will be found in another portion of this book.

Mr. Kase is now engaged in building the Lehigh and Eastern railroad, which is another connecting link in the direct route, passing through the coal fields of Pennsylvania. It connects with the Danville, Hazleton and Wilkes-Barre road at Tomhicken and extends to Port Jarvis. Capitalists of the country and all public-spirited men are beginning to comprehend the vast importance of this direct route from Boston and New York to the great West.

In closing a rapid sketch of the prominent features in the stirring life of Simon P. Kase, it is just and proper to say that in the great industrial enterprises and in the progressive improvements of this region, no man of his age has made a more lasting impression, and that impress in all our future history will remain indelible forever. He is one of those rare specimens of the *genus homo* that are not met at the corner of every street. Once in a while they dash across the common track in their seemingly eccentric course, understood no more by the masses than the origin and mission of a comet. Such men as S. P. Kase do not travel in the beaten path; but ever and anon strike out into new and startling projects that seem to the multitude visionary, impracticable and beyond the reach of human effort. But looking to the end from the beginning and discarding the word "fail" from their vocabulary, they hear but one word and that is " forward," and as such men feel the inspiration of genius or some unseen power impelling them onward in the accomplishment of great purposes opposition or even ridicule becomes new incentive to action, and with a tireless energy they persevere until the world is startled again by their complete success. Looking abroad as he crossed the threshold of manhood he saw with impatience the slow and sober pace of local and general affairs; and instead of waiting for something to " turn up" he proceeded at once with a bold and fearless hand to turn something up. It must not be forgotten however, that such men as he, absorbed in the prosecution of great enterprises and in the ceaseless whirl of important improvements or bold adventures often forget minor matters or lesser details; and this affords a pretext to embarrass their steps and retard their progress; thus hindering instead of aiding in that which must result in a common benefit. Men like Mr. Kase always have been and always will become the common mark for the arrows of detraction. It is the tribute that all who rise above the level must pay to the world, until we reach a higher plane of civilization. Their motives are misrepresented by those of conscious inferiority and the envious predict a failure at every step of their progress. Even final success is poisoned with a bitter ingredient, and the history of inventors, reformers and public benefactors, who have devoted their lives to the general good, is but the history of public ingratitude if not of actual persecution. But time brings all things even, and when the lapse of years has swept away the cobwebs of human prejudice, S. P. Kase will be honored for what he has done for Danville, and his name will be associated with the great public improvements in which he pioneered the way, long after he

> " Hails the dark omnibus,
> That brings no passenger back."

The Israelites.

The Jewish congregation in Danville was organized under a charter granted by the court of Montour county in 1854, with the name of Benai Zion. The charter members were A. Levi, Jacob Loeb, Lewis Lang, Moyer Lyon, Jacob Weil, Solomon Meyer, Jacob Mayer, Jacob Levi, Sandel Dreifuss, Feis Blum and Simon Ellenbogen. The constitution and by-laws constitute a well-written code of laws and regulations. The officers are a president, a treasurer, a secretary and three trustees, all to be chosen annually by the congregation. The president, treasurer and secretary are *ex officio*

an executive committee. No more than one thousand dollars is allowed to be raised by pew rent in any one year. The price of
pews according to location was fixed at $15, $10, and $7 per an-
num. Two dollars must be paid for the privilege of being married
in the Synagogue. It must be remembered however that Israelites
in Danville had a church organization long anterior to 1854, when
they became a chartered body. They had built a frame school-house,
which they continue to use for school purposes. It was built in
1853. The new Synagogue was erected in 1871. Rabbi Jastrow
of Philadelphia conducted the dedicatory services of the new Synagogue. The procession was formed at the house of the president of
the congregation, and proceeded in order bearing the appropriate
symbols of the Jewish religion, according to the instructions given
to the children of Israel. At the portico of the Synagogue, Miss
Bertha Eger presented the keys to the president with a neat and
pertinent address, to which the president made an apt reply, when
he unlocked the door and the procession followed by the crowd entered the audience chamber and witnessed the ceremonies of the
dedication. Rabbi Jastrow preached an eloquent sermon highly
appropriate to the occasion. Rev. Nusbaum the teacher in charge
closed with a brief address, and so ended the interesting ceremonies
of the day.

Going back to 1853 we find that the first rabbi or teacher in
charge of this congregation was Rev. Friendlich. The next was
Rev. Emanuel Oppenheim. He was a man of extensive learning,
not only in the German and Hebrew, but also in the English. He
was a good speaker and a writer of ability in the latter and frequently
contributed to the current literature of the day. Rev. Oppenheim
was highly respected by all classes of the community. He was affable to all and remarkably warm in his friendships. He went to
Pottsville from this place, where he died a few years ago, much regretted by a large circle of friends. He was followed by Rev.
Hommer as teacher in the congregation of Danville. Rev. Heil-
brenner was the next and he was succeeded by Rev. Brandise. Then
came Rev. Simon Gerstman, who was a scholar and a gentleman,
as well as a teacher. He was well versed in the English language
and wrote on various subjects. A few lines, in verse, on the death
of Louis Loeb, from his pen will be found in this book. After him

came Rev. Nusbaum. He was a quiet man and mingled but little with the world, outside of his own people. He was followed by Rev. Friedenthal and he by Rev. Newmark who is the present teacher.

Jacob Leob is president of the congregation and has been, with a brief exception, ever since the organization. H. L. Gross is secretary and Samuel Goldsmith treasurer. The trustees are Moses Bloch, Jacob Goldsmith and Jacob Moyer. There are over twenty families connected with the Jewish congregation Benai Zion.

Y. M. C. A.

The Young Men's Christian Association was organized in Danville, in the Mahoning Presbyterian church on the 21st of June 1872. The officers elected were: President, S. G. Butler ; vice president, John Sweisfort ; secretary, John R. Rote, and librarian, H. H. Yorgy. The managers first chosen were : James M. Coulter : William McCormick, C. F. Lloyd, J. Sweisfort and C. P. Bradway. The society has been active in the work for which it was instituted, and a corresponding degree of success has marked its progress. The organization at present is as follows : President, James M. Coulter ; vice president, J. S. Huber ; secretary, George Swartz ; treasurer, George M. Gearhart ; general secretary, D. C. Hunt ; financial secretary, H. H. Yorgy. The association numbers eighty-one members, all active, earnest members of the several churches in Danville, united for greater efficiency in doing good.

Welsh Congregational Church.

This congregation worships in a neat brick church, on Welsh Hill, just above the Catawissa railroad. It was built in 1853. Rev. J. B. Cook was the pastor for many years. He was a good man and a faithful minister, and died some years ago in the full assurance of a blessed immortality.

Welsh Calvanistic Methodists.

These followers of the celebrated Whitfield, are located near the Catawissa railroad in the Third ward. Their church is small : but comfortable and was built in 1845.

The Welsh Baptist church is located on Spruce street. It is a frame structure and was built in 1870. An effort is now making to rebuild or repair the church.

A. M. E. church, known as "Zion." on York's Hill, is the modest building where worship the Methodists of African decent. Rev. Palmer is the pastor at present.

The Revere House.

This house formerly known as the " Pennsylvania House," is a large frame structure on the corner of Mill and Front streets, near the bridge and convenient to the court-house. John Gulick first opened it as a hotel in 1812, having bought the property from Daniel Montgomery. Philip Goodman kept the " Pennsylvania House " for sometime previous to 1818. In that year he completed the building of his new hotel, now the " Union Hall." In 1829 John Gulick sold the property to John Rhodes. He greatly improved it. He died in 1852. It still belongs to his heirs. Various parties kept the house previous to 1860, among whom was George W. Freeze. In 1866 it was kept by Charles Savage ; in 1868 by Mr. Lindner and in 1870 by Joseph M. Geringer. In March, 1872, James V. Gillaspy took charge of the house and conducted it with marked success to the present time. In 1875 the house was thoroughly rejuvenated inside and outside. Rooms were differently and more conveniently arranged. It was newly plastered, painted, and papered and newly furnished in every department. In March, 1880, the old name of " Pennsylvania House " was taken down by Mr. Gillaspy, and " Revere House " put in its place. It is now known far and wide as the " Revere House." Mr. Gillaspy has added much to the popularity of the house and has won by his urbanity and pleasant accommodations a large share of public patronage. The inviting and home-like comforts afforded at the Revere, can not fail of appreciation by a discriminating public ; as well as its proximity to the court-house and the business center of the town.

Michael Kessler.

A record of the gallant soldiers of Danville would be incomplete, without at least a brief mention of " Old Mike Kessler." In 1847 he joined the "Irish Greens" at Pittsburg and under General Shields served through the Mexican campaign. He was in the bat-

tle of Cero Gordo and also of Contreras, as well as in the forlorn
hope at Molina Del Rey, and finally at the storming of the gates of
Mexico city. With General Scott he entered the "Halls of the
Montezumas," and there remained for nine months. In this war
he lost one of his eyes, but none of his courage as a soldier, nor of
his patriotism, always for his country without regard to what party
for the time administered the government. Accordingly in the
last war he enlisted in the "Guards" under Captain Ephlin, for
nine months, and acted as color sergeant at the battle of Antietam.
Here he was badly wounded and being unable to walk, and his
regiment yielding for a time to a terrific charge, he was forced to
retreat or yield the flag. With a heroism eclipsing the boasted
chivalry of romance, he crawled back, wounded and bleeding without lowering the flag, still keeping it unfurled and defiant in the
face of the coming foe. Though he should fall he was determined
to keep the "stars and stripes" afloat, and he succeeded in saving
both, as the Union forces rallied and charged in turn. In the fearful slaughter at Fredericksburg on the 13th of December, 1862.
Kessler escaped unhurt amid the storms of leaden hail that beat upon
the Union troops. At the battle of Cedar Creek they struck the
old soldier again. This time a shell took off one of his legs, near
the body. He also lost his remaining eye and became totally blind.
And here in our midst, minus a leg and both his eyes, the old hero
of two wars lived for a number of years; kindly cared for by the
Government and his friends it is true; still I often thought what a
priceless sacrifice that man made for our common country. Unable
to walk and darkness unbroken around him; surely he should be
gratefully remembered among the fallen heroes of the Republic. I
often turned aside to pass an hour with him, to hear him tell of
sieges dire, and to see him "shoulder his crutch and show how
fields were won." Long may his memory live in the grateful remembrance of his countrymen, for whose ransom he paid a price
more precious than gold and dearer far than the costliest treasures
of earth.

"Old Mike Kessler" never lost the enthusiasm of patriotism, nor
his ardent devotion to the Republican party. It was his delight to
be taken out to the public gatherings and to listen to the speeches
that harmonized with the war sentiment. On such occasions there

were always good friends to bring "Old Mike," and there was always a seat of honor for him on the platform. Nor was he forgotten on election days. There was always a committee and a carriage to bring him to the polls, and it was always a sure Republican vote. He died a few years ago.

The Consumptives.

LOUIS LOEB, JOSIAH WOLF AND SAMUEL DREIFUSS.

Josiah Wolf was the last survivor of the trio I was wont to see slowly moving about on their canes, and bearing their favorite air cushions under their arms. With a subdued feeling of sadness I could almost daily note the waning powers of life. Samuel Dreifuss, Louis Loeb and Josiah Wolf, all in the prime of life and in the strength of manhood, bowed to the insidious destroyer—consumption. They were all of Jewish origin, and were knit together by the bonds of mutual friendship. Each sought renewed health in milder climes than ours. Samuel Dreifuss crossed the ocean, and breathed the balmy air under the sunny skies of Italy. Louis Loeb traversed the mountains of South America, and Josiah Wolf inhaled the sea breeze in Florida—the land of flowers. But all returned and met again, to die in the old home.

I often noticed them seated together in the cool shade in the summer time—often they were in earnest conversation among themselves. Perhaps they spoke of the *unknown* to which they *knew* they were so rapidly hastening. They had dismissed from their minds the stirring pursuits and the inspiring hopes that once absorbed their attention. They saw the sands of life almost exhausted, and the shadow of the gnomon fall—near, ah! how near the final hour. Perhaps they were interchanging thoughts in regard to the scenes that might lie beyond the dark curtain—the premonitory bell for the rising of which was already tinkling in their ears. Perhaps they spoke of the probabilities as to which of their number would first solve and realize the mysteries of eternity. One thing they knew, and that was that their separation here would be brief, and that soon, very soon they would strike hands on the other shore. Perhaps, too, they sometimes spoke of this bright world, on whose changing scenes their eyes would soon be closed; for the sun of their lives and of their earthly hopes had suddenly sank at high noon, and was already passing through the golden gates of the west. They *knew* that they would all sleep under the snow-drifts before they saw the laughing flowers, or heard the gladsome notes of another spring-time.

They were men of promise and of usefulness in their day and generation; but they have passed away. Peace to their names!

OBITUARY.—Lines to the memory of Louis Loeb, son of Jacob Loeb, Esq., who departed this life on Tuesday, November 15th, 1870, aged 31 years and 6 months.

> If ever departed worth did claim a tear,
> Reader, whoe'er thou art, bestow it here;
> For not to relatives is grief confined;
> All must lament the friend of human kind.
> If modest frankness—if unsullied truth,
> In childhood planted, and matured in youth—
> If tender charity, adorning age
> Deserve a record on memory's page.
> If rigid chastity—devoted love,
> Or calm submission to the God above
> Were faithful tokens of a heart sincere,
> Then oft will his image extort a tear.
> Rest then, blest shade! accept the plaintive lay
> Which affection and friendship love to pay,
> For those who knew thee exult in conscious pride
> That thou hast lived respected, and regretted died.

S. G.

DANVILLE, PA., *November 23d, 1870.*

Col. A. J. Frick.

Col. Frick entered the army for the Union, on the 18th of September, 1861, as captain of infantry in the Eighty-fourth regiment Pennsylvania volunteers attached to the Third army corps. Emulating the noble example of his brother, Doctor Clarence H. Frick, who led the Columbia Guards through the storms of battle in the conquest of Mexico, Col. A. J. Frick led his gallant command in defense of our national heritage—the old flag, the constitution, and the union. He served as captain until October, 1862, participating in the battles of Winchester, Port Republic and second Bull Run. In 1863 he was lieutenant colonel, in the Forty-first regiment of Pennsylvania, during Gen. Lee's invasion of the north. Col. Frick made for himself an honorable record, as a soldier and as an officer.

He is now deputy collector of internal revenue for the Twelfth district of Pennsylvania ; and who, in the distribution of public favors, so well deserve recognition as the soldiers of the Union.

From the record, I extract the following items. The Eighty-fourth regiment in the battle of Winchester, lost in killed and wounded, one third of its men. Company D, commanded by Capt. A. J. Frick, lost, killed W. R. Fowler ; wounded H. Funk, J. M. Price, C. Mummy, T. C. Fowler, C. D. Burns, M. Fitzhams, G. Holcomb, John Prosser, William Prosser, J. C. Teeter, and J. L. Wheeler. The report adds that Capt. Frick was highly spoken of for the gallantry he displayed under the terrible fire of the enemy.

" Winchester " was inscribed on their banner.

Colonel Charles W. Eckman.

Colonel Eckman enlisted as a private soldier, at Danville, in company H, Ninety-third regiment, Pennsylvania volunteers, on the 25th of September, 1861. The regiment soon marched to the front. Eckman was promoted to second lieutenant on the 24th of October in the same year and to first lieutenant on the 25th of July, 1862. On the 21st of October in the same year he rose to the office of captain of his company. He was next promoted to major of the regiment, on the 27th of November, 1864, to lieutenant colonel on the same day, and finally to colonel of the Ninety-third regiment on the 25th of January, 1865. His service in the army extending from the 25th of September, 1861, to June 23, 1865, during which time he participated in all the battles of the Army of the Potomac, and he was also with General Sheridan in Shenandoah Valley. He was a brave soldier, a popular officer, and on every field made an honorable record for himself.

William Keiner.

William Keiner enlisted in the " Danville Rifles," Captain Manly. At Baltimore on his way to the front, he was accidentally shot in the leg by Mat. Johnson, a member of his own company. The bone being shattered, amputation became a necessity, and for some time his life was despaired of. But a robust constitution and a strong will brought him through the dangerous ordeal. He was honorably

12

discharged. This loss severe and life long, is the sacrifice he has made for his country. How many thousands who never paid half that price, plume themselves on supposed superior claims to our common inheritance. Indeed the war, apart from its direct results, has taught us some wholesome lessons. After his recovery and return to Danville, Mr. Keiner engaged in merchandising.

George B. Brown.

George B. Brown is one of the most active business men of Danville. He conducts the oldest (and always popular) book store and news depot, in this place. He is also a leading dentist and is well patronized in his profession. Mr. Brown has trodden some of the rugged steeps in life's uncertain way, and in his own experience has demonstrated a problem that thousands fail to solve. The man, who in order to show a clear record and to enjoy the luxury of a peaceful conscience, will honor claims for which he is no longer legally responsible, must surely be that rarity, seldom found except in books—*an honest man.* Too many, when the clouds have turned their "silver lining," forget or ignore that which has gone beyond the reach of law. Like Job, he came up from the wreck of fortune, to the enjoyment of renewed prosperity, all the brighter, because he met every obligation, dollar for dollar and dime for dime. I mention this, not in flattery ; but because it is an occurrence worthy of note on account of its rarity in this selfish, grasping world of ours.

Mr. Brown has the honor of circulating the first daily newspaper in Danville. It was the Philadelphia *Ledger.* All the important dailies are now kept on his counter. He is also treasurer of the borough and as such his name is inscribed on the water bonds : and the school fund is also in his hands. He has been found faithful to every trust placed in his hands, and they have been many as well as important. At one time he held no less than ten agencies and treasuryships, and all came out correct to a dot.

First National Bank.

The First National Bank was organized on the 25th of January, 1864. in accordance with the provisions of the national banking law. At the first meeting of the stockholders the following board of directors was elected: Samuel Yorks, Jr., George F. Geisinger, C. Loubach, Charles Fenstermacher, William Yorks, Ferd Piper and G. H. Fowler. At a meeting of the board of directors, Samuel Yorks, Jr., was chosen president and W. A. M. Grier, cashier. The substantial character of the stockholders with the ability and known integrity of its officers, secured at its opening the full confidence of the public, which it has steadily maintained to the present time. Its career has been a prosperous one, and it affords one of the safest depositories in the country. On the resignation of W. A. M. Grier, A. P. Fowler was chosen cashier. In 1866 B. R. Gearhart was made teller of the bank, and on the resignation of A. P. Fowler, in 1870, B. R. Gearhart was chosen cashier, and which position he still holds at the present time. S. A. Yorks was made teller some years ago, and still occupies that position. After the death of Samuel Yorks, Jr., in 1878, C. Laubach was elected to the presidency and continued for two years. The present organization of the First National Bank of Danville, is as follows: Thomas Beaver, president; B. R. Gearhart, cashier; S. A. Yorks, teller. The present board of directors are, C. Laubach, I. X. Grier, Dan Morgan, George F. Geisinger, B. R. Gearhart, R. M. Grove and F. C. Eyer.

The bank is conveniently located in the Montgomery building at the corner of Bloom and Mill streets.

The Opera House.

Until recent years, Danville was but indifferently provided with public halls. Concert Hall on Ferry street, a dingy, old, tumble-down, frame structure, was long the place of public gatherings on extra occasions. There, within its somber walls were, sermons, lectures, shows, dances, concerts, fairs and public meeting of all sorts. It is now converted into private dwellings.

Reynolds' Hall on Mill street was also used, but was too small for general purposes. It has now for a number of years been occupied by McMahan & Irland's well-known and popular picture gallery. As an art gallery it is an excellent hall, and it is still in the full tide of successful operation.

Lyons' Hall, is on the third story of his brick building on Mill street. It has at times been used on public occasions.

Moyer Lyons' Hall is in Excelsior block and is also used on some general occasions, but mainly as a club-room. So also is the hall in Kaufman's building on the corner of Mill and Center streets, and perhaps some others.

Thompson's Hall was built about 1859. It was then by far the largest hall in town and was much used for all the purposes to which public halls are usually devoted. It is still in use and is second only to the Opera House.

The Opera House is one of the grandest public buildings in the interior of the State. The want of a suitable hall had been discussed for some time and it took practical shape with William J. Reed, in 1871. He purchased the ground conditionally, on the corner of Mill and Mahoning streets, of Jacob Snyder. There was an understanding that Reed was to do the excavating and Snyder was to invest $6,000 in the building. Accordingly William J. Reed broke ground for the Opera House on the 4th of July, 1871. A company was then organized and a charter was procured from the court, for. as they styled it, "The City Hall Association." After some time it was agreed that the stock should be exchanged for certain portions of the work, Reed having previously agreed to furnish the brick and had also contracted for the stone. C. S. Wetzel of Danville, was the architect and by his counsel and advice, the issue of stock for aid in building, was set aside after certain contracts in that direction had been made by Mr. Reed. Whereupon Mr. Reed, in March 1873, sold his interest and retired. He was certainly the moving spirit in the enterprise. But for him the project would no doubt have failed at that time, and consequently we would be without our grand opera house. On the other hand Jacob Snyder would not have lost his fortune. Still it is an open question whether the sacrifice of Snyder or any one else was really necessary to secure an opera house. There is much in the management of great enterprises that make or mar the fortunes of men. The opera house building is 156 by 84 feet, and is located on the corner of Mill and Mahoning streets. The basement contains the heating and ventilating apparatus. The ground floor is occupied by the post-office, Kramer & Co's treble store fronting on both Mill and Mahoning streets, Dennis Bright's hardware store, Ramsey Child's stove and tinware store, and M. T. McGuire's gas fitting and plumbing establishment. The theater is on the second floor approached by two stairways from Mill street. It is a magnificent chamber. Its appointments, adornments, scenery, and properties are all elegant, costly, and complete. The briliant chandelier sheds a beautiful light over the parquet, the dress circle, and stage ; whilst the sparkling ornaments lend a grandeur to the scene that excites both wonder and admiration. There are fourteen hundred reversible opera chairs upholstered in crimson plush. In one word there is not a theater in the State that excels the Danville opera house in elegance, comfort, or in acoustic qualities. There are also a number of rooms on the second, third, and fourth floors, occupied as lawyers offices, club-rooms, and lodge-rooms.

It is somewhat strange to see a man like Jacob Snyder, a plain, honest farmer, risk all his fortune, the hard earning of a life time, in an enterprise like the building of such a magnificent opera-house, an enterprise so far in advance of the town. and where the large capital invested had to remain partially dead until the town grew up to it. It is nothing to see a speculator hazard the loss or gain of thousands, but for an honest, hard-working farmer like Jacob Snyder to venture all in a project like this, is remarkable. But no doubt he got into it by degrees, and had at last no choice but to involve himself for its completion. Surely Danville owes a debt to Jacob Snyder for the splendid opera-house, that is the pride and boast of its citizens. Let him see that he has not sacrificed himself for the benefit of a thankless community. Don't leave it until he is dead either, and then pay the debt with a monument when the sense of earthly enjoyment has passed away forever.

Montour House.

The Montour House is a large hotel, opposite the court-house. It was originally built by General Daniel Montgomery who kept a store in the corner room. An orchard extended from the building up to Ferry street. Boyd, Colton and Donaldson also kept store there. In 1834 it was first opened as a hotel by Samuel Brady, who gave it its name " The Montour House." In 1846 G. M. Shoop purchased the property, and subsequently the house was kept by W. G. Gaskins Cornelius Garretson. Smith, Kramer, Kirk and Jones. About 1859 James L. Riehl, the present proprietor pur-

chased the Montour House, and it has since been kept by him. The
house has been remodeled and greatly improved and ranks with the
best hotels of the country.   It contains every modern convenience
and is kept in the best possible manner.   For its popularity the
house is much indebted to Samuel Cressman, the gentlemanly clerk,
whose attention and accommodating spirit have made hosts of
friends for the Montour House.   The proprietor, Mr. Riehl, ever
watchful for the welfare of his guests superintends every department
of the establishment, and insures to all, every comfort that could be
desired.

Market.

Like all other small towns, Danville had been supplied with the
produce called "marketing," by the farmers and others who came
at irregular times and huckstered through the various streets and
alleys of the town.   This mode rendered the supply very uncertain
and the prices were still more uncertain.   Through the newspaper
then under my control, I persistently urged the advantages of a
regular market, under the regulations of the town authorities.   The
people began to think about it and finally the council took up the
subject and passed an ordinance for the establishment of a regular
market on Tuesdays, Thursdays and Saturdays, closing at eleven
o'clock A. M. each day.

It is called "curb-stone market."   The wagons backing up to
the pavement and each paying a dime for the privilege on each
market day.   This is collected by the street commissioner, who
makes his returns to the council.

On the 19th of April, 1872, an ordinance was passed, embody-
ing general regulations for the market.

The first section fixes the market days and that Mill street from
Spruce to Mahoning should be used for the market.   It forbids sales
in gross during market hours, except grain and flour.

The second section forbids the hawking or selling of produce on
the streets, except fresh fish and oysters, at any other time or place
than the time and street designated.

The third section forbids under a penalty, the sale of any tainted
or unwholesome article.

The fourth section fixes the tax and orders that the market shall be on the west side of the street from October to May ; and on the east side from May to October. The street is not to be blocked and free crossings shall be maintained and room for business men to load and unload goods.

The fifth section defines the penalty for light weights or short measures.

Under these rules and regulations the market has been successfully conducted to the present time. The street commissioner, at present Mr. Faux, also acts as market inspector.

The Danville market is well supplied by the farmers and producers of Montour and Northumberland counties. Among the regular attendants is Jesse Conway. His inviting assortment always attracts the crowd and he always sells out at an early hour. Howard James is emphatically the "butter man." He is always on hand with the choice, fresh roll butter of the country. C. S. Soper, he of the Washington hills, has converted a barren ridge into a productive garden teeming with the choicest fruits and vegetables in their season. He attends market just when it suits him ; but when he does come, he gets better prices and sells faster than anybody else. Charles Maus, always has a nice lot of fruits and vegetables and finds a ready sale. Mr. Hendricks and Mr. Kirkner are also regular attendants and supply a host of customers. There are many others worthy of mention, who keep the people of Danville supplied with the products of the farm, the garden and the dairy. The market rules are seldom violated, the dime is cheerfully paid and the market is a success. The great want now is a market-house.

Danville.

Danville is laid out with as much regularity as the nature of the ground will admit. The streets run north and south, east and west, with very little variation. They are not as broad as they should be, especially the main avenues of trade. Mill street is laid solid with cobble stones or it is McAdamized. The best blocks of business houses are in Mill street in the Third ward, and the finest residences are on Market street, though some portions of Mahoning, Mulberry, and other streets are very pleasant. With the exception of Mill street there are well shaded pavements and the green foliage in the summer-time adds much to the beauty and the comfort of the place.

The canal runs in a westerly course through the center of town and is spanned on the main streets with neat iron bridges. The public square is on Market street, between Ferry and Pine streets. The water and gas pipes are laid in nearly all the streets; but the sewerage is not complete, and owing to some disagreement with the gas company, there has been no light on the streets for several years. The town, however, has been well governed, and there is about as much safety as in any other place of equal size. Latterly there have been several alarms of fire, that have caused the authorities to discuss the necessity of watchmen or a paid police force.

There have been two additions to the town in late years, "Magill's Addition" on the Bloom road and "Gulick's Addition," on the east. A large number of lots have been sold and improved in these additions. The future extension of the town, must of necesbe mainly eastward, as it is the only direction in which there is suitable room for any considerable extension.

The Fire Department.

The volunteer fire department of Danville is noted for its activity and efficiency. The members are among the most intelligent and respectable citizens of the place.

The Friendship is the oldest organization in the department, having been organized in 1841. It occupies a handsome engine house on Ferry street. Before the water works were built it was furnished with a steam fire engine. This is no longer necessary. Their regular meetings are held on the last Saturday of each month.

The Washington was formed in 1859. They also have a neat and pleasant house. It is located on Market street. Their regular meetings are on the first Saturday of each month.

The Continental was also organized in 1859. Their comfortable house is on Mill street, and their meetings are held on the last Saturday of each month.

The fire department is made up of volunteers, and is under the general control of the town council. The council districted the town and regulated the ringing of the bells by the following schedule:

First district.—All of South ward west of Church street.

Second district.—All of South ward east of Church street.

Third district.—All of North ward east of Pine street and Catawissa railroad.

Fourth district.—All of North ward west of Pine street and Catawissa railroad.

Fire alarm for each district with be as follows :

First.—Commencing with fire alarm and one tap for the First district.

Fire alarm and two taps for the Second district.

Fire alarm and three taps for the Third district.

Fire alarm and four taps for the Fourth district.

My Own Recollections.

In the spring of 1857 there occurred what was known as "the big
strike" at the Montour iron works, then under the management of
J. P. Grove. Some six or seven hundred men in regular order, by
day and by night for more than six weeks, were constantly marching
through the town ; halting for speeches at the court-house, or on the
grounds of the Grove church. They were orderly as a general thing,
did no harm to any one, but marched along merrily singing songs
composed for the occasion. The principal speaker was John Hanna.
He was quite a ready talker with a large vein of humor that kept
the boys wide awake and elicited much applause. True there was
n ot much elegance in his utterances : but there was "mother wit"
and keen sarcasm that made him immensely popular and many
others not connected with the strike, crowded round to hear John
Hanna. Poor fellow, his popularity ruined him. He sank like
many others under the influence of social habits and died almost
forgotten. Andrew J. Thompson was also one of the most prominent leaders of the strike. He afterwards left this place, and has
been dead a number of years. During the "big strike," the men
and their families were supplied with provisions by the farmers of
the surrounding country as well as by the citizens of Danville ; for
in that strike, public sympathy was enlisted very warmly on the side
of the working men. But it finally terminated, in some kind of a
compromise and they returned to work. There have since been
partial strikes on various grounds ; but none so general, or so well
sustained by popular sentiment and "material aid."

From the canal to Mulberry street, there was on each side of Mill
street, a row of low, dingy, frame buildings. Some were reached
by a plank gangway from the sidewalk, as the street was only partially filled up, and the sidewalk was only a narrow and rickety
bridge resting on frail trestles, or scantling stuck in the mud on a
level with the creek that passes under the street at Keiner's store.
There were only three or four brick buildings in that part of the
town, one of which stood on the present crossing of the railroad, in
which Smith B. Thompson resided. But one by one and sometimes
by the half dozen, the fire-fiend swept away the old, wooden buildings, and the solid, elegant brick structures of to-day, took their
places. The brick buildings of Mr. C. Laubach, Moyer Lyon and
Jacob Reed, are all that remain, on either side of Mill street, from
the canal to Mulberry. There was but one iron front in town, and
that was the store of E. W. Conkling, adjoining the old bank building. It was burned with the corner building, Mill and Market
streets, and still lies in unsightly ruins in the main thoroughfare of
the town. J. O. Richardson and C. C. Baldy, kept the only hardware stores in Danville. T. O. Van Allen had a large store of general merchandise on the corner above named, and Richard B. Hul-
lihan, was for many years the genial and popular clerk. Isaiah S.
Thornton kept a shoe store in the Montgomery building; but
Thomas Woods, opposite the opera-house, had and still keeps what
is emphatically known as the "Oldest Shoe Store." M. C. Grier,
J. B. Moore and Dr. William M. Bickley kept the drug stores.
Among the merchants of twenty-five years ago, who are still in
business, are C. Laubach, J. C. Rhodes, P. Baldy, Jr., W. H. Hassanplug, Saul Lyon, Henry L. Gross, and E. Thompson.

Among the physicians were Doctors Magill, Hughes, Simington,
Strawbridge, Snitzler. The lawyers were E. H. Baldy, William C.
Johnson, J. W. Comly, H. A. Childs, John G. Montgomery, B.
K. Rhodes, Paul Leidy. Alexander Jourdan was judge and Daniel
Frazer was sheriff.

Shilo German Reform Church.

The German Reform congregation was organized in 1858, under
the pastoral charge of Rev. D. W. Wolf. Services had been held in

the court-house for some time and the young congregation, composed of twenty members, was organized. In 1859 a new church was built on Bloom street, though it remained unfinished for some years and was not dedicated until December 20, 1862. Rev. D. W. Wolf resigned in 1861, and on the 1st of May, 1862, Rev. J. W. Steinmetz assumed the pastoral charge of the congregation. The church is of brick, 60 by 40 feet, with a pleasant basement. The congregation now numbers more than two hundred. Rev. J. W. Steinmetz resigned the charged. The present pastor in Rev. Mr. Schaffer.

John C. Millhouse.

John C. Millhouse is a son of St. Crispin and a master of his craft. During the war he was with Gen. Burnside in his memorable expedition to North Carolina. At Roanoke and Newburn, he manifested the sterling qualities that crowned the Ninth corps with the garlands of victory, and that finally saved our flag from dishonor, and our free institutions from the maelstrom of destruction. Mr. Millhouse was one of the most valued army correspondents of the *American*, then published by the writer of this volume. Many of the former readers of the *American* will remember, how, in those stormy days, we anxiously looked for his letters, as they always gave us a clear and intelligent view of the situation. Returning home after the great work was done, he resumed his occupation. But fortune did not smile on him as he had reason to expect. Several times his shop with his tools and stock were mysteriously destroyed by fire ; once it was burglarized and the most valuable stock of leather was stolen. But each time with a firm will and patient industry he commenced anew. In 1876 the old shoe shop became a sort of head-quarters for the greenbackers. The working men being in enforced idleness, often met in the shoe shop to discuss the situation, to investigate the cause of business stagnation, and to seek a remedy. Ranged on rickety benches round the wall, through the stormy winter days and long winter nights, the interest never flagged in the great question that involved the well being of themselves and families, as well as the prosperity of the country at large. I often spent a plesent hour in their midst and thus in jingling rhymes rehearsed the story of

"The Old Shoe Shop."

When down the stream of Time afar,
  Some lowly bard may catch the strain
That lingers 'round the old Shoe Shop,
  And sing its glories once again.

He strikes his harp to numbers low,
  Perchance on next Centennial year,
Recalls the scenes of long ago,
  While thousands crowd around to hear.

How village statesmen gathered there,
  In sober ranks around the wall,
And oft display'd more solid sense
  Than those who spoke in Congress Hall.

The chief was known for skillful work,
  And rain or shine, from early dawn,
His gavel rung upon the stone—
  His work was good—his name was John.

And as he drew the wax-end through,
  He drew conclusions bold and strong,
From standard books and careful thought
  Showed where financial laws were wrong.

With one accord the patriot band
  Indorsed his views and gave their own.
Could they have made their country's laws,
  Financial storms had been unknown.

But all are gone to meet no more!
  The tide swept on, they could not stay;
The young have sought a western home,
  The old, perchance, have passed away.

But by the streams or sounding shore,
  In distant lands or on the main,
In day dreams oft these friends of yore
  Will gather 'round the stove again.

Ah, no! they never can forget
  The scenes and friends to mem'ry dear,
While life indures, for they shall grow
  More bright with each departing year.

Like pilgrim shrine, this place is sought
  Since two-score-years had pass'd away,
When, lo! there came a wondering bard—
  'Twas on a bright Autumnal day.

He cross'd the street and gain'd the lawn,
  Where once a gate swung to and fro;
He touched his harp and rais'd his voice,
  And mournful sang in numbers low.

Not one is left with me to view
  This crumbling shop in ruins laid;
And save in dreams they ne'er shall know
  The fearful wreck that time has made.

The window glass and sash are gone,
  Half open stands the crazy door;
The boards are warp'd—the frame is sprung,
  One corner sunk a foot or more.

Along the roof and crumbling eves
  The wasp has built his house of clay,
And through the gaps that time has made,
  The beetle wheels his droning way.

Like Pisa's grand and wond'rous tow'r,
  The chimney seems about to fall;
Its base is gone—its ragged crown
  Leans out some feet beyond the wall.

And there, within the corners dim,
  Many a heedless victim dies,
For there the spiders weave their webs,
  And set their traps to catch the flies.

The mice are gambling on the floor
  And seeking for the paste-horn still,
While undisturbed the cricket sings
  His plaintive song beneath the sill.

And as the logs beneath the floor
  Yield to time and sure decay,
The noisome snail, with horns erect,
  Slowly marks its devious way.

Beneath the stones and in the mould,
  The centipedes by thousands roam:
And in the corners, damp and dark,
  The squalid toad has made its home.

Farewell, old shoe shop! You must go,
  As you, perchance, have gone before;
In changing forms you come and go,
  But we, to life that dies no more!

Well, there may be some romance about a shoeshop on rare oc
casions; but as a general thing there is an everlasting sameness.
The shoemaker's bench is the same old pattern it was an hundred
years ago. You see a low seat, lined with leather conveniently dished,
a drawer containing odds and ends, the bench checkered off with
little compartments, containing pegs, bristles, tacks, a ball of wax
and a piece of broken glass; and what is strange you never see a
new one. They are all old and dingy.

M. S. Ridgeway.

M. S. Ridgeway came to Danville about 1844 and has since been
one of our most valuable and enterprising citizens, except a brief
period when he was manager of a rolling-mill, in Youngstown,
Ohio. Long years as manager of the large iron manufactory originally known as the "Montour Works," tried him to the utmost and
brought out those sterling qualities of character that mark the able
executive, as well as the man. His daily intercourse with the thousands of employees who have been under his charge, is always dignified and courteous, and at the same time firm and exacting where
duty to all is involved. Strangers or casual observers are apt to regard him as somewhat cold and austere. But this seeming may be
the result of constant habit in controlling the varied and oft times
turbulent elements, incident to a large corps of operatives, and in
exacting from each the duties required. On other occasions the
sunny side of his nature is manifested, and no man in the community is more generous or liberal, social or benevolent. No work-
ingman worthy of a favor ever appealed to him in vain, and many
will long remember his substantial efforts in their behalf. The
iron worker before his glowing furnace, will bless the man who introduced a shield, to defend him from the burning heat. Not only
does the improved furnace door defend the worker; but it is also
of great pecuniary advantage to the manufacturer. He who con-
tributes in any degree, to the benefit of mankind, is more worthy
of note than he who conquers millions.

Mr. Ridgeway enjoys, as he justly merits, a wide reputation as a
successful manager of iron works, as well as a complete knowledge
of iron in all its combinations, grades and forms. His son, E. O.
Ridgeway, is making his mark in the same direction.

John P. Leisenring.

John P. Leisenring was a native of Northumberland county. He was born on the 23d of December, 1816, and died at his residence, on Mahoning street, Danville, on the 7th of September, 1870, consequently he was nearly fifty-four years of age. He came to Danville about 1848 and established a picture gallery which soon won the popular favor. He was a strictly honest man and a model of industry. As an artist he was ambitious to keep pace with the rapid improvements in his profession; and by his skill and fair dealing, he kept up a flourishing business in his photographic gallery for more than twenty years. During this time he acquired some property, and found himself in easy circumstances. He was a good citizen, attending to his own business, but was always ready and prompt to aid others, or to contribute to any good cause, civil or religious. In him the suffering and the needy always found a friend. To many other excellent traits of character may be justly added that of " peace-maker." During the latter part of his life, he thought and spoke much of the life which is to come—of that undiscovered country that lies beyond the life that now is, and in his lingering illness of eight months duration, he bore his sufferings with the fortitude and the resignation of a Christian. He was a member of the First Baptist church in this place, but now we trust of the church above. In him I, with many others lost a true and steadfast friend; but our loss for a season, is his gain for ever.

His son, Henry H. Leisenring still continues the business and enjoys an extensive patronage. His gallery is now in the Montgomery building.

The Court-House.

The old court-house was built in ——. Joseph Maus was the contractor, and the cost was $3,980 80—a little less than four thousand dollars. Included in the cost there were $64, for sixty-four gallons of whiskey consumed by the builders, and which is charged in the bill, at one dollar per gallon. The court-house occupied the site of the present structure, the ground having been donated for that purpose, by Gen. William Montgomery. The ground occupied by the jail was donated by Gen. Daniel Montgomery. Those who were employed on the work of the old court-house, under the contractor Joseph Maus, were John Bryson, John Stricker, Edwin Stocking, Alexander Johnson, Benjamin Garretson, Nehemiah Hand, William Lunger, Peter Watts, Peter Snyder. Frederick Harbolt, James Thomas, William Doak, D. Henderson, B. Long and D. Heller.

The new court-house was built in 1871. Mr. O'Malley was the contractor and architect. B. K. Vastine did the brick-work and H. F. Hawke & Co., furnished the massive cut-stone. It is a structure that reflects credit on the county and on all who were concerned in its erection. The county commissioners purchased the adjoining ground, on which the building occupied by the Friendship Fire Company formerly stood; and this addition with the building and surrounding improvements cost about $55,000. The commissioners exercised much care in the work, and with a due regard to public economy, they presented the county with a court-house in which every citizen can feel an honest pride. The first story is occupied by the offices of the commissioners, the prothonotary and clerk of the courts, the register and recorder, the grand jury and the sheriff. The second story reached by two broad stairways, is occupied by the court-room. It is furnished with all the modern appliances of comfort and convenience.

For a number of years a park of deer have sported on the spacious grounds, the whole being inclosed by a tall iron fence.

David N. Kownover.

David N. Kownover was a native of New Jersey, but resided for some years in the northern part of this county. In 1839 he was appointed by the State authorities, superintendent of the North Branch canal, from Northumberland to Wilkes-Barre, an office which he held for thirty years. Soon after his appointment he moved to Danville and resided here until his death, which occurred in August, 1870, when he had about reached the allotted three score and ten years. When the canal passed into the hands of the company, he was reappointed; and his efficiency, sterling integrity and fitness for the place, is best attested by his long retention in a position of so much importance, and one that many others sought so eagerly. His quick perception, good judgment and promptness in action on many occasions saved thousands of dollars both to the State and the company ; whilst his intimate knowledge of human nature enabled him to secure the very best services from those under his control. David N. Kownover was universally respected as an honest, intelligent citizen, faithfully discharging his duties in all the relations of life. Such is the honorable record he has left behind him. I know only two of his sons, Harry and David F., and a daughter married to George S. Sanders. David spells the name with a C, and writes his name David F. Conover. He seems to have inherited much of the sterling qualities of his father. In 1862, while quite a young man, he became a clerk in a large jewelry house in Philadelphia, where, by his own merits, he gradually rose, until he became the head of the firm and the master of a fortune.

Public Schools.

The public schools of Danville are conducted with much care, and a high standard of teachers is required by the board of directors. There are now twenty-eight schools in this place, attended by one thousand five hundred and fifty-four scholars. Seven hundred and ninety-six males and seven hundred and fifty-eight females. The present board of school directors, (three for each of the four wards,) is composed of William C. Johnson, J. C. Rhodes and Dr. J. D. Mansteller of the First ward ; George W. Miles, Samuel Mills and E. J. Curtis, Second ward ; E. Thompson, H. F. Hawke and E. C. Voris, Third ward ; James Vandevender, F. C. Grau and J. R. Philips, Fourth ward. President of the board, J. D. Mansteller ; treasurer, E. Thompson ; secretary, E. J. Curtis.

Rev. M. C. Horine is superintendent of public schools and is said to be one of the most efficient officers who has served the county in that capacity.

The corps of teachers at present engaged in the schools of Danville, is as follows :

F. C. Derr, principal of high school.

Miss Mame Hughes, assistant.

S. M. Gibbs,	Miss H. Alexander,
R. P. Laird,	Miss E. C. Wilson,
Miss Maggie C. Madden,	Miss M. Richardson,
F. Ream,	Miss A. Richardson,
Miss S. Musselman,	Miss L. M. Bloom,

13

Miss M. O. Hughes,	Miss Carrie Matcham,
Miss A. McDermot,	Miss A. M. Whitman,
Mrs. R. B. Maxwell,	Miss Lizzie Coxey,
Miss Annie Hiatt,	Miss Maggie Kramer,
Miss Annie Yerrick,	Miss Ruth Weaver,
Miss A. Irvine,	Miss M. Tillson,
Miss A. Johnson,	Miss Lizzie Antrim,
Miss A. Jones,	Miss Ida V. Grau.

By the common testimony of the community, this corps of teachers have never been surpassed, in this place.

Mystery of the Mine.

In December, 1873, the dead body of Bernard Westdossal was accidentally discovered in an abandoned mine, between this place and Mausdale. The evidences of murder were plain and clear; but no clue to the perpetrator could be found, until years later when a man formerly of this place, was convicted of murder in a western State, who confessed the murder of Westdossal for the sake of his gold watch. Bernard Westdossal had been a lieutenant in the Prussian army, and made some progress in studying for the priesthood: but became reduced in circumstances, came to this country and was selling pictures at the time he was murdered.

Peter Baldy, Sr.

Peter Baldy, senior, came from Northumberland to Danville in 1814. He was a blacksmith but soon engaged in merchandizing and dealing in grain. In 1839 he built the stone, steam mill on Church street. By care and industry, closely watching the corners and being fortunate in his speculations, he amassed a very large fortune, and became one of the wealthiest men in this part of the State. He was the first president of the first bank established in Danville. He was always a substantial supporter of the Protestant Episcopal church to which he belonged from the time of its organization in this place, and left $50,000 to that church, in his will. During the war Mr. Baldy contributed liberally to the comfort of the volunteers of this place: especially to the "Baldy Guards," Captain Ramsey, and the "Fencibles," Captain Shreeve. Nearly twenty years ago, Mr. Baldy retired from active business and spent the evening of life in the quiet of his home on Market street, where he died on the 24th day of November, 1880, at the ripe old age of ninety-two years and nine months, lacking a few days.

Co-operative Iron and Steel Works.

The Co-operative Iron and Steel Works, are among the most enterprising and successful business institutions of Danville. It is true that the principle upon which the works are based, have often failed in practice, but in every case the failure could be traced to mismanagement. There is perhaps only one way to conquor success, and that is in wisely marking out a line of conduct and then placing its execution in the hands of an able and discreet manager. The controlling power must ultimately terminate in a unit; however the elements may be diversified, their combined power must culminate in a single point. Then success depends primarily on wise councils. and finally on the intelligent execution of those councils; but there must be no subsequent interference; only holding the manager responsible for a judicious use of the power placed in his hands. The adverse of this rule has been the ruin of many co-operative institutions. The Co-operative Iron and Steel Works were established in 1871. Some six acres of ground were purchased of Jacob Sechler. Sr., and the stockholders erected their mill on the most approved plan and with all the modern facilities for the manufacture of iron. The capacity is 15,000 tons per annum. Perry Deen was the first president and L. K. Rishel has been secretary, treasurer and general manager since the organization. Peter Baldy, Jr., is president at the present time. J. D. Williams is manager of the mill and Samuel Mills is roller. There is one thing of which the management of the Co-operative can justly boast, and that is, that through all the long years of business depression, their mill never stopped a single day for lack of orders; but steadily moved on through the panic, until the present time when it is in full and successful operation. Ten years of experiment has proved the co-operative system a success. No better rails are made in the country and no rail mill gives more abundant promise of success in the future.

Eagle Foundry.

The Eagle foundry was built on the site of an old iron manufactory, on Ferry street, by Moore & Stewart, in 1837-38. In the latter year Samuel Huber became the chief moulder and he remained there some ten years. In February, 1839, the foundry was totally destroyed by fire. Some two or three years subsequently, the foundry having been re-built, it was operated by Stewart, Biddle & Lloyd. After the lapse of a few years they added a machine-shop and among other things they made a steam engine. Lloyd and Stewart now retired and the firm was Moore & Biddle, in a year or two it was reversed and made Biddle, Moore & Co. This was about 1845 and so it continued until 1850, when it was William Biddle, agent, and so it has been conducted to the present time. Stoves of various patterns, plows, &c., are made at the old Eagle foundry.

M. B. Goodrich.

Maxwell B. Goodrich, for whom the Post of the Grand Army of the Republic in this place, is named, was one of the most gallant and generous hearted among the loyal soldiers, who with our brave and bold went out to battle. He was first lieutenant in company H, Ninety-third regiment, Pennsylvania volunteers, at the time he was mortally wounded in the Wilderness on the 5th of May, 1864; but he lingered until the 4th of June, when he died and was buried with the honors of war in Danville. "That was just like Max Goodrich," said the boys, when W. M. Snyder of company H was killed by a rebel sharpshooter at Williamsburg and Goodrich, who was then a sergeant, stepped out in front and shot the sharpshooter, thus speedily avenging the death of his comrade. And now, every year his well-known grave, in the old Grove church-yard, is strewn with the flowers of May, not only by his surving comrades; but by the hands of ladies fair, who with a kind remembrance of the once noble-hearted Max Goodrich, deck with the garlands of honor, the mound where he sleeps.

Danville Bridge.

On the 2d of January, 1828, a company was chartered by the State to build a bridge across the Susquehanna, at the town of Danville. The company was organized as follows: President, Daniel Montgomery; treasurer, James Loughead; secretary, John Cooper; managers, John C. Boyd, William Colt, Peter Baldy, Sr., William

Boyd, Andrew McReynolds and Robert C. Grier. On the 3d of March in the same year a contract was made for the construction of the bridge, with John P. Schuyler and James Fletcher, who at once commenced the work, and in January, 1829, it was completed : being accepted by the company in February, as finished according to contract. The Governor was notified of the fact, as the State originally held a small amount of stock in the bridge. Daniel Hoffman was elected the first toll collector, at the annual salary of sixty-five dollars. Previous to the 14th day of March, 1846, eleven dividends had been declared, on that day the bridge was swept away by a flood in the river. Daniel Blizard was carried down on a fragment of the bridge and was rescued with great difficulty near the old stone house. Subsequent to that date there was no dividend declared until 1863. After the loss of the bridge in the great freshet of March, 1846, a contract for its rebuilding was made with Chester Evans, and David N. Kownover; but Evans disposed of his interest to Kownover and David N. Kownover alone carried on and finished the work. This second bridge stood the storms and floods until 1875 when it too was swept away by the high water, on the 17th day of March in that year. The bridge was at once rebuilt in the ensuing season. H. F. Hawke & Co. did the stone work and the superstructure was erected by the Smith Bridge Company, of Ohio. The toll collectors from the first opening of the bridge to the present time, were Daniel Hoffman, Rudolph Sechler, E. Mellon, Isaiah S. Thornton and Joseph Hunter. Mr. Joseph Hunter took charge in 1851 and with rare fidelity and very general satisfaction, has discharged the duties of the position for thirty years.

I need not stop to say that this bridge is a great public benefit. Everybody knows it. I need not speak of its substantial character. Everybody feels it.

The bridge is one fourth of a mile in length. It has a pleasant and covered footway on each side, entirely shut out from the roadway.

The officers at present are : President, Thomas Beaver ; treasurer and secretary, E. H. Baldy, Esq.; managers, William H. Magill, Alex. J. Frick, E. W. Conkling, John H. Grove, Amos Vastine, J. Hudson Kase ; toll collector, Joseph Hunter.

Planing Mills.

The first planing-mill in Danville, was Duncan C. Hartman's, in the brick building that was originally built for a wollen factory, by Doctor Petrikin. This was in 1839. It was burnt. About 1857 Levi Berger built a large planing-mill, by the canal in the rear of Reed's brick building at the north-east corner of the canal bridge, on Mill street. Mr. Burger furnished his mill with the most approved machinery and did a very large business until 1872, when this mill too, with all its valuable contents, was totally destroyed by fire. In 1869 Voris, Heigh & Gregg built a large planing-mill by the canal on Ferry street.

Manufactories.

Danville is a manufacturing center of great importance. Its abundant material and facilities for transportation to and from all points of the compass, are unsurpassed. Iron ore, coal, and limesone in inexhaustable quantities are stored all around it, and we are blessed with all the advantages that could be desired, for the extensive manufacture of iron in all its forms. Nature has been lavish with her gifts, and the enterprise of our people, has largely developed the abundant resources of this locality. The iron works established here with its army of operatives, have also opened a wide door for other manufactories, as well as a market for surrounding farmers and producers. The ground for a variety of manufactories that might be carried on here with large profits, is not yet occupied; but the necessities of the future will inevitably plant them here. Capital seeking remunerative investment will surely be attracted to this place when its advantages are fully understood. Not only nail, wire, axe, and other factories connected with the iron trade; but such as are designed to supply the wants of the thousands who are workers in iron. These supplies could be manufactured here and furnished to the operatives at less cost than they now pay for the same articles. It is therefore the interest of every working man to encourage the location of all kinds of manufactories in this place. Especially would a cotton-mill or some establishment employing boys and girls, prove a great blessing to the " street children " and their parents, as well as to the community in general. Productive labor with a combination of interests alone can build up a town. Simply buying and selling does not add a penny to the value of an article, or to the wealth of the community. It is creating an article or increasing its value that makes your wealth, builds your cities, and moves the world.

I say, therefore, with a full knowledge of the situation, and with full confidence, to my best friend: if you wish to invest capital in any department of industry, Danville is one of the most promising fields in the State.

Montour Iron and Steel Works.

In the whole wide range of subjects connected with the past history of Danville, this immense establishment is the most important in a business point of view, and is at the same time the most difficult to trace through all its extensions and its changes of owners, operators and managers. To note its history in detail from 1838 to the present time would be a history in itself, and would require a volume larger than this to give a full and complete idea of its origin and its progress through the sunshine and shadow of more than forty years. It is to be hoped that before the past is entirely buried in forgetfulness, and while there are still living witnesses of its beginning, rise and progress, some one possessing the ability will search the old records, tax the memory of its pioneers and give us a complete history of this great enterprise, with a note of each owner, operator and manager. In a work like this, a general sketch is all that can be expected, and this sketch is as nearly correct as the facts can be gathered at this day. The charcoal furnace, No. 1, was built by B. Patterson in 1838. It stood beyond the Mahoning steam mill of to-day and near the railroad crossing. It has now entirely disappeared. About 1840, Chambers built the twin furnaces, Nos. 2 and 3. These were among the very first in the country, that made iron with anthracite coal. Benjamin Perry was the leading spirit in the production of anthracite iron. Furnace No. 4 was not built until 1845. The Montour Iron Company owned the works and they were for some time represented by the firm of Murdock, Leavitt & Co. This firm consisted of U. A. Murdock, Edward Leavitt, Jesse Oakley and David Wetmore. Henry Brevoort was resident superintendent. The rolling-mill was built in 1844. (A. G. Voris was a general agent and builder, who was for many years connected with the works, as builder, purchasing material, selling iron and having the renting of the dwellings in charge.) T. O. Van Alen built the store-house, now known as the company store in 1844 and conducted the store and the flouring mill until about 1850 when he sold to Conely, Grove & Co. He was also resident agent for a time. The rolling-mill was completed in 1845 and here the first T rail was made. The U rail had been made before this date ; but to Danville belongs the honor of having on the 8th day of October, 1845, produced the first T rail that was ever made—a rail that now connects the Atlantic and Pacific oceans and checkers with iron roadways every civilized country in the world. In 1843 the furnaces were leased to Benjamin Perry, Alexander Garretson, Cornelius Garretson and William Jennison. Their contract was for two years. Harris was the manager at the rolling-mill in its first operation and was succeeded by M. S. Ridgeway, the manager at the present time. The foundry and machine shop was established by Heyward & Snyder in 1839, but they were purchased by the company in 1852. From 1847 to 1849 the rolling-mill was operated by Ridgeway, Allen, Heath and Stroh. The resident agent of the company at that time was Warren Murdock. He occupied the position until the advent of the Grove Bros., about 1850 or 1851. Peter and John Grove managed the works until 1857. During their *regime* the new mill was built, adding much to its extent and capacity, which is now 45,000 tons of iron rails per annum. In 1857 the entire works passed into the hands of I. S. Waterman, Thomas Beaver, William Neal and Washington Lee, as trustees for the creditors of the Montour Iron Company. They operated the works as trustees until 1859 when the entire interest in the whole concern was purchased by Waterman & Beaver. They also purchased the real estate with all the franchises of the company and changed the name to the Pennsylvania Iron Works. They operated the works with great success and general satisfaction. In 1868 Thomas Beaver, Dan Morgan, C. Mulligan, George F. Geisinger and Dan Edwards operated and shared the profits of the works. This combination was successful and continued until 1874. In 1876 Thomas Beaver sold his interest to I. S. Waterman, retaining by purchase the mansion house on the hill, with twenty acres of ground.

In 1880 I. S. Waterman sold the whole establishment to the Reading Railroad Company and the works have since been conducted in the interest of that corporation. As before remarked it is very difficult to get the changes exactly, as scarcely any two men agree on the exact date of occurrences that should be correctly stated in a work like this. The reader may rest assured however, that in the main our sketch is correct and reliable.

It only remains to add a few notes which a sense of justice seems to demand. Of the proprietors who preceded Thomas Beaver, I know nothing personally; but of Mr. Beaver everybody in Danville can speak confidently, he having resided here for the last twenty-three years. Among the enterprising men of business, who have directed their energies to the development of our natural resources, and who have most notably contributed to the substantial interests of Danville, is Thomas Beaver. His life affords a noble example of human capabilities under the influence of our free American institutions, and the abundant material afforded to intelligent industry, without regard to accidental circumstances. In his early boyhood, Mr. Beaver worked on a farm at two dollars and fifty cents a month. He afterwards engaged in merchandising and visited Philadelphia to purchase his goods before he was eighteen years old. Through the energy and the executive ability that has characterized him through life, he succeeded until he became one of the prominent merchants of the city, and finally joint proprietor of one of the largest establishments in the State; employing more than a thousand men and producing more than one hundred tons of iron rails in a single day, in connection with a store in which he employed more than forty clerks and during his proprietorship sold goods to the amount of between eight and nine millions of dollars. No man could be better adapted to meet the requirements of his important and responsible position. requiring quick perception, comprehensive thought and at the same time a watchful care of the most minute details. Of course he amassed a fortune; one half of all his profits, on a fair calculation, he donated to charitable, educational and religious purposes, and what is equally rare he knows how to enjoy the blessings of wealth not only in the personal comfort it affords; but in adding to the happiness of others, in quiet acts of true benevolence, that always return to bless the giver.

The name of the works has been changed to the " Montour Iron
and Steel Works." The organization is as follows : President, W.
E. C. Coxe of Reading. Pa. ; general manager, F. P. Howe, Danville ; treasurer, S. W. Ingersoll, of Philadelphia. Mr. Coxe is
well known by our people he having formerly resided here. during
his connection with the works, some sixteen years ago. He also
took an active part in the local affairs of the town and acted as marshal on several public occasions. Mr. Howe is managing the works
with general satisfaction and great success. The chief operators in
the various departments are Dan Morgan superintendent of the blast
furnaces. He has occupied that position for many years, and is
more particularly noted in another portion of this book. M. S.
Ridway, manage ; P. J. Adams has been in the machine shop about
as long as any other ; and in an establishment like this, long years of
employment is a test of industry and skill. George Lovett is the superintendent of labor, and time keeper, a position of responsibility
requiring activity and constant watchfulness. William Cruikshank
is the moulder, a position formerly occupied by the genial Henry
Gearhart. Captain Gaskins occupies his old place at the weigh
scales, Joseph Bryant at the stock scales. There are many others
filling important positions that it would be a pleasure to name. A.
W. McCoy is chief clerk in the office. C. M. Mock also holds a
responsible clerkship in the principal office. Samuel S. Gulick keeps
a record in a minor office near the machine shops. J. Boyd Gearhart, M. C. Gearhart, John Walize and many engineers, heaters and
workers whose names are unknown to the writer whose brain and
muscle keep the works in motion, deserve at least a passing note.
The extent of the Montour iron and steel works, can be imagined by
the fact that in the rolling-mills, furnaces. mines and machine shops
there are thirty-nine stationary steam-engines and four locomotives.
The works are now (February, 1881,) running to their full capacity
night and day. They are crowded with orders and all the army of
iron-workers have constant employment.

    J. R. Philips looks after the heating, J. R. Lunger takes his place
at night. and John Marks that of Ridgway. E. C. Voris is veteran
among the patterns. E. O. Ridgway is roller and Hiram Antrim
runs the flouring-mill.

Marble and Stone Cutting.

The marble and stone cutting business in Danville is carried on by H. F. Hawke & Co., and so well has this firm met the public demands that they have no opposition in their line of business and those who would venture on a rival establishment would find " Jordan a hard road to travel." Col. A. J. Frick is the partner of Mr. Hawke in the firm. Their marble-yard is at the old stand formerly occupied by Peter Hughes, deceased, and their stone-yard is at the intersection of Ferry street and the Lackawanna railroad. Mr. Hawke is a practical workman of long experience and is complete master of the business in all its details. His skill and taste in designing and in execution is known all over the country and large corps of marble and stone cutters are kept in constant employment. The artistic work of this establishment is seen in the Opera House in the Grove church and numerous buildings here and elsewhere, as well as in the cemeteries all around us. The works were established in 1869 and have proved a complete success and their work adorns many of the most celebrated buildings throughout the State.

Stone cutting is not only a trade, a mechanic art but a science, just as much as many others that are dignified with the honor. Here comes a strolling adventurer, who proposes to walk a wire, to tame a horse, or to sell a nostrum. He comes as a " Professor," too. Professor about as much as the porter at a railroad depot. or the locomotive of a wheelbarrow. But if any man among the sons or toil is entitled to the distinction, it is he, who master of his art, whatever it may be, excels in producing the useful and the beautiful. And none has a stronger claim than the sculptor, or the ornamental worker in stone. No matter whether he hews, chisels and shapes the human form, the monuments of the dead, or ornaments to adorn the abodes of the living. The man who shapes the solid rock into forms of beauty and the various styles of architecture, is a professor, and should rank as such, for he is as far above the montebank who assumes the title, as the pyramids of Egypt are above the sands of the desert. I have been led to these remarks by the artistic skill displayed by Mr. Hawke, contractor and proprietor of the Danville Stone Works. His work for the Asylum, the Grove church, and the new Opera House, are beautiful specimens of the sculptor's skill.

Of course much is due to the designer, but equal credit belongs to the man who with chisel and mallet, clicking away from morning till night, gives form and beauty to the design. He brings out the conception from the rough stone, and presents in reality that which only lived in the brain of the architect.

Columbia Furnaces.

The Grove Brothers were natives of Lebanon county, who by energy, perseverance and the intelligent use of small means and large brains, rose to the front rank among the iron manufacturers of the country. The bond of brotherhood between them was close and enduring as life. Unity of purpose and concert of action, no doubt contributed much to their success. In addition to this they studied the nature of iron and the most economical modes of its manufacture, as a science. In 1840 they bought a furnace that had been built by Mr. Patterson in 1839, and operated it very successfully. In 1860 they added a very large furnace, with great improvements, giving them a capacity of 12,000 tons a year, of the first quality. These furnaces have near at hand, iron ore, coal, limestone and every facility for the extensive and economical production of pig iron. Three of the brothers have passed away and the second generation is now, (profiting by the lessons and examples of those who went before) judiciously following in their footsteps. Two of the brothers remain (one is here) to temper the ardor and to direct the energies of the younger members of the firm. Some years ago, Grove Brothers built a magnificent mansion, to which reference is made in another portion of this book. The furnaces are on Mahoning street and connected with the railroads by proper sidings for the reception of stock and the shipment of iron. They have a very fine office near the furnaces. With Michael and John I was best acquainted. They were affable in their manners and social in their nature John especially was a man of remarkable intelligence. Though he was not a politician in the ordinary acceptance of the word and took no public part in political contests beyond the exercise of the ballot : yet he seemed to have the clearest and most comprehensive views of the Government, its history, its foreign and domestic relations, its finances and the policy demanded by the duties of the hour. Many who read these lines will no doubt remember his lucid, off-hand expositions of public questions, and his sound judgment touching the probabilities of the future.

Early Schools.

Of our early schools, Mr. Frazer says: The people of Danville have ever manifested a deep and abiding interest in the education of their children. Some time about 1790, whilst the village was yet unknown as a distinct organization, but included in the very comprehensive and more widely known organization of Mahoning, a school-house was erected on the grounds of the Grove church, a few yards east of the old church edifice, where the children of the forefathers of the border settlement received the rudiments of their education. The names of the teachers have all passed into oblivion, save that of Master Gibson, but neither the date of his service nor their duration can now be ascertained nearer than that it was during the last decade of the last century. Subsequently, when the population of Danville became sufficiently numerous to support a village school, the building at the Grove church was found to be too remote for them, and Gen. William Montgomery, with commendable liberality, donated a lot for school purposes, on his town plan, which seems to have been bounded by the great road leading from his house to the river, called Mill street, on the southeast, by the river on the southwest, by Factory street on the northwest, and the Mahoning on the north, and being a part of his farm.

His deed of dedication, dated February 1, 1802, recites that "the said William Montgomery, for and in consideration of his desire to promote the good of the people of Danville and the points adjacent, hath granted, confirmed and quit-claimed unto a majority of the inhabitants of said village, that certain lot marked twenty-two on the plan annexed, called the plat of the west end of Danville, for the purpose of erecting thereon a school-house and academy for the instruction of youth in reading English, writing, arithmetic, the mathematics and music, and whatever other branches of literature may be thought conducive to the general interests of said town and vicinity."

A frame school building, about twenty feet square and one-story high, was erected on this lot, by voluntary contributions, in 1804.

The gable end fronted on the alley midway between Mill and Factory streets, with a door and two windows; and three windows on each side. The writing desks fronted the sides, so that the backs of the pupils who occupied them, were turned to the interior of the room. The smaller students were seated on benches in the middle of the room, running parallel with the writing desks. All the seats were common wooden benches, destitute of backs. The entire arrangement of the school-room was extremely inconvenient, and so continued many years.

The school near the church having been discontinued, the first school in the new building was taught by the venerable Andrew Forsyth, who continued it for years, until advancing age admonished him to relinquish it, much to the regret of his patrons and pupils. Few, very few of his old pupils survive, but those few retain pleasing recollections of their worthy and revered teacher.

Mr. Forsyth was succeeded in the school by John Moore. He was a competent and popular teacher, but was averse to occupying his time in so unprofitable and thankless a vocation, and soon abandoned it for the more profitable one of merchandising, which he successfully pursued for many long years, and deceased in 1870, at the good old age of eighty, greatly regretted by his old pupils and the entire community.

All these schools, until the present school system was adopted, were wholly supported by voluntary subscriptions made by the parents or guardians of the pupils and were renewable quarter yearly. They were essentially private institutions, and continued just so long as the teacher and his employers mutually agreed, and no longer, yet they were not much more subject to change than are those under the present admirable system of the public schools.

Insurance Companies.

There are two insurance companies located in Danville. First the Farmers' Mutual Fire Insurance Company of Middle Pennsylvania. This company was organized on the 21st of June, 1859, and is conducted strictly on the mutual principle. It has paid out nearly three hundred thousand dollars for losses, and yet for more than twenty years it has made only five moderate assessments on the premium notes of its members. William Follmer is president ; Samuel

Snyder vice president and P. Johnson secretary and treasurer. There is no doubt that the company, mainly owes its extraordinary success to the watchful care and the executive ability of Mr. Johnson. His long experience and efficiency as secretary and treasurer have steadily and surely led the way, through all the financial fluctuations of more than a score of years, to the prosperity that marked its progress up to the present time. On the first day of January, 1880, its financial condition was reported as follows:

Amount of property insured, ...	$10,659,974 00
Amount of premium notes in force, . .	517,020 80
Cash in treasurer's hands, ...	$209 51
Net amount due from agents on premiums, . . .	1,353 86
Gross amount due on assessments including No. 5.	21,096 64
	$22,660 01
Liabilities.	$11,478 53
Amount paid for losses during past year,	14,752 28

The office is located over the book-store of E. W. Conkling & Co.

The Danville Mutual Fire Insurance Company is located in the same place. The officers at this time are G. M. Shoop, president; C. Laubach, vice president and treasurer, and W. H. Ammerman, secretary.

The following was the condition of the company at the last report:

Amount at risk January 1, 1880. .	$569,853 00
Cash surplus January 1, 1880,	$13,903 93
Premium notes in force,	34,676 63
Available assets,	$48,580 56
Total amount of losses paid since organization, . . .	$17,051 46

The efficiency of secretary Ammerman is also worthy of the highest commendation.

H. B. Strickland.

One of the most substantial and successful teachers of music in this place, is Henry B. Strickland. Of modest pretentions and unobtrusive manners, yet most thorough in the rudiments as well as in the higher departments of musical science. In addition to these sterling qualities, he has the faculty of imparting instruction to the youngest student, as well as to the more advanced, in a clear and comprehensive manner, so as to make a lasting impression. As a composer he has taken an honorable place. Some of his published productions rank deservedly high among musicians of culture ; and all bear the stamp of a high order of talent. Mr. Strickland was a hard working miner in his earlier years ; but his natural genius, with a brief period in one of the noted musical institutions of the country have placed him in the front rank of instructors in the science. As a vocalist he has few equals in this locality, and he is equally at home on the piano or the organ. He has made his mark on the musical history of this place, a mark that will long remain to guide the lovers of " the concordance of sweet sounds," when the more flashy work of others is forgotten. He is now the organist of St. Joseph's Catholic church, and is also a dealer in music and musical instruments. on Mill street.

Dennis Bright.

Another of our brave soldiers was Dennis Bright. Though retiring in his disposition he has nevertheless acted a prominent part in our local history. He is a native of this county and son of Peter Bright of Valley township, and originally from Reading. When the war broke out, Dennis was in the State of Indiana, where he enlisted in the Fifteenth regiment of Indiana volunteers. For meritorious services he was soon promoted to a lieutenancy. At Cheat Mountain he was severely wounded and for a time disabled. When partially recovered he was detailed on recruiting service ; and was afterwards promoted to assistant adjutant general, with the rank of captain on the staff of Gen. Wagner. At the close of the war he returned to his old home and engaged in the business of oil refining in Danville. In the fall of 1871 he was elected to the State Legislature, in the district composed of Montour and Northumberland counties. This was certainly a tribute to his personal·worth, as the majority in the district is largely against the Republican party of which he was the nominee ; and he was the first Republican member that ever appeared in the Legislature from Montour county. Unobtrusive in his manners, he was not a noisy ; but a watchful, working member, exercising sound, practical judgment on all subjects and securing the legislation desired by his constituents. More than all, amid the bold corruption of the time, his honesty and fidelity to duty were never questioned, and no shadow of suspicion ever fell upon his name.

In his political sentiments he has always been a Republican, though never of choice a politician. He is now engaged in the hardware trade, in the opera-house block, and is one of the substantial business men of Danville.

Catholic Church.

In view of the great number of members of the Catholic church, with their families. who came here as iron workers on the establishment of the Montour works, the authorities of the church located a mission in Danville about the year 1847. It was placed under the pastoral charge of Rev. J. P. Hannigan. who labored successfully in organizing a congregation. Soon after the arrival of Rev. Hannigan. the frame church at the railroad on Center street was built. After some time the pastor was succeeded by Rev. Joseph O'Keefe, and he by Rev. Hugh Kenney. How long they respectively ministered to their people in this place, I have not ascertained ; but when I arrived in Danville, in 1855, Rev. Michael Sheridan, successor to Rev. H. Kenney was in charge of the congregation. Rev. Sheridan went to Ashland, where he officiated as pastor of the church in that place, until his death some time ago. On the departure of the Rev. Sheridan, Rev. Edward Murray took his place in Danville. He was a pleasant gentleman, affable in his manners and was much respected ; Rev. Arthur McGinnis was next in order. The new brick church was built during his pastorate. He was a man of extensive culture, a pleasant companion and a faithful minister. He visited Europe in 1871 during his ministry in Danville and seemed much invigorated on his return ; but subsequently died suddenly

14

while reading in his library. His death produced a profound sensation, not only in this place, but in Catholic circles all over the country, as he occupied a high position in the confidence of the church and in the respect of the public. The funeral ceremonies, both here and also in Philadelphia where his remains were entombed, were of the most solemn and imposing character.

The brick church on the corner of Ferry and Center streets was built on a lot which they purchased of Mr. Joseph Diehl. The ground was bought in September, 1857; but the church was not completed until 1869. The church building is sixty-one by one hundred and seventeen feet. It has a tower one hundred and five feet high, which is surmounted by a large, gilt cross. The style of architecture is called Romanesque. The auditorium will seat fourteen hundred, nor is it too large, as there are more than two thousand communicants, a larger membership than all other churches in Danville combined. The new church was dedicated on the 25th of July, 1869. Rev. O'Connor former bishop of Pittsburg and since a member of the Society of Jesus, preached the dedication sermon. In his exordium he paid a glowing tribute to the congregation for the taste and liberality displayed in the church edifice. His sermon was an able and interesting exposition of the appropriate text he had chosen. This was the first time I had witnessed the ceremony of dedicating a Catholic church, and by their courtesy occupied a place where I had the best opportunity for seeing and hearing the interesting ceremony of the occasion. Quite a number of the clergy were present clad in the rich vesture enjoined by the church. Rt. Rev. Bishop Shanahan of Harrisburg consecrated the church and the altar. High mass was celebrated by Rt. Rev. Bishop O'Hara of Scranton. Rev. Barry was master of ceremonies. There was something peculiarly impressive in the dignified bearing and kindly though penetrating eye of this young priest, and I regret to learn that he has since died. The church itself is an imposing structure and on that day was decorated with paintings and flowers in a chaste and beautiful manner. The image of the Saviour surmounted the altar and the lamb at the base, with all the adornments, could not fail to produce an effect, at once sublime and lasting. The music was grand. One female voice was surpassingly lovely.

In July, 1873, Rev. Thomas McGovern assumed charge of the

church in Danville, and in which he remains. During his pastorate a magnificent organ was procured for the church. There was a grand musical concert and introductory ceremonies, under the direction of the pastor, as the deep tones of the organ for the first time, filled the church. The concert was a success financially as well as musically. Prof. M. J. Cross presided at the organ, at the opening; but Prof. H. B. Strickland has been and is still the regular organist. Through the efforts of Rev. McGovern a bell, weighing more than four thousand pounds was placed in the tower, on Saturday, November 6, 1880. It is one of the finest, if not the finest toned bell in this place. Rev. Thomas McGovern is not only a man of marked ability, but possesses more energy and executive power than any of his predecessors. As a controvertialist he is a dangerous opponent, and seems to be armed at every point to battle for the church and to defend the faith he professes. Yet he is liberal and generous, courteous and pleasant to all; and holds an honorable place in the respect of the community at large. He is a fine speaker and on special occasions always attracts a crowd of those outside of his own church. The Sunday school is attended by more than four hundred scholars and is superintended by the pastor.

Oddities.

"Old Gabe" was an African and wood sawyer. Why they called him "Gabe" is a mystery as his name was Jim Gray. He was a good type of his race, in its primitive state. He once inquired for a letter at the post office. "What name?" said the post master. "Why mine to be sure," said Gabe, "ef hits for me de name'll be on de upper side, an' ef hit ain't hit wont be dar." But long years have passed away since he meandered through the town with his saw-horse on his back, carefully watching the wood-piles in his way.

There was another colored individual for a long time employed at the Montour House. His name was Clarke; but they called him "Black Bill." At the time gents' shawls were first worn, one of the town editors bought one of a peculiar pattern. For a live joke some of the gents up town, bought one of the same pattern for Black Bill, and sent him on a pretended errand to the printing office. But the editor took the wind out of that sail, by wrapping his shawl about him and walking up town by the side of Bill. The delight of Bill was to indulge in *hifaluten*. Meeting another colored man named Green, on the canal bridge one cold morning Bill inquired, "How's your complexion dis mo'nin'?" "Easy dar now," said Green, "go way wid your gramatics." Bill rose on his dignity and replied: "Don't you try to graduate your moral noxification 'bout me. How de diameter of cerebellum gatiate any how. Can't you expectorate when a gemman suhnoxicates; tell me dat: you fisticated specimentor of noncomposity?" Bill left for Scranton. He was a jovial happy mortal and was faithful to every trust, but never troubled himself about to-morrow.

The Enterprise Works.

The "Enterprise Foundry and Machine Works" are located on Ferry street, between the canal and Mulberry street. They were first erected in 1872 by James Cruikshank, J. W. Moyer, Robert Moore, and Thomas C. Curry, under the firm of "Cruikshank, Moyer & Co." The whole structure with all its valuable contents was totally destroyed by fire in the fall of 1873. But the parties, true to the name they had adopted, rebuilt on a larger scale, in the summer of 1874. The main building is 104 by 45, the boiler-house is 45 by 24 feet, attached to these is a large blacksmith shop and other necessary buildings. About two years ago Mr. Moore left the concern, and only Cruikshank, Moyer, and Curry are now in the firm; but the title of the firm continues as formerly. "Cruikshank, Moyer & Co." The foundry is especially superintended by Mr. Moyer, a practical founder of large experience. Castings weighing seven tons have been cast in the Enterprise foundry, and the capacity at a single casting is nine tons. In the extensive machine department, steam engines are made, also rolling-mill, blast furnace, saw and grist-mill machinery and railroad and bridge castings. These works have been carried on very successfully and their work is shipped to all points of the compass. The three partners are all practical men, the one a founder and the other two machinists and and each a master workman. This fact has no doubt secured the excellence and the consequent popularity of their work. The Enterprise Foundry and Machine Works of this firm have added very materially to the current of business in this locality. It is kept in full operation and bids fair for a long and prosperous future. Where men of sterling integrity and practical skill, lead the way, success must follow.

Noted Murder Trial.

In May, 1857 Catharine Ann Clark, wife of William J. Clark, died after a painful and somewhat peculiar illness. Before she was buried suspicion arose that there was something wrong. This was strengthened by the fact that there was a reported intimacy between William J. Clark and Mary Twiggs. It was also known that David Twiggs, the husband of Mary, had died in the same mysterious manner, a few weeks previous. Add to this the fact that Clark had purchased both arsenic and strychnine, at the drug store of Chalfant & Huges a short time before, and that the corpse indicated death by arsenic. All these circumstances pointed to Clark as the poisoner of his wife. Upon this he was arrested and lodged in jail. A coronor's jury made inquiry into the matter, the body of David Twiggs was exhumed, a portion of the stomach and contents of each of the dead, was secured for analysis. Doctor Simington had attended Mrs. Clark and also analyzed the contents of the stomach. At the trial in February, 1858, he testified to the finding of arsenic as did also Doctor Snitzler, Doctor Strawbridge, and Doctor Magill. After a trial fairly conducted by the counsel, the court and the jury, he was convicted of murder in the first degree, and sentenced on the 19th day of February. He persisted in his innocence to the last and died with a solemn denial on his lips. Mary Twiggs was tried in May, 1858 and was condemned on the same general testimony. She was also hung, while she protested that she was innocent of the crime. The first execution in Montour county was William J. Clark and the second his accomplice, Mary Twiggs. Subsequently William McGinly killed Thomas Shevland with a knife. He was tried and convicted ; but he made his escape from prision and has never been heard of since.

Our School Houses.

Danville is furnished with at least three of the most complete school buildings in the State. The people of this place have always felt a warm interest in the subject of popular education, and have employed every agency to advance and sustain our public schools. The care and taste exercised in the construction of our school buildings, is in keeping with that which is exercised in selecting teachers and watching the education of the young. The school-building in the Third ward, is a fair sample of all, and a brief description of this imposing structure, will answer for those of the First and Fourth wards, only they are much larger.

The size of the building is ——

At either side a wide door opens into a central hall, from which two splendid stairways lead to the second story; each floor being divided into two rooms, very large, high ceilings, well ventilated and heated by two large heaters located in the basement. The primary department is in the west wing on the first floor. We have never seen, either in city or country, fixtures and furniture better adapted to the purpose. There are twenty-eight desks in each room, and fifty-six very neat little chairs, immovably fixed on iron pedestals, and suited to the size of the scholars. In the center of each desk, imbeded in the lid, is an inkstand that can only be moved with a key. The chairs and desks are all of maple wood, nicely varnished and polished, with metal supports firmly screwed to the floor. The four rooms are all furnished alike, only the desks and chairs in each room are suited to the size of the pupils. The wood work of the interior is neatly and handsomely painted and grained to match the furniture. This complete and artistic part of the work was executed by Mr. M. B. Munson, and attests the skill with which he handles the brush.

The brick work was done by Mr. C. Books, and is one of the most substantial and finished jobs of the kind that can be found in our place. Look at those neat, yet massive walls, and you will indorse our opinion.

The construction of this grand edifice was in the hands of Mr. Robert McCoy, contractor and builder, of this place, and every part was designed by him and finished under his personal supervision.

This, as well as other structures erected by Mr. McCoy, places him among the first architects of this part of the State ; and while the children enjoy the benefits of pleasant, convenient, and healthy school-rooms, he may well feel an honest pride in the building itself, as the result of his skill and experience in the science of architecture.

There are twenty-eight schools in the borough of Danville, with an average number of seventeen hundred scholars.

F. C. Derr is principal of the high school and has been for a num- of years. There are twelve school directors in the town, three for each ward by special act of the Legislature.

Rev. Horine is superintendant of schools for this county at the present time. The school term is ten months in each year.

Peter Yerrick.

Among the soldiers who endured the hardships and encountered the dangers of the Mexican campaign, was Peter Yerrick, cousin to the writer. Although badly wounded at Molino del Rey, he escaped with his life. He first enlisted in the United States army in 1838, for five years, at the expiration of the term, he was honorably discharged. During his service he was chiefly employed on the western frontier, guarding the lives and property of the pioneers, on that extensive border. His experience in those days was wild and romantic. In 1846, when war was declared against Mexico, the old spirit was revived, and Veteran Yerrick first intended to join the "Columbia Guards," especially as Captain Wilson was anxious to avail himself of his experience, in the position of orderly sergeant of the Guards. But some misunderstanding having arisen, he preferred the sterner discipline of the regular army in which he again enlisted. He served under Colonel McIntosh and went with General Taylor as far as Saltillo, and then joined the army of General Scott, fighting his way to Mexico's capital. In all the battles that marked the course of General Scott's triumphant march to the city of the Aztecs, Yerrick bore a prominent part. As stated he was severely wounded at the storming of Molina del Rey, and when the city was taken, he was carried within the walls where he remained six months. He was then honorably discharged on account of wounds received in battle. He reached his home in Danville in May, 1848.

In the late war he again followed the old flag. Among the excellent traits of his character, is an unquestioning patriotism. He is for his country ever ready to defend its honor, without caring what political party may be in power. The stirring scenes of his active life, his thrilling adventures on the plains, the dangers of the siege and the battle, the memory of his comrades who fell by the way— all interwoven with the woof of his life, would fill a volume. He now resides somewhere in the west. May the evening of his days be peaceful and pleasant, as the sunshine, when storms are over and gone.

Agricultural Societies.

These institutions are now organized generally through the farming districts of the country. Though it cannot be denied that where they have existed for some time, there is a noted decline in the interest formerly manifested in the annual exhibitions. The causes of the decline are readily ascertained.

To realize the full benefit of these exhibitions, there should be some system or programme adopted for an interchange of ideas and experiences in the production of the articles presented. But little *real* information is gained by merely glancing at a fine animal, large vegetables, or any other product ; and just as little by reading the cards attached. Let it be arranged for every producer in his turn to tell his neighbors exactly how it was done. Let them compare notes, and thus get at the true design of these exhibitions. If the object were simply a season of enjoyment, seeing your neighbors, looking at curiosities, and enjoying the races, then are these fairs generally conducted properly. But the true design is to *benefit the farmer and the mechanic*, to improve the products of the soil and the workshop. For instance, here is a bag of superior wheat. Farmers admire it, and walk away knowing no more about it, except that it "looked very nice." Why not have the farmer that produced it, at a stated time, take his station by the bag, and tell his neighbors where the seed was from, in what kind of soil it was raised, what are its peculiarities, when was it sown, how was the ground prepared, what fertilizer was used, how much to the acre, and how much did it yield? In a word, all his experience, including also what would likely prove a failure in its cultivation, and so of other articles. If it is a general frolic, trials of speed and sight-seeing, it amounts to nothing. If it imparts solid and useful instruction, thus promoting the industrial interests of the country, it will be productive of much good, and the true object of agricultural exhibitions will be attained.

The first knowledge I have of any organization to promote the interests of agriculture in this section, was a public meeting called in the old court-house, on the 18th of February, 1856, to organize the Montour County Agricultural Society. The following officers were elected: Thomas R. Hull, president; vice presidents, Philip F. Maus, Valley; C. Garretson, Danville; Robert Patterson, Liberty; P. Wagner, Limestone; D. Wilson, Anthony; E. Haas, Derry; J. Sheep, West Hemlock; G. Shick, Mayberry; William McNinch, Cooper; Jacob Sechler, Sr., Mahoning. Secretary, James McCormick; corresponding secretary, Dr. C. H. Frick; librarian, B. K. Rhodes and treasurer, D. M. Boyd. The board of managers were John Best, George Smith, James G. McKee, James McMahan, Jr., A. B. Cummings, Jacob Sheep, A. F. Russel, Stephen Roberts, William Henry, William Yorks, Jacob Cornelison, Edward Morison, J. M. Best, Mayberry Gearhart, Joseph Levers, John Hibler, Samuel D. Alexander, Robert Blee, William Snyder. On motion the meeting adjourned to meet at the call of the managers. E. Wilson, secretary.

The fair, in that year was held at the mouth of Mahoning creek, and there was a fine display of stock and vegetables as well as mechanical and art productions. The annual fair was subsequently held at Washingtonville. In the course of time, however some difference arose between the town and a portion of the country. The result was a split and the organization of another society, known as the Northern Montour Agricultural Society. The headquarters of the latter is at Washingtonville, where the annual fairs are held. The Montour County Agricultural Society holds its meetings and fairs in Danville. This society purchased a piece of ground, from Waterman & Beaver, on the Mausdale road. It has been fenced and a good track has been made. The exhibitions are very creditable; but it cannot be denied, that the general interest in these institutions has been on the decline for some years.

Danville House.

This is a large brick building on the corner of Market and Ferry streets. In 1848 it was first opened as a hotel by John Deen, Jr., and he kept it until 1861. Mr. Deen was quite a popular "host," and built up an extensive patronage. George W. Freeze then left the "Pennsylvania" and took the Danville House, and in 1863 he was succeeded by Charles Savage. Then came Wolf & Wilhelm in 1865. It was next kept for a brief period by John Whitman who was followed by Heim & Snyder. The next in order was Charles Wilhelm, then it was Wilhelm & Brother, the brother being Frederick Wilhelm, who was drowned accidently, with his little son, while washing a carriage in the river. Wilhelm & Brother also kept a livery stable in connection with the hotel. The house is now and has been unoccupied for some time. The cause is found in the fact that it is out of the direct current of trade and travel. The frequent changes of proprietors has also operated against it. It is a large and comfortable house, with every convenience that could be desired in a country town.

Michael Sanders.

Michael Sanders was long and favorably known to the people of Danville, and held many positions of public trust, all of which he filled with honesty and fidelity. On the 1st of November, 1872, he met a terrible death. On that fatal night his residence, in the Second Ward of Danville caught fire from a coal oil lamp, and was totally consumed. He was tax collector at that time, and ventured into the burning building to save the money and papers belonging to the public. The floor gave way, he went down in the crash and never returned alive. Over-powered by the flames he sacrificed his life in fidelity to a public trust. He was seventy-two years of age. Michael Sanders was a good man, a christian by practice as well a profession.

Twenty-five Years Ago.

Twenty-five years ago, I pitched my tent in Danville. Some were stormy and some were wasted years. They are gone beyond the reach of human redemption. And yet this theater of many of my personal misfortunes, is still more like home to me than any other spot in all the wide world. Here I have ever found friends, warm-hearted and true, whose hearts and whose hands were never closed against me. And if I have many sins to be forgiven during those long eventful years, I can only plead my ceaseless devotion to the welfare of Danville and the prosperity of its people. And now as I look back from this waymark, I gaze in wonder on the changes that have passed over it in the last quarter of a century. Great iron manufactories have grown greater, while others sprang up into active life. New industries in the various departments of trade, arose and joined the onward march of progress. New elements of advancing civilization have come to improve society and to bless its people. Prominent men in the front ranks of business or professional life, have fallen by the way, some in the prime of life and others like the leaves of autumn. What a mighty roll the dead of twenty-five years presents, as we recall the names of those we knew so full of life and hope, and who now so quietly sleep with the dead. Yonder stern and busy man, intent on gain, and on whom the marks of time are seen, was a careless, rollicking schoolboy, twenty-five years ago. That stately matron passing down Mill street, was then a joyous, merry school-girl, whose sunny smile and sparkling eyes marked life's golden period, when cares are unknown, when the the stern, cold realities of life, to her were but the roseate dream of a bright and cloudless future. Yes, change is written on all things around us, and on nothing more indellibly than on ourselves.

Within the last twenty-five years gas was introduced, costly water works were built, railroads and iron works have been multiplied, the asylum, the opera-house, seven large churches, three model school-houses, a new court-house and many palatial residences have been erected. Danville, then but a country village, now presents the solid and elegant proportions of an inland city.

Mt. Lebanon.

Mt. Lebanon is the title I have given to the beautiful knoll and palatial residence built by the Grove Brothers a few years ago. Mt. Lebanon, where the tall cedars grow, no less luxuriantly than those that made the beams of the temple. Crowned with the magnificent mansion, and overlooking the town of Danville, it is one of the most charming places ever read or dreamed of, in the annals of history or romance. The enclosure surrounded by an impenetrable hedge, contains many broad acres, and is dotted all over with the rarest shrubbery, gardens and flowers, intersected with pleasant walks and carriage ways. The mansion occupying the summit of the knoll, commands a panoramic view of the river, the town and the hills that gird it roundabout. It is of massive though artistic proportions, and is furnished with all the appliances that can minister to the comfort and enjoyment of its occupants. Its architectural beauty and picturesque location on the summit of Mt. Lebanon, has attracted the admiring gaze of thousands as they have passed on the iron rail; and we can almost imagine the tales and the poetry of future bards, who centuries hence, may delve amid its ruins, or with reverence view the stately pile, and out of the dim and misty past, weave in song the "legends of forgotten lore" of mouldering castles, and of those whose footfalls once echoed through its sounding corridors and lofty halls. But we do not intend to "steal their thunder," so we shall close by advising all who may visit Danville, especially in the summer time, to take a view of Mt. Lebanon; and if they admire the beauty of art and nature in harmony combined, they will share the pleasure we have enjoyed.

The Oil Works.

The Danville Oil Refinery is located on the canal betweeen Church and Ferry streets in the Third ward. It was established in 1865 by John G. Hiler and Charles L. Sholes. The capacity was about thirty barrels a week, but the works have since been much enlarged and improved. After conducting the oil refinery for about two years, they sold the establishment to William T. Ramsey and Charles W. Eckman. They sold to Dennis Bright and he to Messrs. Baily. Mr. Crane was also concerned in the works for some time. At present the firm is S. Baily & Co. The capacity of the Danville Oil Refinery is about three hundred barrels a month. Messrs. S. Baily & Co., are practical men and scrupulously guard the safety of consumers by carefully testing all their burning oils. These works have been a great convenience to the place, and aid very materially in swelling the growing volume of business in Danville.

Late in 1880, the Danville Oil Works, were purchased by the Standard Oil Company.

South Danville

South Danville, was laid out a few years ago, under the superintendence of William F. Gearhart, one of the owners of the ground. South Danville commences at the southern end of the river bridge and follows the continuation of Mill street, to the brow of the hill and down the river to the boundary of Riverside. For beauty and for value in a business point of view, South Danville is not excelled in any quarter, from the head-waters of the Susquehanna to the Chesapeake bay. It occupies the plane of a gentle slope, from the southern eminence, down to the river bank, and is admirably adapted to fruit culture, as well as the whirl and stir of active business, thus combining every advantage that could be desired. The station, passenger and freight, of the Danville and Hazelton railroad are in South Danville. There is a fifty foot street on each side of the railroad, and the lots are laid out on each side, in regular order. Many pleasant homes adorned with beauty and taste, have been planted in South Danville. Its educational facilities and its local government are all that could be desired. A charming location like this, with its proximity to the town of Danville, invites the citizen of taste and culture, and many of its pleasant sites are filling up as business places or suburban homes. Mainly to the enterprise of William F. Gearhart, we owe the town of South Danville, and the success that marks its progress.

Telegraphing.

The first telegraph office in Danville was opened in the spring of 1850 by the "Susquehanna, North and West Branch Telegraph Company." The line commenced at Hazleton, where it connected with the Philadelphia and Wilkes-Barre line. The new line was run across the mountain to Berwick, then down the river to Espy, Bloomsburg and Danville. From this place it continued down to Northumberland and up the West Branch to Lock Haven and from there to Bellefonte, thus connecting us with all the world. The Danville office was in the second story of the Montgomery building, over M. C. Grier's, now J. W. Philip's drug-store, and George B.

Ayers was the first operator. The first regular message over the wire was in April, 1850; and it was a remarkable coincidence that two events of so much importance to Danville came in one flash of lightning. The one event was the fact of our telegraphic communication, and the other was the news contained in the dispatch: namely that the Legislature had finally passed the bill creating Montour county. The dispatch was from Valentine Best then in the Senate, to his brother Alexander, then postmaster at Danville. When the dispatch was handed to the postmaster, he read it carefully, then looked up with doubt and surprise, exclaiming, "Why that's not Valentine's writing," and handed it back to the messenger.

Doctor Goel of Philadelphia, was the leading spirit in the establishment of the telegraph in this place. M. C. Grier was also prominently connected with the enterprise. Some years later the office was in Grier's drug store and R. M. Cathcart was the operator, later still, it was George M. Gearhart. The "Western Union" subsequently established an office in Conkling's book-store. It was afterwards in Allabach's jewelry store. The operator was latterly William John Arms. The Reading Railroad Company also planted an office on Mill street, in the room occupied by George G. Reed's store, then the Reading express office in charge of C. N. Kight. The operator was R. M. Pegg. These are now united in the express office in Torrence's building where Mr. Kight has the Reading express office, and William J. Arms is the operator. The railroad companies also have each a telegraph office at their several depots. Mr. Van Buskirk is the operator at the Lackawanna, Mr. Faust at the Catawissa and he is also assisted by Mr. Matchin and Mr. Campbell. At the D. H. & W. station in South Danville, Mr. John K. Kinter is the operator. The American Union Company has just erected a new line and located an office in Reed's store. Miss E. Shaw is the operator.

Danville Foundry.

The Danville iron foundry was built by Daniel DeLong, in 1872. It is located in East Danville near the Lackawanna railroad. The building is 56 by 84 feet and is covered with a slate roof. Its capacity is a casting of seven tons at one heat. It is solidly built and with its blacksmith and pattern shops is one of the most complete iron establishments in Danville.

Trinity M. E. Church.

This is one of the latest additions to the church edifices of Danville. The necessity for its building grew out of the large and growing congregation in St. Paul's, and an actual want of room. A sort of mission was first established north of the canal, which was the nucleus of the new congregation. The mission was placed in charge of Rev. McCord and soon preparations were made for the erection of a new church building. A lot was purchased of Michael Walize, on the corner of Ferry and Center streets, immediately opposte the new Catholic church, and the building was commenced. M. S. Ridgway, Captain Lovett and others, not members of the church, took an active part and contributed liberally in rearing the church. Thomas Beaver was the largest contributor. His contribution was counted by thousands of dollars. As the financial troubles of the country came with the stoppage of the iron works and consequent want of employment, the congregation was unable to meet the heavy debt ; which the continuance of good times would have enabled them to meet, and their beautiful house, costing nearly thirty thousand dollars was sold by the sheriff for an unpaid balance of eight thousand dollars. It was bought by Thomas Beaver at that figure. Afterwards Rev. I. H. Torrence, thought it to be his duty to bear a part of the burden, and purchased one half interest of Mr. Beaver. Next Mr. Thomas Beaver donated his half ($4,000) to the church ; but Rev. Torrence being unable to do so, held his ($4,000) against it ; freely offering the same at cost to the church. In the mean time the church was occupied as usual by the congregation. Subsequently to bring matters into definite shape the church was again sold and Rev. Torrence became the owner in fee simple. Rev. Torrence gives the congregation the use of the church and has offered to transfer it to the congregation on the payment of his net claim.

It is a large brick edifice built in modern style. The inside appointments are unexceptionable. The audience chamber, with its tasty arrangements and stained glass, produces a grand effect. There is nothing gaudy or showy, and yet its adornments are admirable. The pulpit and surroundings are of walnut, finely finished.

The seats are of the same material and are arranged in a semi-circular form, thus every auditor faces the pulpit. In addition to the auditorium there is also a spacious basement, well ordered and comfortable. This is used for lectures, prayer meetings and Sabbath school. There is also a church parlor, well furnished and carpeted, designed for social meetings. It also has a kitchen attached, with cooking apparatus for the use of festivals and similar gatherings. In fact this beautiful structure contains every desirable accommodation and modern convenience. We venture to say that there is not a church in Danville, so handsome or so well arranged for comfort and convenience as Trinity M. E. church. The property is valued at $30,000.

Rev. McCord was the first pastor of Trinity church. He was succeeded by Rev. Van Fossen, who abandoned the ministry and studied law, afterwards removing to Colorado. Rev. J. P. Moore, was next appointed to Trinity church. Rev. Moore was an eloquent speaker, a true christian, a wise counselor and a steadfast friend. He was followed by Rev. Stephenson and he by Rev. Strawinski, the present pastor.

City Hotel.

The ground occupied by the City hotel was purchased by Joseph Cornelison about 1820, and in 1830 he erected the house he called the " White Swan." Many will remember the oval sign in front, with the picture of a bird that bore a strong resemblance to a goose. The name of the artist is lost and so is the swan on the oval sign. Here too the post-office was kept for a time. Joseph Cornelison conducted the White Swan hotel, until his death which occurred in 1852. His son, Jacob Cornelison then became proprietor of the White Swan and kept it until his death in 1865. It was afterwards kept by William Smith and others until 1870, when Adam Geringer purchased the property. In 1872 Mr. Geringer moved the White Swan building to the rear where it remains in modest, though not useless retirement. In that year Mr. Geringer erected the present hotel. The design was by C. S. Wetzel : but many arrangements, additions and conveniences were by the proprietor himself. The building is of brick 41 feet on Mill street and 80 feet on Penn street.

It is three stories high above a spacious and well-ventilated basement, in which the bar and restaurant are kept. This department is superintended by John K. Geringer. The house contains a large number of sleeping chambers nicely furnished and well ventilated. The dining-room is eighty feet in length with every modern convenience for a large number of guests. The office, sample-rooms, gents' parlor and other apartments are all arranged in the most convenient order. The ladies' parlor is on the second floor front, with a neat and pleasant balcony extending over the main entrance. In a word, the City hotel, located in a central part of the town, near the opera-house and the principal business houses; presents in all its departments, a convenient, cheerful and pleasant home to all its guests. John K. Geringer assisted by Charles S. Geringer usually presides at the office, and the proprietor personally supervises every department, looking after the comfort of every guest that comes under his roof. First-class accommodations, reasonable rates and careful attention, have given the City hotel a reputation second to none. The excellence of its *cuisine* and its inviting table are known and appreciated. In a word the City hotel, in its location, appointments and its management is all that could be desired, and merits the extensive patronage it receives.

Doctor R. S. Simington.

Doctor R. S. Simington came to Danville in 1854, a new fledged M. D., and has been remarkably successful in his profession. Some years ago he built a comfortable residence in a very pleasant location on the public square at the north-west corner of Market and Ferry streets, where he still resides. He was surgeon of the Ninety-third regiment Pennsylvania volunteers, during the war, and served with distinction. His skillful treatment and watchful care of the soldier boys, not only won their confidence, but their lasting friendship. Nor were his sterling qualities and professional services limited to his own regiment ; but others also were often heard to say, as they were carried to the rear when wounded, "Take me to that sandy whiskered doctor, of the Ninety-third."" At the close of the war he returned to Danville and resumed his extensive practice, in which he is still engaged.

15

In 1866 Doctor Simington was elected and served as burgess of Danville. He was afterwards elected associate judge in the court of Montour county by a very flattering vote, and after serving five years he was re-elected to the judgeship by a decided majority. He is yet in the prime of life and is making a life record alike useful and honorable.

Prominent Citizens.

Under this head, reference is made to some of the prominent men of to-day. But comparatively few could be mentioned in a work like this; enough only to give distant readers, or the future inhabitants some idea of Danville, professionally or in a business point of view, as it is in the beginning of 1881.

Doctor I Pursel came from Northumberland county some years ago and has since practiced his profession with marked success. The judgement of the community assigns him a place in the front rank of an excellent corps of physicians.

Doctor James D. Strawbridge, one of our most prominent physicians was a surgeon in the United States army during the civil war and reached the highest point of honor in being made surgeon of a corps. He was captured by the confederates and for some time was a prisoner of war in the city of Richmond. A little episode during his service in the army, was his contest with General McClernand, in which the haughty general came off second best. It occurred in this wise: Doctor Strawbridge in his solicitude for the sick and wounded on one occasion, chose a neighboring mansion as an hospital, which General McClernand also chose for his own headquarters. The contest almost resulted in blows, so fierce and determined were they for the possession of the mansion, the one in behalf of the sick and suffering soldiers and the other for his own selfish gratification. Enough that Doctor Strawbridge gained the point and "held the fort," notwithstanding the bluster of the doughty general.

After the war Doctor Strawbridge was elected and served in the Congress of the United States, and has since resumed his extensive practice, his main *forte* being surgery, in which he has won a high reputation and is frequently called to distant places to perform important surgical operations.

Charles S. Wetzel is emphatically the architect in this region, and has designed many of the most elegant buildings in the central portion of the State. At home, the opera house, the Grove mansion, the palatial residences of the Baldy's on Market street, as well as many others attest his taste and skill. Mr. Wetzel came from Lewisburg to Danville some years ago.

William J. Thomas is the leading painter and paper-hanger in Danville. Many public and private buildings both here and elsewhere attest his skill and taste in the decorative art.

Emanuel Peters affords an example of what patient industry will do. Honest, persevering, faithful and industrious, he has worked his way steadily up to what is known as "comfortable circumstances." I knew him when he carried his stock in trade on a push cart; now he keeps an establishment on Mill street, drives a spanking team and don't call the King his cousin.

Rev. Irvin H. Torrence resides on a farm on the opposite side of the river; but is so closely identified with Danville folks and Danville interests, that our local history would be incomplete without at least a brief mention. He is, and has for a number of years been secretary of the Pennsylvania Bible Society, an appointment made by the several churches of the State and sanctioned by his own church: a responsible position for which no man in the connection is more eminently qualified in all respects. He is progressive in his nature and somewhat aggressive in his life-work. He would just as soon preach on the canal bridge as in the Cathedral at Milan, provided a Methodist preacher could be heard in that magnificent pile. Rev. Torrence is a ready speaker, has a fine address, has traveled through Europe and is a good scholar in the science of human nature.

G. M. Shoop, (senior of the firm of G. M. Shoop & Son,) one of the substantial men of Danville, is an extensive manufacturer and dealer in lumber, Pennsylvania and West Virginia oak, car lumber, walnut, hickory, ash, and poplar. Mr. Shoop is an enterprising business man, whose active aid is freely given in every good work. Though an earnest and influential politician he has never been an office-seeker, and with the exception of postmaster has held none, preferring the pursuits of private citizenship.

Benjamin G. Welsh, is one of the *live* men of Danville. Though at present residing in Riverside, his business movements have been mainly in Danville for a number of years. He has been prominently connected with the manufacture of iron, and is now agitating the project of a street railway. In past years he bore a full share in pushing forward the business interests of Danville; but latterly he has directed his efforts to the improvement of Riverside. He is a man of enterprise, who has done much for the moral as well as the material advancement of Riverside, and who will yet more substantially make his impression, on the future of Danville. He is a local preacher in the Methodist connection, and is yet in the prime of life.

R. H. Woolley is the most extensive dealer in coal, in this place. He is sales agent for Cunningham & Co.'s, Wilkes-Barre coal, and disposes of immense quantities of the "black diamonds," in supplying a large and increasing demand. His office is on Mill street, opposite the opera-house where the clerks, J. W. Sheriff and M. M. Rhodes are always busy receiving orders and keeping the records of the office. Sometime ago they had a square block of coal, originally weighing several tons, in front of the office; but one night a gang of drunken Goths or Vandals, imagining themselves to be "coal breakers" under a full head of steam: tilted it over breaking it into all sizes from lump to lime-burners' coal. But the business goes on all the same.

Doctor George J. Grauel, a thorough scholar and a leading physician of Danville, was born May 25, 1825, in Felda, Electorate of Fessia, now a province of Prussia. He passed through the common schools of his native place and entered the Gymnasium in 1836. Passed his *abiturient* in 1845; studied in the Universities of Strasburg, Gottingen and Werzburg: graduating in medicine at Gottingen in 1848. In 1853 he came to America; subsequently graduating at the Medical College of New York. He then practiced medicine two years in the city of New York, after which he practiced for seven years in Lehigh county, Pa., and in 1862 came to Danville, where his learning and high credentials at once gave him a leading position, which he continues to hold.

Daniel Ramsey came to Danville in September, 1832, and took charge of the steam mill. This was a substantial mill built of stone in 1825, and was burnt some years ago. Mr. Ramsey was a practical miller and conducted that establishment with universal satisfaction, until 1852. At the end of twenty years he embarked in merchandising in his own brick building where he now resides, pleasantly enjoying the evening of his days.

Ned Buntline, the *nom de plume* of E. Z. Judson, who has gained some notoriety as a writer, lecturer and hunter in the wilds of America, spent his boyhood and school-going days in Danville.

George F. Geisinger has been identified with the iron interest for a number of years, and continues to be one of the prominent and active business men of Danville.

Alfred Creveling is one of our most enterprising citizens. Building iron works and operating them even in the season of depression, he persevered and now is at the head of the Glendower Iron Works. He came from Columbia county and this place is much indebted to him for his capital and his energy in building up the town, up towards its business capabilities.

T. O. Van Alen has long been identified with the business interests of Danville. With the first development of the iron manufacture in this place, he was actively connected, and aided materially in its permanent and successful establishment. He is now conducting a nail factory at Northumberland which he built some years ago. It is a notable fact that Mr. Van Alen kept the factory in operation through all the late money depression that silenced so many manufactories in every department of industry.

Baptist Church.

The Baptist church of Danville, was organized on the 13th of November, 1842. The meetings were held in the court-house for about a year subsequent to the organization, during which period, a frame church was built on Pine street, not far from the river. It was dedicated on the 5th of January, 1844. In 1863 it was removed to give place to the new brick church, which is a large and elegant building. As near as can be ascertained the pastors in their regular order of service, were Reverends J. S. Miller, W. T. Bunker, John H. Worrall, A. D. Nichols, Ira Foster, O. L. Hall, A. B. Still, T Jones, G. W. Scott, I. C. Winn, John S. Miller, the second time, J. John Mostyn, J. E. Bradley, and now Rev. Mr. Sweet.

Jacob Reed, during his life-time was the leading man in the Baptist church, financially and religiously.

The Company Store.

This institution has long been known as " The Company Store," even through all the years when it was owned by Waterman & Beaver it was called " The Company Store," all the same. It is an immense concern. The building one hundred and seventy-five feet in depth, with ninety feet front and is full of goods from the cellar to the attic. The capital invested ranges from fifty to one hundred thousand dollars. It is now owned by the " Montour Iron and Steel Company," and is superintended by William K. Holloway who has at present twenty-four clerks in the store. Under the former *regime* has had as many as forty clerks, all busy as bees in a clover field. The annual sales now amount to $250.000, under the proprietorship of Messrs. Waterman & Beaver the annual sales were as high as $500,000. The immense sales and the manifold departments it includes, require the most complete system and exact management for the successful government of the establishment. I may remark here, that the large sales are not due to the men employed at the iron works, so far as their trade is controlled, either expressed or implied by their employers. They are perfectly free to deal wherever interest or inclination may lead them. But prices being as low as at any other store in town, giving the purchaser a much greater variety from which to make a selection, the result is, that the cash sales to those who have no connection with the iron works, are very large. The store opens at 7, A. M., and closes at 7, P. M.

The merchant tailoring and clothing department is in charge of Thomas W. Scott, a "boss cutter," from John Wanamaker's establishment in Philadelphia. The chief book-keeper is Jacob C. Miller : and Harry J. Crossly has charge of current accounts. Samuel H. Boyer is at the head of the dry goods department and Samuel Ross of the grocery : Joel Hinckley of the hardware and Jasper B. Gearhart of the provision department. John Ricketts is chief among the boots and shoes.

The efficiency of William K. Holloway, the superintendent, his wonderful executive ability and his fidelity to a great trust, are best attested by his retention for twenty years, by all the parties who have owned the establishment during that period. He was only one year at the counter when he was promoted to time-keeper and superintendent of accounts. Next he rose to cashier which he held for twelve years. For the last three years he has had charge of the store, as superintendent, which position he occupies at the present time.

Joel Hinckley, always at his post, has had charge of his department for twenty-one years. This tells its own story. Samuel H. Boyer in charge of the dry-goods department, and Samuel Ross in the grocery division, have also occupied positions in the store for a number of years, and have made a good record in their respective *roles*. Webster Rhoads officiates in the notion department. Harry J. Crossly is a very popular clerk, although his position brings him in more direct contact with the employees. Jasper B. Gearhart deals mainly with the farmers and producers, and seems to enjoy their confidence while he guards the interest of the store with jealous care. Among the clerks are Charles E. Swartz, Lewis Rodenhafer, F. P. Murray, John Gibson and others, all of whom are experts or they would not be there.

National Iron Foundry.

This foundry, near the Columbia furnaces, was originally built by Peter Baldy, Sr., about 1839, and was first operated by Belson, Williams & Gardley. For some cause they failed and it passed into the hands of O'Connor & Rice. They also failed and R. C. Russel took charge of the work. After a brief period of time he sold to Hancock & Carr, who soon transferred it to John Hibler. The several parties named conducted the establishment for twenty-five years. In 1854 Samuel Huber, who had acted as foreman in the Eagle foundry for a number of years, leased the National iron foundry and operated it until 1859, when it was totally destroyed by fire. In the spring of the same year he had taken Samuel Boudman into partnership, and who after the fire abandoned the enterprise. But Mr. S. Huber, with the energy and spirit that has always characterized him, bought the ground of Mr. Baldy, rebuilt the foundry more complete than it had been before and again embarked in the business, successfully conducting it alone, until the 1st of April, 1868, when his son, J. S. Huber, became a partner under the firm

of S. Huber & Son. They carried on the business with entire satisfaction until the 19th of January, 1877, when C. C. Huber,
another son, was taken into the firm, when it became S. Huber &
Sons. Subsequently W. H. Huber, the third son, was also added
to the firm, and so it remains to the present time.

Some years ago Mr. S. Huber, the senior of the firm, turned his
attention to the construction of an improved plow, in which he was
completely successful. His invention was patented and the Huber
plow, made at this foundry, is now a popular favorite over a wide
region of country. Hundreds have gone far and near and still the
demand is increasing. It is the province of the historian to note the
facts and especially those that relate to the productive industry of
the locality, without pausing to inquire into the relative merits of
the invention. Stoves and a great variety of castings are also made
at this foundry.

Could I do so, without seeming flattery, or the danger of tran-
scending my limits, I would like to add a commendatory word in
relation to the members of this firm. As citizens, neighbors, friends
and business men, they are always reliable. With S. Huber, the
father, and J. S. Huber, the eldest son, I am best acquainted, and I
take pleasure in bearing this testimony to them, as honest men and
true Christians. They have each erected a handsome residence on
Mulberry, one of the most beautiful streets of Danville. These
homes are surrounded with all the charms that rural taste can add to
the enjoyment of life. About three years ago, Mrs. J. S. Huber
opened the "Shoe Bazar," on Mill street, especially for ladies,
misses and children, which has become, and in fact it at once became, one of the prominent business establishments of Danville.

Railroads.

Danville is well provided with railroads. There are no less than
three running in every direction and connecting at all points with
the great iron checker work reaching every nook and corner of the
country. The first railroad built through the town of Danville was
the

Catawissa, now a branch of the Reading railroad, and strange to
say it was laid with rails manufactured in England. So much for
low wages in England and low tariff in America. The location of

this road, to those who are acquainted with the topography of the country presents something of a curiosity. The natural course would seem to cross the river at Catawissa, then down the North Branch and pass through this place from a point near Gulick Grove, up Mahoning creek to Mansdale. Why it was bent up to Rupert can only be accounted for on the supposition that it was to accommodate the people of Bloomsburg. It is said that it was done mainly through the influence of Hon. Charles R. Buckalew. This location has placed the Danville depot on the hill above the town, though that quarter has since been pretty well built up. In fact railroads should have their freight depots outside of town. The Catawissa railroad was put in operation in 1853, and it is a remarkable fact, that during the twenty-seven years it has been operated, doing a heavy freight and passenger business, carrying hundreds and thousands over its lofty bridges and through the wild mountain gorges on its tortuous track, not a single passenger has ever been killed on the Catawissa railroad. This speaks volumes in favor of its management; and this high honor is shared alike by its superintendents, conductors, engineers, brakemen, telegraphers and all its employees. I was best acquainted with Superintendent Nichols. He was a man of much executive ability and was admirably adapted to his responsible position. Mr. Ellis, the agent at this place is spoken of in the highest terms, for his fidelity, his urbanity and the watchful care he bestows on every department of his responsible duties.

The telegraphic operator and others connected with the station, also share the public commendation. The depot building is a nuisance.

The Lackawanna and Bloomsburg, or Del. L. & W.—This railroad extends from Northumberland to Scranton, a distance of eighty miles. The depot at Danville is an improvement on that of the Catawissa railroad at this place still it is considerably short of what it should be. The ladies' parlor especially, looks too much like a bar-room in a country tavern. I have seen the ladies' room, at towns much smaller than Danville, carpeted, furnished with mirrors and elegant sofas, that contrast strangely with the bare floor and wooden benches provided for the ladies at this place. But suppose we must wait our time. This defect however, is made up by the courteous treatment and ever watchful care of those in charge. A. Mont.

Gearhart, is the agent and dispatcher in charge of the station at
Danville ; and if there is a more faithful officer or one more obliging
to the public, I have not found him in my travels. His assistant, Mr.
Van Buskirk is also worthy of the place. The same can be said of
all the gentlemanly attaches of this station. There are four through
passenger trains every day and a heavy freight is carried over this
road, chiefly coal. iron rails, pig-iron and ore. In 1856 a strong
effort was made by some of our citizens to have the link of this road
between Rupert and Northumberland constructed ; but it was not
built until a few years subsequent to that period. But if our people
finally contributed as much to the desired extension, as they exacted
for the right of way, is a question. The Lackawanna and Bloomsburg railroad, now the Delaware, Lackawanna and Western. was
our second railroad, and marked an important era, in the history of
our town. As it took its passengers on the first down train at Danville, and approached Northumberland, the hind-wheels of the last
stage-coach, disappeared as it slowly pulled in Kapp's yard there to
rot in the sun and to bounce over the highway, nevermore.

Danville, Hazleton & Wilkes-barre Railroad.—This is the latest
addition to the railroads of Danville. It is now operated by the Pennsylvania Railroad Company and extends from Sunbury to Tomhicken, a distance of fifty-four miles. This is one of the most important railroads in the country, as it forms a link in a direct line from
New York to the great West. The completion of the Lehigh and
Eastern will complete the chain. from San Francisco to Boston. For
the construction of this road we are indebted to S. P. Kase. Through
his indomitable energy. and against all obstacles thrown in his way
that interest or malice could invent, he persevered and its completion
is a proud triumph of his enterprising and daring spirit.

The depot of this road is in South Danville. It is quite a respectable building, and Mr. J. B. Kinter, the agent is a gentleman much
respected, not only for his faithfulness to the interests intrusted to
him but for his qualities as a man. His attention to the public his
accommodating spirit and his known integrity have made him hosts
of friends.

Doctor William H. Magill.

Dr. Wm. H. Magill came to Danville in 1817 and has, up to a recent period been the leading physician of this place, as well as in the surrounding country. He has now retired from the active duties of his profession. He married a daughter of Gen. Daniel Montgomery, and they both now enjoy a calm and serene old age in their pleasant home on Market street. They will be long and gratefully remembered not only on account of their devotion to religion ; but for their steadfast practice of its benign principles. Not only on account of professional skill, but for that unostentatious charity that makes it doubly blessed Obedient to the prompting of humanity, they ever responded to the calls of want and distress, with a sentiment of liberality, that includes all within its wide embrace. Many in this community will bless their names when they are gone—bless them for their active sympathy, and keep their memory fresh and green. Weak and sinful as human nature is, few are so depraved as to forget those who ministered to them in the hour of need.

Glendower Iron Works.

The ground occupied by the old Rough and Ready rolling mill was originally intended for a nail factory. A building for that purpose had been partially erected and then abandoned. For years the roof on a frame-like stilts, without siding, stood idle and useless. It seemed as if some genius had begun at the top to build downwards and had never reached the foundation.

In 1847 William Hancock and John Foley changed it into a rolling-mill for the manufacture of merchant iron. The enterprise was rather unpromising until 1850 when they converted it into a rail mill. Then their prosperity began. After eight years of remarkable success. Mr. Foley retired and Mr. Hancock became sole proprietor. This was in 1858. Mr. Foley soon after left for Europe. Sometime during the war and after the return of Mr. Foley from Europe, he again became a partner with Mr. Hancock. In 1866 Mr. Foley again sold his interest to Mr. Hancock and moved to Baltimore where he died some years ago.

The first of the Danville Furnaces was built in 1870 by Hancock &

Creveling. The second and larger furnace was subsequently erected. These furnaces were superintended by George W. Miles, a skillful and successful manager. The capacity of the Danville Furnaces is 15,000 tons per annum.

In 1867 the National Iron Company was formed, superseding the Rough and Ready. Of this company William Hancock was president at first and afterwards William Painter; P. C. Brink was vice-president and Benjamin G. Welch was secretary, treasurer and general manager.

This organization continued until 1871, when the Danville Furnaces were purchased. The new rolling-mill had been erected in 1870. George W. Miles continued the superintendence of the furnaces under the National Iron Company. John G. Hiler was manager at the new rolling-mill, and Joseph H. Springer at the old Rough and Ready rail-mill. In 1873 owing to large expenditures and heavy losses, the company was compelled to go into bankruptcy. After the works had lain idle some time they were purchased by the heirs of William Hancock, deceased, in 1874, under a mortgage sale; upon which the Hancock Iron and Steel Company was organized. Doctor J. D. Gosh was chosen president and B. G. Welch, secretary, treasurer and general manager. This company existed only about six months, when the works were again idle until 1877, when they were leased by A. Creveling who operated them until June, 1879, when A. Creveling and George W. Miles purchased the works—the old Rough and Ready property, John Roach purchasing the part lying north of the canal. A. Creveling and George W. Miles then organized the Glendower Iron Works, with A. Creveling, president; H. Levis, treasurer and George W. Miles, secretary and general manager. They have kept the works in successful operation to the present time. The capacity of the works is 20,000 tons.

On the 10th of October, 1879, Creveling, Miles, and H. Levis bought Chulasky furnace three miles down the river, under the firm of Creveling, Miles, & Co., (limited.) They put Chulasky furnace in blast on the 6th of November, 1879, and it has been in successful blast up to present time. Mr. Roach moved the new mill to Chester.

Local Government.

By an act of the State Legislature, Danville was organized as a borough on the seventh day of February, 1849. The act creating the corporation was signed by Governor Wm. F. Johnston.

The first burgess was Dr. Wm. H. Magill. The first town council, composed of five members, was as follows: George S. Sanders, George Bassett, Valentine Best, Frank E. Rouch and E. H. Baldy. The first council meeting was held in the office of E. H. Baldy, Esq., and the first business transacted was the election of E. H. Baldy, Esq., as clerk of the council. Edward Young was chosen the first street commissioner at a salary of twenty dollars a year. Thomas Jameson was the first constable. The officers and members of the council were duly sworn by William Kitchen, Esq. On the 22d of May, in that year, the first dog tax was levied in the borough of Danville. Some of the citizens could not see the justice of the act, and there were remonstrances and considerable complaint on the part of those who had several dogs on hand. In the same year, the bill of Edward Young, street commissioner, for laborers employed on the streets, amounted to $11,59 41½, which was accepted and paid. The Friendship Fire Company represented to the council that the hose was old and rotten, and requested seven hundred feet of new hose, which was ordered.

A contract was also made with James F. Deen for an engine capable of supplying the Friendship Hose Company. The price was to be $800. It was constructed and ordered to be given in charge of the company. At this period the fire apparatus came under the general direction of the borough.

On the 24th of December, 1849, the council passed a resolution making application to the State Legislature for the erection of a new county, to be called Montour, with the county seat at Danville. It was also resolved to furnish the new county with necessary buildings. The new county was granted in 1851, and the borough of Danville well and truly redeemed every promise it made.

Of the members and council during the first year of the borough, a note may be proper. The burgess, Dr. Wm. H. Magill, still resides here.

Edward Young, the first street commissioner, is still a resident of

Danville. He has also been burgess and filled a variety of public offices with great satisfaction to the people. His popularity attests his worth as a man and as a citizen. Thomas Jameson, the first high constable, is dead He was for years one of the most active and enterprising citizens of Danville, and joined in many public improvements. He left a reputation for honesty, united with a large degree of liberality and goodness of heart. He had a keen appreciation of wit, and could enjoy or perpetrate a joke with equal pleasure. He was burgess in 1852. Wm. Kitchen, Esq., by whom these first officers were sworn, is also dead.

On the 29th of March, 1850, a new council was organized, though not all new members, several having been re-elected. Dr. Wm. H. Magill was re-chosen as burgess and Valentine Best as a member of the council. The new members were Dr. Isaac Hughes, George B. Brown, Thomas Woods and William Morgan. Valentine Best was chosen clerk, and M. C. Grier was elected treasurer.

The meetings of the council at this time were held in the office of Valentine Best. Edward Young was the tax collector for 1850.

On the 4th of April, 1851, the council met for organization. At the previous March election Thomas Chalfant had been chosen burgess, and the following were returned and took their seats as members of the council: James F. Deen, John Rockafeller, J. C. Rhodes and A. F. Russel. William Clark was appointed high constable, and B. W. Wapples, street commissioner. He built the first canal bridge on Ferry street.

In the Spring of 1852, Thomas Jameson was elected burgess, with the following council: George S. Sanders, John Deen, Jr., G. W. Boyer, and George W. Bryan. The latter was chosen clerk. In this year Sydney S. Easton filled up Northumberland street, which was an improvement or no small magnitude.

In 1853, Joseph D. Hahn was elected burgess. The council were Daniel Ramsey, P. Hofer, David Jones and James Gaskins. William G. Gaskins was chosen clerk.

Robert Moore was chosen burgess in the spring of 1854. The council were John Deen, Jr., John Turner, William Hancock, James G. Maxwell and Robert McCoy.

In 1855, William Henrie, of the Union Hall hotel, was elected burgess. The council were Smith B. Thompson, David Jones, Isaiah

S. Thornton, Frank E. Rouch and Isaac Ammerman. In this year the borough limits were greatly enlarged and particularly defined, including, as it now does within its boundary, 996 acres. A census was also ordered by the council, under which the inhabitants were enumerated, and the same was reported at the close of the year. Population, 5,427.

In 1856, David Clark was elected burgess. The council consisted of Jacob Sechler, John Best, John Arms. William Mowrer, and Paul Leidy, Esq.

Jacob Seidel was chosen burgess in 1857, with the following council: Jacob Sechler, Charles Leighow, Joseph R. Philips, Samuel Hamor and John Patton.

In 1858, Dr. Clarence H. Frick, was elected burgess. The council that year was composed of William Mowrer. David Jones, Gideon Boyer, George S. Sanders. and Frederick Lammers.

Christian Laubach was chosen burgess in the spring of 1859, with the following council: D. N. Kownover, Joseph Diehl, B. K. Vastine, D. M. Boyd and William Cook.

In 1860, J. C. Rhodes was made burgess. The council were William Cook, W. G. Patton, B. K. Vastine, Emanuel Houpt and Michael C. Grier.

E. C. Voris was burgess in 1861: the members of the council were Reuben Voris, David James, Joseph Flanegan, William Morgan and D. M. Boyd.

In the year 1862, Isaac Rank was chosen burgess, with the following council: Jacob Aten, William Mowrer, Charles W. Childs, David Grove and James L. Riehl.

B. K. Vastine was made burgess in the spring of 1863. Council—James L. Riehl. William Twist, William Lewis, John G. Hiler and John Rockafeller.

In 1864. E. W. Conkling became burgess. Council—James L. Riehl, John G. Hiler, Joseph Diehl, C. Laubach and William Lewis.

In 1865, John G. Thompson was chosen burgess, and the following were the council: Henry Harris, Dan Morgan, D. DeLong. William Henrie and Jacob Aten.

. Doctor R. S. Simington was elected burgess in 1866, and the council were Dan Morgan, Francis Naylor, D. DeLong, William Henrie and Charles H. Waters.

In 1867, George Bassett was made burgess. Previous to the election, the borough had been divided into four wards, the First, Second. Third and Fourth. Before that time there had been two wards —the South and the North—with five members of council, each elected for one year. The change provided for four wards and twelve councilmen, three from each ward to serve for the first year, one third of them to serve one year, one third two years and the other three years; and also providing for the election of one councilman each year from each ward. Under the law. the following council was elected for 1867: James Cornelison, John A. Winner, C. W. Childs, William Henrie, David Clark, James Kelly. Samuel Lewis, M. D. L. Sechler, Joseph Sechler, Thompson Foster, John G. Thompson and E. Thompson.

In 1868, Robert McCoy was chosen burgess, and the following four new members of council elected to take the place of the four who had been elected for one year, viz: James L. Riehl, C. S. Books, Geo. W. Reay and David Grove.

In 1869, A. J. Ammerman was elected burgess, and the new members of council were Wm. Henrie, J. S. Vastine, John R. Lunger and Franklin Boyer.

D. S. Bloom was burgess in 1870; the new members of council— Wm. Buckley, Hickman Frame, M. D. L. Sechler and Samuel Lewis.

Thomas Maxwell was elected burgess in 1871, with new councilmen as follows: H. M. Schoch, G. W. Miles, George Lovett and Jacob Sweisfort.

The burgess in 1872 was Oscar Ephlin, and the new members of council, elected or re-elected, Geo. W. Reay, Henry Vincent. Jacob Schuster and J. L. Riehl.

Edward Young was chosen burgess in 1873; councilmen, new or re elected, Wm. Buckley. N. Hofer, Joseph W. Keely and Thomas Coxey.

In 1874, J. R. Philips was elected burgess; new councilmen— Jas. Vandling, Jas. Auld, W. D. Williams and David Clark.

Charley Kaufman was chosen burgess in 1875, and the new members of council were M. D. L. Sechler, Wm. T. Ramsey, J. R. Philips and J. W. Von Nieda.

In 1876, the Centennial year, Henry M. Schoch was elected burgess; new councilmen—J. D. Williams, David Ruckle, Wm. K.

Holloway and Wm. R. Williams. Isaac Ammerman was elected at a special election to fill the vacancy occasioned by the resignation of James Auld, who had been chosen county commissioner.

In 1877, Wm. C. Walker was chosen burgess. New councilmen—David Clark, C. A. Heath, A. B. Patton, and John A. Wands.

James Foster was chosen burgess in 1878; new councilmen—J. W. Keely, Stephen Johnson, Jas. Welsh and Thompson Foster.

1879, Jas. Foster, burgess; new councilmen—William Angle 1 year; P. Johnson 3 years, and S. Trumbower, Jacob Goldsmith, H. B. Strickland and Lewis Rodenhofer 1 year.

1880, Joseph Hunter, burgess; new councilmen, Wm. Angle, Wm. Keiner, Hugh Pursel, Nicholas Hofer.

1881, Joseph Hunter re-elected burgess; new councilmen—A. G. Voris,— P. Keefer, Henry L. Gross, Jas. Welsh.

William G. Gaskins was clerk to the council for twenty years and was succeeded by Capt. George Lovett in 1874. In 1879 J. Sweisfort was chosen clerk and he was succeeded by Charles M. Zuber, the present clerk. Among the street commissioners in the last decade were Emanuel Peters, Daniel McClow, William C. Walker, Oliver Lenhart and Mr. Faux. The street commissioner is also *ex officio*, collector of the market tax, and presumedly a sort of inspector of that institution.

The council is generally selected very judiciously and consequently enjoys the public confidence, as the citizens feel assured that in view of a common interest that body will move cautiously and economise where that virtue can be exercised with mutual advantage. The council of 1880 is especially regarded as an able and judicious body.

Danville Iron Works.

This was a rolling-mill built by William Faux some ten years ago, on Church street near the canal. Several other parties were at different times concerned in its operation. In 1877 Mr. Faux moved all the machinery to Pueblo, Colorado, on twenty-eight railroad cars, where he operated it for a time and then moved it to Denver. This establishment was familiarly known as "Cock Robin." Being requested to write something for the *Pueblo Chieftain*, published in that place, I sent them the following:

16

A Twilight Reverie.

We miss the Danville Rolling-Mill,
　　We miss its cheerful glow
Upon that arid plain where nought
　　But iron seem'd to grow.

We miss its bugle call, so shrill,
　　It seem'd to shake the ground;
Old Montour and Mnemoloton
　　Echoing back the sound.

We miss its corps of workingmen
　　Of muscle and of brain,
Who wrought the rails from molten ore,
　　Nor fear'd the fiery rain.

'Mid all the storms of panic years
　　It moved on brave and bold,
While Faux so nobly cheer'd them on,
　　And paid them all in gold.

Silent, sad and desolate now
　　The scene so bright and fair,
Like ruins old, of castle gray,
　　In silence mold'ring there.

So pass away the things of Time—
　　They pass beyond our ken.
So pass away on noiseless wing
　　The fleeting lives of men.

Yes, time itself must yield at last,
　　For years like men must die,
And with the cent'ries grim and old
　　In dust of ages lie.

But we may hope those works again,
　　Will rise in all their pride,
And prosper more, in years to come,
　　By fair Pueblo's side.

Danville Gas Company.

The Danville Gas Company was organized in 1858 under a charter granted by the Legislature of Pennsylvania. A contract was made with Dr. Danowsky of Allentown, for the erection of the works. In the autumn of that year gas was first introduced in Danville. The works are located on East Market street. About seven miles of pipe are laid; but owing to some misunderstanding, or on account of the price. gas has not been used by the borough for a number of years. The stock is nearly all owned by H. P. Baldy, who acts as president. secretary, treasurer, and board of directors.

County Officers for 1881.

The officers of Montour county at the present time are as follows :

President Judge of the Court—Hon. William Elwell.

Associate Judges—Hon. R. S. Simington and Hon. Thomas Butler.

Prothonotary and Clerk of the Court—W. M. Gearhart.

Sheriff—Jacob Shelhart.

District Attorney—L. K. Mowrer.

Court Crier—Samuel Blue.

Register and Recorder—William C. Johnston.

County Treasurer—George W. Peifer.

County Surveyor—George W. West.

Justices of the Peace—First ward, John W. Miles : Second ward, J. F. Gulick ; Third ward, J. P. Bare; Fourth ward, J. R. Philips.

Simon Krebs came to Danville from Tamaqua some years ago and engaged in the wholesale liquor trade. He has been one of the active, enterprising men of this locality. In 1872 he took the contract for laying ten miles of iron pipe for the new water works, for $87.500, which he completed according to contract. He afterwards became a partner in running the Danville Furnaces. Mr. Krebs also built a handsome residence on Mahoning street and has contributed a full share in building up the town and advancing its general welfare.

Dan Morgan.

Dan Morgan came to Danville about 1851 and at once took a leading position among the iron manufacturers of this region : that position he has maintained for thirty years. He has during all those years successfully managed the large blast furnaces of the Montour Works, and in addition, for a time also, superintended the Chulasky furnace, three miles down the river. From 1868 to 1874 he held an interest in the iron works as stated in the history of that concern. Mr. Morgan is a thorough master of the business, understanding the composition and the nature of iron in all its combinations; thus qualifying him for its production. Mr. Morgan has taken rank among those on whom fortune has bestowed her favors. Thoughtful, liberal and helpful, he both enjoys and dispenses the blessings of life. He built a pleasant and commodious residence on Bloom street, where he now resides.

Capt. Samuel Hibler, one of those who from this place responded to the call for volunteers in the time of peril, nobly performed his duty as a loyal soldier of the Union. He was in the 7th Pennsylvania Cavalry and operated mainly in Kentucky and other Southern States. His company presented him with a splendid sword as a token of regard; and finally he was placed in command of his regiment and led the gallant Seventh in some of their bloodiest battles. His brother John recruited a company and was also a brave soldier fighting the battles of his country, and finally yielded up his life for the cause. There are some sad circumstances connected with his death. Enough that he died the death of a hero, amid the horrors of the rebel prison at Andersonville.

Capt. George Lovett.

Among the bravest of the brave who joined the Union army in the civil war was Capt. George Lovett. An ardent patriot and with an intelligent appreciation of the great issue involved in the struggle, he was ever ready to hazard his life for the cause of right—to vindicate the honor of the old flag and to save the heritage of the American people. He first enlisted as a private soldier in the "Danville Fencibles," in 1862. This company was attached to the 132d regiment. P. V. At the battle of Antietam, Lovett was wounded by a minnie ball, but he kept his post while the blood streamed over his face, until the day was won. On the expiration of his term of enlistment, he re enlisted in the 187th regiment and was promoted to the office of captain. In this regiment he led his company through all the battles of the Wilderness in Gen. Grant's memorable campaign of 1864. Capt Lovett was in the battles at Petersburg, Fort Hill and the Welden Railroad. At Fort Hill he was severely wounded in the left arm, by which he was disabled for a time, and from which he still suffers : however he returned to his post where he remained until the close of the war. He was also injured in the hands by the premature discharge of a cannon in firing a salute on an occasion of public rejoicing. Capt. Lovett is now superintendent of labor at the Montour Iron and Steel Company's Works, and wherever his lot may be cast, his services in the time of trial will always entitle him to the consideration of the public.

Danville contains the usual secret societies and benevolent institutions, the "Free Masons," "Odd Fellows," "Knights of Pythias," "Red Men," "Druids," "American Mechanics," "Sons of America," and "Free Sons of Israel." There is also a post of the "Grand Army of the Republic," designated "Goodrich Post, No. 22." It is named for Sergeant Goodrich, a brave soldier of Danville who was killed in the civil war.

Jacob Sechler.

Jacob Sechler was the son of John Sechler, who bought the tract of land, south-east in the Montgomery purchase, and partly included in the borough of Danville. John Sechler was one of the early settlers of this place, and his son Jacob, the subject of this notice, was born here on the 9th of October, 1790. He served in the "Danville Blues" in the last war with England, and was the last survivor of that patriotic company. But, whether in war or peace, Jacob Sechler made an honorable record in life. He was noted, through all his long and useful career, for all the sterling qualities that marked the noble band of pioneers, and through all the changing scenes of almost a century he maintained an honorable reputation down to the close of life. He left a number of sons, who are among the active and influential citizens of to-day; evidencing in their lives that they inherited the industry and the honesty that marked the old pioneer. Jacob Sechler died the calm and peaceful death of the christian, on the 26th day of December, 1880, aged ninety-two years and two months.

"So dies a wave along the shore."

Great Day.

One of the great popular demonstrations in Danville, was the last rally of the Republicans on the eve of Lincoln's second election. It was on Saturday, the 5th of November, 1864.

The procession was arranged and conducted by *Chief Marshal*—Lieut. Dennis Bright. *Assistant Marshals*—W. E. C. Coxe, William Aten, O. H. Ostrander, Lieut. E. W. Roderick, Dr. George Yeomans, Stephen A. Johnson, Maj. Charles Eckman, Lieut. M. Rosenstein.

The magnificence of the immense cavalcade, the numerous banners, flags and tasteful decorations, with the martial strains of Stoes' silver cornet band and Sechler's brass band, gave the demonstration a brilliancy unsurpassed by any other, in the annals of Danville.

The most gorgeous spectacle in the magnificent pageant was the triumphal car, containing a charming representative of the Goddess of Liberty, and a lady, in full costume, representing each State of the Union. The Goddess of Liberty was robed in the National colors. Her head was adorned with a brilliant tiara—she bore a staff surmounted with a liberty cap, and occupied an elevated position on the car. She acted her part with peculiar grace, eliciting the universal admiration of the thousands that witnessed the inspiring scene.

The ladies representing the States were tastefully adorned in red, white and blue—dresses white, sashes red and caps blue, ornamented with a star, and surmounted with a beautiful white plume, tipped with red. Each lady wore a badge across the breast, upon which was printed the respective State she represented. They each bore a small flag, and they were seated in a triumphal car, decorated with evergreens in the most artistic manner, while the goddess occupied the center of the group, elevated on a pedestal. Messrs. Derr and Von Neida acted as ensigns. This was truly the *chef d'œuvre* of the great occasion, and on their route elicited the heartiest cheers, waving of handkerchiefs, flags and every other token of delight.

And while the storms of hail and driving snow deterred many from participating in the ceremonies of the day, it not only proved the patriotism, but gave a character of heroism to the ladies as they braved the storm and waved their starry flags amid the falling snow.

The following is the list of ladies, with the State each represented :

GODDESS OF LIBERTY :

Miss Lou. Hill.

Pennsylvania—Mollie Magill.
New York—Emma Butler.
Ohio—Malissa Brown.
Indiana—Clara Rockafeller.
Illinois—Ella Painter.
Wisconsin—Lydia Housel.
Iowa—Lillie Cook.
Maine—Clara Beaver.
New Hampshire—Clara Faux.
Vermont—Kate Carey.
Connecticut—Libbie Critz.
Massachusetts—Mary Gulick.
Texas—Mollie J. Waples.
North Carolina—Emma A. Laubach.
South Carolina—Libbie Rank.
Georgia—Gussie Pratt.
Louisiana—Fanny Bordner.
Kentucky—Emma Woods.
Tennessee—Ruth Basset.
Maryland—Alice Rockafeller.
Alabama—Martha B. Laubach.
Missouri—M. W. Beaver.
Virginia—Libbie Faux.
California—Mary Gibbs.
Mississippi—Malinda Cleaver.
Florida—Laura Flanegan.
Rhode Island—Aggie Easton.
Michigan—Abbie Bright.
Oregon—Emma Sechler.
Delaware—Ada Pratt.
New Jersey—Ella Heath.
West Virginia—Alice Wilson.
Nevada—Mary Brobst.
Minnesota—Annie M. Hefler.

Arkansas—Harriet Garrett.
Kansas—Mary Bealand.

TERRITORIES.

Nebraska—Hannah Eger.
Colorado—Mary Lovett.
Washington—Mary A. Thomas.
Dacotah—Emma A. Brower.

EQUESTRIENNES.

Another attractive feature in the procession was the ladies on horse-back.

Miss Pitner was dressed in red, Miss Jennie Koons in white and Mrs. D. Gearhart in blue.

Miss Mary Appleman, Miss Mary Pursel and Miss Lucy Everett—all skillful riders—occupied a prominent place in the cavalade.

The procession was one of great length—composed of carriages and wagons, filled with *voters* as well as ladies. The wagons were handsomely decorated with wreaths, flags and banners.

THE SPEECHES.

When the procession arrived on the grounds, the meeting was organized with the following officers :

PRESIDENT :

Thomas Beaver, Esq.

VICE PRESIDENTS :

William Hancock,	Charles C. Baldy,
Isaac Rank,	Rev. John Cook,
John Grove,	Joseph Diehl,
John Titley,	W. H. Hassenplug,
G. M. Shoop,	Dan Morgan,
Rev. Mr. Barnitz,	Samuel Ware,
William Twist,	Charles Hock,
Dr. William H. Magill,	Philip Maus,
George A. Frick,	Cornelius Styer,
Thompson Foster,	And others.

William Lewis,   L. O. VanAlen.

The addresses delivered by Hon. William H. Armstrong and Clinton Lloyd, Esq., of Lycoming, were eloquent.

Mr. Lloyd is one of the most effective speakers in the State.

Mr. Armstrong is known as a man of marked ability, and his address was one of great power, and was delivered amid the plaudits of the vast assemblage.

In the evening many buildings were illuminated and tastefully decorated. Fireworks added to the brilliancy of the scene and the enthusiasm was unbounded. Thus ended one of the memorable days in the annals of Danville. The Democrats also had a brilliant demonstration in that campaign ; but I can find no record of particulars, or I would take pleasure in transcribing them for this page.

Emanuel Evangelical Church.

Sometime after 1860, a Rev. Mr. Stokes established a mission in Danville, in connection with the Evangelical church. He preached for some time in Thompson's Hall. He was succeeded by Rev. Davis in gathering a modest membership with a view to the organization of a congregation, and the erection of a church building. Accordingly a neat frame church was built on Front street, in 1869. Rev. Davis was succeeded by Rev. Detwiler and he by Rev. Buck. Rev. Raidebaugh next took charge of the congregation. After him came Rev. Orwig, then Rev. Raidebaugh the second time. He was followed by Rev. Hunter and he by Rev. Hornberger the present pastor.

Rev. Raidebaugh with whom I am best acquainted, is an active worker, and in addition to his ministerial labors. published a small weekly paper called " The Temperance Star," which had a wide circulation.

Random Notes.

The Hospital for the Insane at Danville was partially consumed by fire on the night of March 5, 1881. Every effort was made to save the building and the hundreds of inmates. All the patients were saved and about one third of the building. Preparations are making for rebuilding ; in the mean time a portion of the patients remain in the uninjured part of the Hospital, and another portion is in the Hospital at Warren.

The lower portion or Western extension of Danville, is facetiously called "Swampoodle." Why it is thus designated is a mystery as the place is innocent of any swamp and is one of the most delightful locations in the town; affording a charming view of the river, South Danville, Riverside, the railroads on either side of the Susquehanna, the canal, Montour Ridge and the cultivated grounds between the river and Mahoning creek. It is a pleasant place and should be known as West Danville or West End.

Among the older inhabitants of this place was John Faust. He bought a tract of land on the Eastern border of Danville, being a part of Gen. Daniel Montgomery's tract, and a portion of which is included in the borough. Mr. Faust married a Miss Bickley of Reading, and first built a small house and a distillery. He afterwards built the large brick house that stands near the upper end of Market street. He died at a good old age some years ago, and many of his descendants still remain in Danville.

Dan Cameron, a somewhat eccentric, old time resident of Danville, was a great pedestrian and if living now would doubtless strip the belt from some of the noted walkists of the present day. Dan Cameron walked from Harrisburg to Danville in a day and considered it a small achievement.

Samuel Gulick owned a farm in the eastern part of Danville; which had been a portion of the Daniel Montgomery tract and adjoining the farm of John Faust. A large part of this farm with a portion of the Faust farm, now constitutes what is known as "Gulick's addition to the borough of Danville." Two of his sons, John F. and Charles still reside on the place, Samuel having bought a farm adjoining Riverside, now resides over the river. Samuel Gulick, Sr., died a few years ago, leaving a handsome property, as well as the record of an honest life, as the heritage of his children.

A beautiful memorial window, in memory of J. D. Gosh, M. D., deceased, has been placed in Trinity Lutheran church by his mother.

Mr. Vanann is master mechanic and general superintendent of the machine shops at the Montour Iron and Steel Works. Mr. Leighow is millwright and has been for years past. E. C. Voris and P. J. Adams have been the longest continuous attachees of these works, extending over a period of nearly forty years. Frank Naylor was long the roll-turner. He died in March, 1881. He was an excellent mechanic and a good man in every sense of the word. E. O. Ridgway is boss roller. His experience here, in Ohio, Colorado and San Francisco has made him master of the iron business. James A. Gibson is also a roller worthy of note. J. R. Philips at the head of the heating department is the right man in the right place. He is also a justice of the peace and an active citizen. John R. Lunger takes his place at night and John Marks that of Ridgway. They both stand deservedly high. In a word these works, from Mr. Howe, the general manager, to the least in authority, are conducted by an excellent corps of superintendents, clerks and attachees.

M. D. Lafayette Sechler, grandson of John Sechler, one of the old settlers of Danville, still resides in the old homestead within the borough limits. There he was born about the time of Gen. Lafayette's triumphal visit to America and for him he was named. There he has always lived and in our local affairs contributed a full share as an officer and as a citizen.

They have torn down the Episcopal church built in 1828, preparatory to the erection of a more elegant structure. For this purpose P. Baldy, Sr., left in his last will the sum of fifty thousand dollars. The new church is designed to be a magnificent building.

Progressing.

It is certainly very cheering to see our goodly town waking up and shaking off the dust of inaction and the rust of fogyism It is seemingly just realizing the importance of its manifold local advantages. And though respectable fossils may be unwillingly disturbed ; yet the reward will come alike to all. On every hand, and in a multitude of enterprises, both old and new, we see the evidences of new life and spirit among our people. We see it in the growth of business establishments—in the enlargement of the old and the building of the new. There seems to be a wholesome energy and vigor among our people unknown before, save by a few. But if our town has not been quite as rapid in its advancement as some others, it has been more substantial. True its valuable resources were for years measurably unimproved, but it was for want of public spirit, and not for want of natural advantages.

The day is dawning upon us, when our young men need not seek other localities to find the aids that Danville has failed to afford. We have, it is true, a number of young men of our place who are now out in the world, manfully fighting the battles of life, and who occupy an honorable position in communities they have chosen, but in order to move " upward and onward," we can not deny they were compelled to leave the old home. Heretofore, a young man reared in Danville, unless specially favored, was forced to join his fortune with those who were further advanced. Now, with a few of the older citizens they are manifesting themselves in our midst. They seem to see the superior advantages of building up and improving their own locality. Their influence is seen and felt in every public enterprise springing up around us, and in every movement that tends towards our local prosperity. We see it in our manufactories and increased facilities of transportation. We see it in our prosperous railroads— in the building up of Riverside and South Danville—in the Opera House, and in the elegant residences that begin to adorn our streets. We see it in our contemplated public improvements, and in the individual enterprise manifested on every hand. Danville is evidently waking up to her true interests and to her importance as one of the great business centers of the State. And who will say that the time may not come when our vast deposits of iron, coal and limestone, with the increasing energy of our people, will make Danville all it ought to be in view of its natural advantages.

To the enterprising capitalist, the skilled mechanic and the man of enterprise in any department of labor adapted to our place, there is no better and no richer field than that which Danville affords at the present time. It presents superior advantages to the western towns of which we hear so much—towns that sometimes grow up as if by magic, and crumble away for want of a solid basis. Here we have the material and the means of transportation at hand to every market in the country ; and as our mineral resources are inexhaustible, our progress will be permanent and substantial.

The Maus Family.

Philip Maus a native of Prussia, was born in 1731. He came to Philadelphia in 1741, when only ten years of age. In 1750 he left school and was apprenticed to a stocking weaver. In due course of time he entered business on his own account and was married, when about twenty-five years of age to Frances Heap. Being prosperous in business he became wealthy ; but expended nearly all his wealth in the cause of the country during the Revolutionary war. He had purchased some lands on the Mahoning creek adjoining Montgomery's purchase, and came to this place in 1772. Gen. William Montgomery, his brother Daniel and four others were then the only settlers in what is now Danville. After the Indian troubles, Mr. Maus and his family moved to Mahoning. He was one of Nature's noblemen, and when provision failed in the infant settlement, Philip Maus bought many barrels of flour and also 200 bushels of wheat, had it hauled to this place and distributed among the destitute. In 1800 he built the stone mill at Mausdale, which is now successfully managed by his great-grandson P. E. Maus. After a long and useful life, Philip Maus, the old pioneer, died April 27, 1815. He was succeeded by his son Joseph who also died at a ripe old age, a few years ago. Philip F. Maus his son, now resides in the old homestead, and is bordering on threescore and ten. Charles, Jackson and David Maus, a branch of the old stock, are now among the active and influential men of the county. I close this brief note with the remark that the Maus family has done much for this place and deserves honorable mention among the pioneers of the past and the worthy men of the present.

Caste.

Generally speaking, the people of Danville in their social aspect are like those of other manufacturing towns of Pennsylvania. Like others, they manifest a variety of degrees in the scale. This is a necessary result of intellectual culture and of moral practice, and is right and proper. Social distinctions are an absolute condition of civilized society, advanced beyond its pioneer state. But, unfortunately, there is another rule of *caste* no less imperious that is creeping into the social fabric of Danville. This is a law founded on false and pernicious principles, naturally growing out of the weakness of human nature. Its influence is alike corrupting to all classes of society. It is the assumed superiority founded on wealth or its seeming, or on the foolish pride of family. There are those whose ancestral blood has perhaps crept through intellectual imbeciles or

moral delinquents ever since the flood, who arrogate to themselves
an air of superiority and practice an exclusiveness, because they
either acquired or inherited the title to a little more wealth than
others who excel them in mental culture or in moral principles.
And it is a remarkable fact, that in conceding this empty claim, the
world pays but little regard to the means by which wealth is acquired. Some there are who obtained it through means that are
universally condemned; and yet the respect rendered to the possession of wealth, and for its sake alone, is scarcely less general. How
many there are, whose riches alone, give value to their opinions?
How many can you call to mind whose names have only a moneyed
value and whose counsels have a metallic ring? How many whose
judgment is valued according to the houses, lands and bank stock
they call their own? How many who wield a controlling influence
in the community, and whose wisdom would turn to foolishness in
the crucible of poverty? Whilst there seems to be a natural inclination to arrogance and presumption on the one hand, there is also
unfortunately a natural tendency to play the sycophant on the other.
Degenerated human nature, has never yet and never will abandon
the worships of the Golden Calf, and by its practice, even in its
most enlightened condition, still declares "These be thy gods, O
Israel."

Distinctions in society, springing from this source, cannot fail to
corrupt its subjects, to contract the mind, and to dwarf the better
feelings of the heart. It requires no stretch of thought or profound
judgment to recognize at a glance, those who have become enervated,
vain and corrupted through this source. On the other hand the worthy
poor are discouraged and are liable to estimate themselves as far below
their proper worth. The weaker, or the more careless, seeing society
thus constituted, accept the situation as "the course of human
events" and plunge still further down the scale. Who knows how
many have yielded to temptations on the ruinous concession of their
own inferiority, and thus missed the mark of excellence to which
they might have attained? Forgetting that "The rank is but the
guinea's stamp, the man's the gold for all that."

The following, in relation to the iron ores of Danville, is from Rogers' Geological Report, a work of the highest authority on the subject :

From the Narrows to the gap of Mahoning creek at Danville, the length of outcrop of the two ores on the south side of the mountain does not exceed about half a mile. That of the hard ore is considerably the longest, and as the iron sandstone containing it outcrops much higher on the ridge than the other ore, the quantity of this exposed above the water-level exceeds that of the latter many times. In this part of the ridge, the average length of the slope or breast of the iron sandstone ore, above the water-level alone, is probably more than 200 yards ; that of the fossiliferous ore is materially less, while, for reasons already shown, the depth of breast of the soft and partially decomposed ore may not average more than 30 or 40 yards. The position of the hard ore, in the vicinity of the gorge of the Mahoning, is shown in our transverse section of the ridge at that place. By inspecting the vertical section which I have introduced of the iron sandstone formation, analyzed in detail, the reader will perceive that while the red sandstone members include two or three excessively ponderous layers, rich enough in iron to be applicable as iron ores, the thickest of these—the only bed, indeed, which is of sufficient magnitude to be wrought at the present day—accompanies the lower bed of sandstone, and has dimensions varying from 14 to 18 inches. But there is another formation here developed, in which beds of iron ore are discoverable. This is the Surgent older or lower slate, this stratum possessing in Montour ridge a thickness of about 700 feet. Its ore has the form of a very ferruginous sandstone in one or two thin and continuous layers, occupying a horizon, near the middle of the formation, between 350 and 400 feet below its superior limit. Scarcely any difference is perceptible either in aspect or composition between the ore now referred to and that of the iron sandstone. It is a sandstone with a large proportion of peroxide of iron diffused among the particles, and, like the other bed, includes numerous small flat fragments, or pebbles of greenish slate, which by their disintegration leave the surfaces of the blocks, wherever the weather has had access, pitted with little elongated

holes, forming one of the most distinctive features of these two ores.
This ore-bed of the lower slate outcrops near the summit of the ridge
on the east side of the Mahoning Gap at Danville, arching the anticlinal axis at an elevation of about 300 feet above the bed of this
transverse valley. Traced east and west from the Notch, the over-
lying slate saddles it, and conceals it from view wherever the mountain is low and narrow, but wherever the anticlinal rises—or where
ever, in other words, the wave in the strata increases in breadth and
height—the ore no longer closes over the axis, but forms two separate lines of outcrop, one on each gentle declivity between the summit and the shoulder, formed by the outcrop of the iron sandstone.
In the vicinity of Danville, the thickness of this layer of ore is not
such as to make it of much importance, so long as the thicker and
therefore cheaper beds furnish an ample supply. Judging from the
fragments at the point of outcrop, I infer its size to be between 6
and 8 inches. The facility and cost of mining it will of course de-
pend upon several conditions connected with the dip and depth of
covering, and will vary with each locality.

Our section of the strata at the Mahoning Gap represents the entire mass of the mountain as consisting there of the two Surgent
slates and their included iron sandstone, while the calcareous or ore
shales, with their fossiliferous ore, rest low at the north and south
base. The upper beds of the Levant white sandstone have not
been lifted to the level of the bed of the Notch, though their depth
beneath it cannot be considerable. This proves a sinking of the axis
from opposite the Narrows to this point; but when the ridge is examined still further east, it becomes apparent that between the Mahoning and Hemlock the anticlinal rises and swells again, causing
the hard ore of the slate to diverge into two outcrops, and the belts
of the iron sandstone to recede. About half way between those two
streams is probably the neighborhood in which the section of the
mountain has its greatest expansion, and the two belts of the iron
sandstone are furthest asunder.

Let us now, before advancing any further east, attempt an estimate of the quantity of iron ore above the water level within a given
length—say one mile of outcrop—in the vicinity of Danville.

I shall reject from my present calculation both the ore of the older
slate and the compact unchanged fossiliferous ore ; the former as

being too thin and deeply covered to be profitably mined, and the latter as too poor in iron, and too calcareous, to be, under existing circumstances, adapted to the smelting furnace.

If we assume the soft fossiliferous ore of this neighborhood to have an average thickness of from 16 to 18 inches, which is probably not far from the truth, we may consider each square yard of its surface to represent about one ton of weight of ore. Let us now adopt the estimate I have already given of the depth to which the ore stratum has been converted into this soft ore, and accept 30 yards as the limit. Each yard of length along the outcrop will then be equivalent to 30 tons of the ore, and one mile of outcrop should supply about 52,800 tons. This amount, it will be understood, is irrespective of elevation above the water-level. Turning now to the hard or siliceous ore of the iron sandstone, we shall find one mile of the outcrop bed to offer a far more enormous quantity of available ore. It is obvious that the whole of the bed is convertible to use, since the composition of the ore is such as to make it fit for the furnace without it undergoing any solvent action, of which, indeed, it is scarcely susceptible. The only limit to the depth to which it may be profitably wrought, is the cost of mining it, and since this element is materially increased the moment we pass below the water-level of the locality, it will be expedient to restrict our present estimate to the quantity of the ore above this natural line. It has been stated that in the vicinity of the Mahoning Gap, the average length of slope or breast belonging to the iron sandstone is about 200 yards; on the south side it is somewhat greater, while on the north side it is probably as much less. This is equivalent to 200 tons of ore to each yard of the outcrop, the ore bed being from 14 to 16 inches thick. One mile of length of outcrop will therefore yield 352,000 tons of the ore above the water level. All that portion which is in this position is therefore nearly seven times as great as the similar part of the soft fossiliferous ore. The two ore beds together represent more than 400,000 tons in a single mile of outcrop; but as from the anticlinal form of the mountain, there is a double line of outcrop for each kind of ore, it is clear that one mile of length of ridge must contain, upon the supposition of no deep ravines or notches intervening, the amazing quantity of 800,000 tons of ore. It is to be remarked that in the foregoing statement I exclude the considera-

17

tion of the ravines, which interrupt at frequent intervals the general line of the outcrop of the strata, and reduce materially the amount of ore above the water-level.

An abatement of one eighth from the quantity as above computed, on the supposition of a perfectly continuous outcrop, will probably more than compensate for the amount thus lost. With this reduction we shall still have, in one mile of the ridge, 700,000 tons of good ore.

The ore estate attached to the Montour Iron Works of Danville, embraces, if I have been correctly informed, a total length of outcrop of the iron sandstone ore of 2,200 yards, equivalent alone to 385,000 tons; the whole quantity of the soft fossiliferous ore I estimate at 45,000 tons; making the entire amount of ore available under existing circumstances 430,000 tons. Such is the apparently enormous extent of the mineral wealth of this favored locality.

Nonsense.

Those who have no taste for nonsense can skip this chapter. It is placed here because it is connected with the work, and will tend to show the difficulties encountered in gathering the material necessary for its completion.

On visiting an octogenarian, he mistook me for a tax-collector or some other unwelcome person. He was very deaf, and on being requested to *tax* his memory in relation to his connection with a noted incident, he replied that he didn't owe any " tax." On explaining to him that it was about the early *settlement* of Danville, he said he had no "settlement" to make and " wouldn't pay a cent." When told it was for a *book*, he said he never had any such book. "Go," said he, " I'm tired of people coming round with books and maps and all kinds of humbugs." Sadly I left no wiser and no better. Perhaps not quite as good.

A pleasant old lady was visited next, when the following dialogue took place :

You have lived here a good while ?

" O, yes, longer as that."

When did you come to Danville?

" It vas de time we moved here from Tulpehocken."

You don't remember the exact period?

"O, yes, I mind it goot."

Do you remember of anything important—anything that happened about the time you came, by which we could fix the date?

"O yes, it most the time when our Johnny vas born."

Ah, now we have it. How old is Johnny now?

"He's no olt at all. He's deat."

Could you tell me when he died?

"Yes. It vas about four o'clock in de afternoon."

I don't mean the hour, I mean the year.

"Vy it vas in de same year as he vas born."

I left discouraged, as the old lady with a bland smile kindly said:
"Come again ven you vant some more dings to set in your book."

Old Towns.

Of old Indian towns and scenery in this vicinity, Mr. Wolfinger says:

Nishmekkachlo.—This town stood on the south side of Montour's ridge, and somewhere about midway between our present towns of Northumberland and Danville—exact spot unknown to the writer of this sketch. I am inclined to think it was the residence of Manawyhickon, a distinguished Delaware chief who ruled over the Indians of these parts before the great Shikellamy and Sassoonan chiefs made their appearance at Shohomokin or Shaumoking the old Indian town on the present site of Sunbury. since our old writer informs us that Manawyhickon lived somewhere on the North Branch, not far from Shaumoking.

Mahoning.—This town stood near the mouth of Mahoning creek, on its west side, a little below where the public bridge crosses the said creek, and about a mile below the present town of Danville, in Montour county.

Montour ridge, a pretty high and beautifully formed elevation of earth, runs northeastward from a point near Northumberland, but leaves a nice valley of beautiful land between its base and the North Branch of the Susquehanna river. This valley, as we approach Danville from Northumberland, gets narrower until it ends in what is called "The Narrows"—grounds just wide enough for the public road to pass conveniently along the foot of the ridge. It was at the eastern end of these narrows where the Indian town of Mahoning stood. Montour ridge at this point presents to the eye of the beholder a high, bold and imposing appearance, and becomes more and more so until just on the north side of Danville it terminates very suddenly, with a high, wall-like face, towards the east, and then sweeping sharply around it runs north for several miles with the same high wall-like face on the west side of the small and narrow, but beautiful valley of Mahoning and its creek of the same name. Every traveler who visits Danville looks with admiration upon this high, bluffy and picturesque termination of Montour ridge and is delighted with the rich and beautiful dark green foliage of its thickly grown evergreen, pine and spruce trees that crown its top and sides, (excepting a cleared or bare spot just north of Danville) and towards the close of every sunny day throw a dark, rich shade over the snug little valley at its base. Its scenery looks wild and romantic even in our day, but must have been far wilder and grander when the Indians roamed over the ridge in the pursuit of wild turkeys and deer or speared the fish that sported in the waters close by.

Montour ridge at Danville looks as if Noah's deluge or some other great commotion of our earth's waters had burst a passage way through the ridge at this point, and so made this valley, for the ridge itself quickly reappears again with a sloping but nearly an equally elevated face on the east side of Danville, and then runs on the eastward to beyond the town of Bloomsburg, in Columbia county, where it gradually slopes down and disappears. Mahoning was therefore, a choice spot for an Indian town and a town of more than common note among the Indians.

Toby Town—This town, so called after a large and powerful Indian by the name of Toby, stood on " Toby Run," a little above the insane asylum, about two miles above Danville. But whether it stood on the banks of the Susquehanna river near the mouth of Toby run, or on top of the high ridge of earth there along the river, I am not able to say. I passed along there in my boyhood days on my road to and from Reading, and heard various stories about Toby and his town, but can give no satisfactory account of them.

Classawango—This town stood still further up the river, but on the south side, and about half way between Danville and the town of Catawissa, but I cannot state where it stood. Who can?

This beautiful suburban town is one of the most delightful places in this section of the State. It was laid out some ten or twelve years ago, mainly on the farm of Mr. Gearhart and Fanx's addition. The survey was made by O. H. Ostrander. Lots were rapidly sold and many improvements were made. The neatness and taste of the dwellings and their surroundings add much to the pleasant appearance of the location. Already it has a borough organization, its churches, school-rooms and all the institutions of a full grown town. The charming location of Riverside combines the elements of beauty and convenience with a highly favorable place for business. It adjoins South Danville, is convenient to the railroad depot on the D. W. & Hazelton railroad, and is surrounded by all that ministers to a pleasant home. With the broad Susquehanna river in front, the lively town of Danville on the opposite shore and the picturesque hills that mark the bold scenery around it, Riverside affords the most delightful place for a country residence. No doubt when our merchants and other active men of to-day, have made their fortunes and retired to enjoy the evening of life, you will find their elegant mansions in Riverside or South Danville.

Danville Institute.

This was an institution of learning established and conducted by J. M. Kelso, A. M., present Principal of the Danville Academy. It was located in the Montgomery building, corner of Mill and Bloom streets. The "Institute" enjoyed a high reputation for the thorough and substantial character of its course of instruction, not only in its immediate locality; but among the best educators in the country. The young men instructed in the Danville Institute, were pronounced among the best prepared for a collegiate course of study.

In June, 1860, occurred the most noted annual examination, occupying three days. The hall was decorated with laurel and a profusion of beautiful flowers. A school examination! what an important epoch in the happy period of girlhood or boyhood! It constitutes a sunny waymark to which the weary traveler on the dusty road of life will often look back with a bounding heart. How often will each one in that happy throng turn back to drink again at the pure fountain of inspiration that gladdened the rosy hour of morning, and again to catch the thrill of the merry voices whose echoes will float on and on, until the shadows of evening come. Invested with peculiar interest were the passing scenes to those whose "school-going" days were over. To them it was an eventful period. And to them the fair young brow will never grow old, to memory dear, no darksome shadow will ever eclipse the light of that sparkling eye, nor cloud of sorrow shroud that joyous smile. In the memory of each the little school companion will linger forever in the form of a child. The following classes were under the special instruction of the Principal—John M. Kelso, A. M. :

Natural Philosophy.
1.

E. M. Biddle,	Emma Woods,
M. D. Brown,	J. M. Jennison.

Latin, Third.
3.

C. D. Biddle,	E. V. Lotier,
G. W. Mowrer,	B. F. Cox,
C. W. Sholes.	

English Grammar, First.
5.

E. M. Biddle,	J. M. Jennison,
C. D. Biddle,	G. W. Mowrer,
J. H. Grove,	B. F. Cox,
J. B. Grier.	M. D. Brown,
P. H. Grove,	M. J. Baldy,
C. Gardner.	

Algebra.
7.

E. M. Biddle.	A. M. Russell,
C. D. Biddle,	M. Moynehan,
G. W. Mowrer,	F. D. Brown,
M. D. Brown.	

Geography, First.
11.

A. M. Russell,	C. D. Biddle,

P. H. Grove,
R. M. Grove,
J. H. Grove,
Augustus Taylor,
James Frazier,
Lafayette Unger,
A. M. Diehl,
Michael Moynehan,
E. A. Laubach,

M. J. Baldy,
Peninah Bright,
H. E. Sechler,
E. J. Curry,
Elizabeth Rishel,
Stephen Ridgway,
C. W. Sholes,
Andrew Schroth,
Sarah Ketcham.

Latin, Second.

17

P. H. Grove,
J. H. Grove,

J. H. Kase,
R. M. Grove,

A. M. Diehl.

Latin, First.

10.

J. B. Grier,

J. M. Jennison.

Geometry.

13.

E. M. Biddle,

G. W. Mowrer,

F. D. Brown.

University Arithmetic.

14.

J. M. Jennison,
J. B. Grier,
A. M. Russell,
J. H. Kase,
C. D. Biddle,

P. H. Grove,
G. W. Mowrer,
M. D. Brown,
Emma Woods,
Sarah Ketcham,

F. D. Brown.

Reading.

19.

A. M. Russell,
C. D. Biddle,
P. H. Grove,
R. M. Grove,

James Frazier,
J. H. Grove,
A. Taylor,
A. M. Diehl,

Henry Wireman,
E. Kaufman,
E. A. Laubach,
M. M. Grier,
H. E. Sechler,
C. Gardner.
P. Bright,
E. J. Curry,

E. Rishel,
E. V. Lotier,
E. Woods,
M. Henrie,
S. Ridgway.
C. W. Sholes,
S. Ketcham,
A. Scroth,

C. L. Martin.

Intellectual Arithmetic.

18.

C. D. Biddle,
P. H. Grove,
J. B. Grier,
E. M. Biddle,
G. W. Mowrer,

A. M. Russel,
L. Unger,
E. A. Laubach,
M. D. Brown,
M. J. Baldy,

E. Woods.

The following classes were under the charge of Miss M. Hughes :

Geography, Second.

2

C. H. Brady,
J. C. Grove,
D. Levi,
W. Thatcher,
E. Kaufman,
J. Seidel,
D. Richards.
J. Mowrer,

W. Lyon.
E. Lyon,
J. Sechler,
M. M. Grier.
M. J. Waples,
E. Harder,
L. Wolf,
E. V. Lotier.

Geography, Third,

K. Baldy,
A. E. Beaver,
K. Beaver,
E. H. Baldy,
A. Imogene Brower,

E. Laubach,
E. Williams.
T. Blue,
C. H. Stover,
W. Roberts.

Arithmetic.

6.

C. B. Brady,

K. Baldy,

J. B. Grier.   E. M. Biddle.
A. M. Russell,   J. M. Jennings,
M. J. Baldy,   J. H. Kase,
                L. Unger.

Third Reader.

8.

J. C. Grove,   J. Seidel,
E. H. Baldy,   D. Richards,
D. Levi,   C. Savage,
J. Sechler,   L. Kirk,
C. H. Brady,   M. J. Waples,
J. Mowrer,   L. Wolf,
P. Bright,   E. Harder.

Arithmetic.

9.

R. M. Grove,   A. M. Diehl,
S. Ridgway,   C. W. Sholes,

E. Kauffman,   M. J. Baldy,
M. M. Grier,   E. V. Lotier,
E. Curry,   E. Laubach,
P. Bright,   M. Moynerhan,

J. Grove.

Arithmetic.

12.

J. Grove,   E. Kaufman,
A. M. Diehl,   C. Sholes,
J. H. Kase,   J. Frazier,
R. M. Grove,   E. Curry,
H. Wireman,   E. Rissel,
S. Ridgway,   P. Bright,
M. Moynehan,   E. V. Lotier,

J. M. Jennison.

English Grammar.

18.

A. M. Russel,   C. Sholes,
A. M. Diehl,   E. A. Laubach,
R. M Grove,   P. Bright,
J. H. Kase,   E. Curry,
H. Wireman,   E. Rishel,
M. Moynehan,   M. Henrie,
E. Kaufman,   S. J. Ketchum,
S. Ridgway,   E. Woods,

L. Unger,

First Reader.

W. Russel,   J. Mitchell.

The classes were thoroughly examined in their several branches of study, and afforded a pleasing evidence of the systematic course, the order, the complete and rapid progress of the pupils which gave to the Danville Institute its high reputation. It is proper as well as just to the Principal to remark that the same advantages are now afforded at the Danville Academy.

Business.

It is proper in a work like this to take at least a hasty glance at the business operations of Danville at the present time. A single glance will show the enterprising and progressive spirit of our people. All our great iron works, which are the mainspring of life and activity, are in full operation. Night and day the busy workers with ceaseless energy, are converting the ore into iron, and fashioning it into finished rails. But other branches of trade are no less essential to the growth and general prosperity of Danville. Professional men, merchants, traders, mechanics, artisans and laborers, all contribute to local as well as general prosperity and happiness. So we honor the patient worker in every department of industry, as each and all contribute a share in securing the blessings of life. Let us then take a cursory glance at our leading business establishments and in so doing, as near as possible, give expression to popular sentiment.

There are twenty-two dry goods stores in Danville; fifteen of groceries and fruits; three hardware stores; three gents' furnishing goods; five millinery and trimming stores; five clothing stores; seven drug stores; six cigar stores; three jewelry stores; two book stores; four confectioneries, and fourteen miscellaneous. Among the business houses are the following:

J. Doster & Son are the leading dealers in furniture and are doing a very large business, in town and the surrounding country. Their cabinet warerooms are on Mill street.

William C. Davis conducts the most extensive confectionery and ice creamery in Danville or in this quarter of the State. The popularity of his ice cream extends to all the surrounding towns, and accordingly he ships large quantities, daily by railroad. His facilities for its manufacture are ample for the large demands at home and abroad. His assortment of confections and fruits of all kinds, with courteous attention, have made his rooms a popular resort, and himself one of the *live* business men of Danville.

Kramer & Co. are doing a very extensive trade in their treble store, in the Opera House block. This is the largest store in town, that is conducted by individual enterprise. It contains a very large stock of dry goods and notions, embracing the latest styles and patterns of dress goods and fancy articles. The housekeeping grocery and provision departments are complete. They have an extensive

country trade and consequently are always supplied with fresh produce to supply the wants of the town. Will G. Kramer is the general superintendent and knows how to popularize a business establishment.

We have six excellent drug stores : but this does not indicate an
unhealthy town. But our druggists sell a great variety of useful
and fancy articles.

J. W. Philips is proprietor of the well known drug store, known
as "Grier's old drug store," in the Montgomery Building.

James C. Sechler's drug store, in Chalfant's building, merits
special note in connection with the general business of Danville.
Mr. Sechler has had practical experience in his profession for fourteen years and for the last eight years has occupied his present location and met with deserved success. His drug store is well supplied. His attention is courteous, his carefulness proverbial, his
medicines selected with judgment and he holds an honorable place
among the enterprising business men of Danville.

Dr. Jordan keeps the "Cottage drug store" on East Market
street.

Dr. S. Y. Thompson keeps a first class drug store in Ramsey's
building.

R. D. Magill, opposite the Opera House, keeps one of the leading drug stores in this place.

Mr. McKinn manages the Dr. Gosh or Centennial drug store
opposite the old bank.

Geo. W. Fisher has a fine drug store in Kaufman's building, opposite the Company store.

H. M. Schoch has built up an extensive trade at his large and
excellent dry goods and grocery store, on Mill street. His store is
to-day among the very best in Danville.

WILLIAM H. HASSANPLUG came to Danville more than thirty years
ago. He was a clerk for some years and afterwards had a store in
Reynold's building. Subsequently he had charge of the dry goods
department in the company store, where in purchasing and disposing
of hundreds of thousands of dollars worth of goods he became thoroughly acquainted with the trade, and his selections are therefore
judiciously made. He now has a large double store in Sechler's
building on Mill street, where he does a large business especially in
dry goods, and boots and shoes.

Mrs. J. S. Huber's " Boston Shoe Bazar," is the most elegant establishment of the kind in this quarter of the State. It is located in Loeb's block on Mill street. Mrs. Huber deals exclusively in ladies', misses and children's wear. She keeps a large stock in great variety embracing the latest styles and is extensively patronized by the *elite* as well as others in town and in the surrounding country. This is our pioneer store in that department of trade.

Gomer Thomas, is the most extensive dealer in music and musical instruments, not only in this place but in this section of the State. His place is on Mill street, sign of the Golden Base Viol. He sells pianos and organs at figures that insure the largest sales—a complete musical bazar embracing every variety of instruments, with all the popular sheet music as soon as published. His judgment can always be relied on, as he is himself a musician of some prominence, having devoted some attention to teaching and also made his mark as a composer. A number of his compositions have been published and rank deservedly high in the class to which they belong. He is still on the sunny side of life and by exercising his talents, could attain an honorable position among the composers of the day.

RAMSEY CHILDS is one of the successful business men of Danville. He started in modest style on a small scale ; now he has one of the largest stove, sheet-iron and tinware establishments in town. He is located in the Opera House block, where by industry and fair dealing he has built up an extensive trade.

WILL G. BROWN, in the retail tobacco and segar trade, leads the way. His place is in Schuster's building opposite the City Hotel. He keeps all qualities, sorts and brands of the weed, maerschaums, pipes and holders, together with a variety of curiosities. In a word this is the most popular segar store in town and Will G. Brown is a popular, young business man, whose excellent qualities will never fail to gather around him, a host of friends. It is a pleasure to speak of those whose sterling principles are sure to redeem our prophesies of the future.

A. M. Diehl's " New York Tea Store " in Mr. Lyon's block on Mill street, is the most complete fine grocery and fruit store in Danville. His catalogue embraces an extensive variety of home and tropical fruits, fancy confections, spices and the rarest brands of teas, coffees and sugars, giving his patrons, all the advantages enjoyed in the cities, in hundreds of articles that had never been kept in this place. He has built up an extensive trade, especially in the finer assortment of goods in his line.

Seidel Brother is a firm eminently worthy of mention in these pages. They are in the line of dry goods and notions, on Mill street, near the Montgomery building. Their house is known as the " Boston Store." They keep a good selection. The senior member of the firm is engaged in a wholesale house in the city and this gives them a peculiar advantage in selecting the right goods at the right time. They do a large business and add materially to the general trade of Danville.

I. T. Patton agent, has built up an excellent trade in the dry goods, grocery and provision line, on Wolf's old corner.

Sheldon & Co., in the Brown building adjoining the Opera House, have one of the largest stores in Danville and they are doing a very heavy business in general merchandizing. Their extensive trade keeps a large force of clerks constantly employed. Their selections of dress goods, ladies' and gent's furnishing goods, notions and housekeeping goods are full and complete and Sheldon & Co., contribute materially to the tide that marks the progress of Danville.

Jacob Loeb, an old and substantial resident of Danville, keeps a snug grocery and does a snug business in his own building on Mill street.

Brief Notes.

In looking over the town of Danville to-day, we find quite a number of *live* business men apart from those engaged in manufacturing. It would be pleasant to note many of the leading business men in the various pursuits that give life and form to the current of trade, and that mark the line of local progress, but space will not permit.

James McCormick runs a line of omnibuses to meet the passenger trains on all the railroads passing this place.—Alfred B. Patton runs a local express. Both are great public conveniences.—Elwood Garrett is and has been for eighteen years the ever reliable bill poster of Danville.—A. M. Diehl's New York Tea Store presents a new feature in its splendid assortment of home and tropical fruits.—William G. Brown has a museum of rare curiosities in his segar store opposite the City Hotel.—William C. Walker has served as street com-

missioner, chief of the fire department, burgess and councilman.—
George B. Brown has held ten offices and agencies all at the same
time.—Mrs. S. J. Huber's "Boston Shoe Bazar," exclusively devoted
to ladies, misses and children, was another step towards the coming
city.—Thomas Woods & Son have the oldest shoe store in town,
opposite the opera-house.—There are seven first class drug stores in
town, and yet it is a remarkably healthy place.—Moyer Lyon is the
oldest butcher in town. He has built two elegant blocks of brick
buildings on Mill street.—J. Doster & Son lead in the furniture trade.
—The leading sewing machine agency, is the Singer Manufacturing
Company, Mr. McClosky agent, Mill street.—William C. Young insurance agent, in the Montgomery building, and Harry Vincent opposite the opera-house.

Conclusion.

And now, more than a long century has passed away and after the
fluctuating tide of a hundred years from the lone hut of the pioneer
to the stately mansions and the great iron manufactories that control the pulse of business life ; here we are to-day ; in the full tide of
local prosperity ; possessing the elements of growth and prosperity,
that cannot fail to stimulate our men of enterprise to develop more
and more the innate wealth and power of this locality, until Danville shall occupy the high place as a manufacturing and commercial
center, attainable through the gifts of nature and the force of human
intelligence. But to reach the goal desired, we must profit by the
lessons of wisdom we read in the book of experience. True, there
are causes of local depression that lie beyond our reach, but in others,
both the "cause and the antidote" are indigenous. The philo-
sophic fact must be recognized that whilst capital is the motive power, labor produces all the wealth of the world. Both are essential
to the prosperity of this or any other locality. Idle hands and idle
capital are equally reprehensible. The man who becomes rich and
hoards up his money with miserly greed, or fails to use it in giving
employment, is an idler as low in the scale as the loafer, and as useless as the tramp. Then let the men of wealth look into the face of
their responsibilities. Let them remember that their hoarded thousands were drawn from the common current that keeps the arm of
labor in motion, and that buried wealth is robbery of the public.

Let them throw it out into the current of trade ; build up new enter-prises of local industry, giving employment to the honest toiler, the mechanic and the artisan, who, in turn, will aid not only in build-ing up a city, but in giving a stronger and healthier tone to public sentiment. The man of wealth is but a steward of God in the world ; and if in a spirit of selfishness, like the rich fool of whom we read, he considers it his own, and hoards it up, or employs it in adding house to house ; buying when others are forced to sell, and selling when others are forced to buy, clutching the utmost penny until the palsy of death unlocks his iron fingers, he becomes a hindrance in the way of local prosperity, whatever his pretentions may be.

Whatever of local advancement we enjoy we owe to the working men and the *live* men of business, who build and control our manu-facturies. They are workers who contribute to make labor and capi-tal productive. It is the arm of labor that forges out the real wealth of the country ; but capital wisely employed, is no less essential. Hoarded wealth, like the dead sea, never turns a wheel nor drives a forge. The active stream must do the work.

Then let the old man of to-day fall asleep in peace and with the light of hope in his farewell glance on the scenes of his earthly toil ; knowing that those who come after him will come up chastened from the season of depression and reap all the advantages God has given us in the hills and streams around us, where inexhaustible sources of wealth conspire to make this a teeming centre of trade, where the strong foundations of local prosperity may be securely laid.

Let the active men of to-day, in a wider sphere and a more com-prehensive spirit, combined with the energy and courage of their fathers, grasp the advantages before them and much may yet be done before their sun of life shall set. to elevate this place up towards the fulness of its capabilities.

Let the boys of to-day, with an eye to their future and fast ap-proaching responsibilities, arm themselves with all the nobler quali-ties of mind and heart, to fight and win the battles of life. Let them resolve now in the morning years of their lives, to take their places when the time shall come, in the ranks of progress to advance the standard their fathers reared, up to the summit of local prosperity, moral, mental and physical, in all that tends to the growth, the honor and happiness of the future city of Danville.

APPENDIX.

[THE following articles, selected from the miscellaneous writings of the author, are appended at the request of friends who desire their preservation in a more durable form than the columns of a newspaper.]

HOME.

HOW many volumes of touching pathos have been written in memory of *home* and its returnless joys. How the wierd spirit lingers around its hallowed endearments. and how oft in the stillness of night it recalls the burning hopes whose diamond flash illumined every rising wave in the dawn of life's bright morning! How the stricken heart of the lone wanderer, far away from the unforgotten scenes of childhood, ever turns from the present to commune with the loved ones who gathered around the family hearth, or bowed before its consecrated altar! Where are now the golden links of the household band—the joyous group whose echoing notes of glee still mingle with the voices of the night? Some estranged and alone are struggling in the battle of life, and some have gone to the city of the dead.

In dreams we read again the sweet memorials of the past—again the pilgrim beside the dusty road revisits the cot of his birth—again he treads his native hills. decked with a richer foliage and canopied with a brighter sky. Even the wayward man of sin and sorrow, though steeped in poverty and crime to the very lips, will sometimes pause in his mad career to revel again in the memory of the fadeless joys that cluster around the home of his childhood. Oh yes, and the crowning glory in that bright vision will be the image of his mother.

The exile may love the country of his adoption, yet the fondest affections of his heart will cling forever to the land of his birth. No lapse of time, no change of circumstances, nor streams of joy, nor floods of sorrow can blot the primeval record, nor cool the patriotic fervor of his heart. Under all the varied scenes of life he presents the evidences of his origin, the characteristics and the love of his native land.

Far away from the home of his boyhood, the aged pilgrim lies down to die, but in the farewell hour of his life, he turns to read again the gilded pages of youth and recalls once more the glowing scenes under the roof-tree or the village green.

Who has not heard of the old Welshman who had wandered to the western wilds of America, and who for half a century had forgotten the language of Wales ; but who in the final death struggle, as memory traveled back to his far off home and paused amid his native hills, the language of his childhood returned once more and in its pure accents the hallowed name of his mother was mingled with his dying prayer. The old man was a child again and of such is the kingdom of heaven.

Home! Oh is it not a potent word? A word that thrills the burdened soul of the far voyager, even as his bark of life is moored in the port of death,—a word that ever wakes and tunes a chord of undying melody in the throbbing heart of Nature's child, throughout all her vast domains.

Heart Memories.

There is enshrined in every human heart, the bright dream of youth, the golden hope of childhood. And there the memory of those first impressions, pure desires and cloudless joys will live forever. Sorrow and misfortune may fling their dark shadows around our pathway : disappointment and anguish may chill the better feeling of our nature : crime may weave its sombre folds around the heart ; the wild storms of passion may sweep its chords ; dishonor and shame may shroud its altar ; but all these can never blot from its tablets the record of childhood's hours—its first impressions, its budding affections, its dream-like joys. Nor can the pride and pomp of power, or wealth, or fame extinguish the light of its inner chambers. No, never. The felon doomed to die, turns back once more when the star of hope has set, to read the *one* bright page, in the light of life's young morning. The aged christian too, as the evening twilight gathers around him, and as he waits in patience and in hope for the Reaper—death : still turns to catch the gleam of its far off rays, and in the light of a living faith he trusts in a renewal of youth, in a more enduring form beyond the grave. Oh yes, there is, in the depth of every human heart, one warm and sunny spot where nestle the images of early love and the sweet remembrances of childhood's home. There they will remain even to the final hour with all the bright memories that cluster around that gladsome period—unchanged forever—the one pure and hallowed spot in life's uncertain way—the star of a darksome world—the earth type of joys to come.

Wealth, its use.

The highest degree of happiness wealth can bestow on its possessor is derived from the happiness conferred upon others. This is a proposition susceptible of proof, strong and clear as words of Holy Writ. The man who so administers his estate, and so conducts his stewardship as to do the most good to others, alone enjoys the means bestowed upon him. The man who hords up his gains, like a greedy dog that hides his bone, never enjoys a single moment of happiness, though he may count his wealth by thousands or millions of dollars. He never realizes a single feeling of contentment, which is better than gold. He gropes his way through the world like a miserable coward, suspicious of all around him, and almost afraid to sleep lest a sixpence might slip from his grasp or take wings and fly away. He is opposed to all improvements that tend to the comfort or convenience of those around him, for the enjoyment of the poor is a real annoyance to him. He frowns a cold and chilling frown on the children of want. The sob of anguish is music to him. The tears of sorrow and the cry of the hungry find no responsive chord in his callous heart. Dead to every ennobling sentiment of humanity, and wrapt in the mantle of supreme selfishness, he drags his soulless carcass through the world, down to the grave, still grasping his gold and clutching for more, until the palsy of death unlocks his iron fingers. When he sees the sure approach of death, in his desperation he hides his treasures in the earth, or resolves to give his thousands to the church or some worthy cause, in the hope of appeasing the Almighty. And this is called "giving to the Lord,"—given alas, because the poor mortal could hold it no longer. For him no tears are shed. No flowers strewn by the hands of those he blest deck the mound where he sleeps. The cold marble may mark the spot and remind the world that his death was the only blessing he ever conferred on the community in which he lived.

See the wealthy miser in the marts of trade. Note his wary and suspicious eye. His character is stamped upon his brow. Mark the nervous twitching of his fingers. You can not mistake the miser. His features are almost as cold and unimpressible as the molten god he worships. See him again as he stealthily counts his gold. With a grim delight he clutches the shining metal. Transformed to a demon he gloats over his hidden treasures and prostitutes all semblance of manhood to the senseless idol on whose polluted shrine he lays the sacrifice of his soul, yielding all the hopes and the aspirations of an immortal life to the tyrant power of his unhallowed passion. Nay more, to swell the sum he would coin his heart and drop his blood for dimes.

But there are rich men in our own community who have made a noble record for themselves—who have ever lent a willing heart and an open hand to every movement designed to advance the physical, mental and moral welfare of the community; nay more, who have ministered to the wants of the poor and gladdened the hearts of the needy—the poor, from the inner shrine of whose greatful hearts the incense of gratitude ascends to heaven to-day. Would you enjoy the benedictions of the FATHER above, send up the blessings of his children below!

That Old Book—The Bible.

" I also will show mine opinion."

We are not a theologian, nor do we make any special pretension to a knowledge of metaphysical science, claiming only the philosophy of common sense as applied to manifest truth. We leave at present the wide realm of speculation and the fairy world of imagination, as well as the various systems of religious faith based on human creeds. But all this, with the errors of its adherents in works or in weakness of faith, does not affect the truth itself. Alike impotent is the power of the learned skeptic who wields the pen of treason against the royal Truth in whose light he " lives and moves and has his being." Nay more, the power that nurtured him—that shields him and crowns his life with the blessings of civilization.

What, then, is Truth? How shall we find it? What are our relations to the past, the present, and the future? How shall we best prepare to meet our responsibilities as reasonable beings? These are questions a thousand fold more important to us than the rise and fall of all the creeds that human wisdom ever devised, or all the speculations that ever sprang from the brain of the metaphysician.

We may have been taught in childhood that the Scriptures are of Divine origin. Not in a general sense like the works of creation, but the result of special revelation, given as a rule of life, directly from God to man. The child accepts this faith implicitly, not as a conclusion drawn from the merits of the Book or the facts in the case, but on the guarantee of its parents or religious teachers. The truth of the volume is accepted as a matter of history, its teachings as a rule of life and as a chart to guide the way to heaven. As the child grows up and comes in contact with the world, and finds that practically this rule is the exception, and as he meets the conflicting ideas of men and the various shades of religious faith—all professedly based on the Bible—as he meets the subtle insinuations of the skeptic or the bold assertions of the atheist, he begins to look for the foundations that support the faith of his childhood. On the assumption that man is a reasonable being, he begins to reason: "Here am I, an atom in the wide universe. From whence am I, and where am I going? All around me such as I are sinking into the grave, beyond which is the land of the unknown. Reason tells me that I, too, must shortly go down to the city of the dead. And what then? Will I lose my identity and mingle with the senseless clods? Will the spirit that animates me go out forever in darkness, like the blaze of a rocket or the flash of a meteor? Can it be that this atom of matchless mechanism, with all its wonderful powers, was designed only for the brief space of human life?—that the powers of mind so vast in their range, with the principle of vitality, shall pass away with the breath of mortal life? *No, it can not be.* Nature recoils from the thought, and reason, in view of the known laws of being, declares it impossible. Then, if I am to live hereafter, and if our brief existence here is but passing through the vestibule that leads to a life beyond, the Bible must be true. For reason, linking these teachings with that which is known of life and death, logically leads to the conclusion that this is not all of life. Reason travels with revelation to the confines of earth and sanctions its truths as far as the finite mind can go, and from known facts implies the truth of those that lie beyond."

But it must not be forgotten that with the faith, gratuitously accepted in childhood, conscience was also educated and prepared to pilot the way when the hand of parental guidance was withdrawn, or when reason failed. And here is a jewel of untold wealth inherited by the child of instruction—an inherent power to judge the true and the right from error and wrong. Not, indeed, an innate principle of competent judgment without religious culture or the knowledge of Divine law, as revealed in the Bible. Conscience is a faculty of the human mind, capable of development, and will prove quick and sure to judge right and wrong only as it is rightly educated. St. Paul persecuted the saints "in all good conscience," for so his conscience had been educated, but when enlightened he found that its judgment had been erroneous. Its rightful culture is therefore a great advantage to the child of religious training when called to meet the sharp corners of the world and to retain a foothold on the rock of Truth.

It is true, the power of reason is limited; it can no more deny than affirm that which is unknown, but it can infer much of the future from the known of the past. Reason can comprehend the principle of righteousness taught in the Bible—and in the Bible alone—and their redeeming influence in the world. Reason can comprehend its matchless system of morals, as the light and life of every age and the source of every law of justice, mercy and truth. Point out a spot on the map of the wide world where the teachings of the Bible are unknown, and reason will point out to you a place of intellectual and moral darkness, destitute of all the peaceful and ennobling qualities of mind and heart that render life and society desirable. This fact alone irresistibly leads to the conclusion that the Bible is true.

There are men in our own community, too, who doubt or affect to doubt the truth of revelation. As the boy with his first cigar imagines himself "a man," so do men appear, who are "wise above what is written." The geologist will point to a rock and make the truth of science a lie. The speculator will picture a dreamless sleep or a world of fancy, beautiful but delusive as the mirage of the desert. The philosopher will light a taper, and in its feeble shimmer deny the light of the noonday sun, and with finite reason attempt to measure the mysteries, the powers and the transcendant glories of the eternal world. But take away, if you please, all books, all science, all philosophy—leave but the BIBLE—and by that unerring chart the Christian pilgrim will solve the problem of life.

Night.

What a comprehensive theme is night! Grand, peculiar and sublime are its inspirations! Who can measure its influence on our physical, mental or moral nature? Who can fathom the wonders of sleep or solve the mystery of its dreams? There lies the body, unconscious as its kindred clods of the field, and yet allied to a living soul—an immortal mind—that by the power of a strange enchantment, creates and peoples a world of its own—a mystic world of shadowy dreams that dissolve like the mists of the morning.

> " How beautiful is Death!
> Death and his brother Sleep—
> One pale as yonder waning moon,
> With lips of lurid blue ;
> The other rosy as the morn,
> When throned on ocean's wave,
> She sheds her blushes o'er the world."

And how the wierd voices of the night stir the deep waters of the soul as they float on the breeze like the far-off notes of dying melody. Ah! yes ; the most wonderful achievements of science, the most brilliant gems of poetry, and the most profound teachings of the metaphysician and theologian, have been the result of thoughts in the night. When the curtain of darkness shuts the outer world from view, we turn within to explore the world of mind. Freed from the thousand distractions of the day, we seek a more intimate acquaintance with ourselves. The past, the present and the future are all before us. Memory brings her treasures up from the storehouse of the past and imagination essays to unfold the future. Though darkness surrounds us, yet all the world is before us, and from the shadows we may look up and count the jewels of the skies as they sparkle in the azure drapery of heaven—but vision finds a limit there. Imagination may travel on—pass the burning zone of far Saturn to the outer pathway of more distant Uranus—but imagination, too, must pause on the threshhold of a universe unknown, the mighty space that science never trod. No peaceful vales nor misty mountains mark the far beyond. No voice or sound, even to fancy's

ear, ever broke the dead, eternal solitude that lies beyond the tele-
scopic power of science.   Faith alone can pierce the gloom and
pass beyond the outer range where science halts and fancy dies.
The faith of the Christian, guided by the chart of revelation, leaves
planets, stars and worlds behind, as it sweeps across the mighty
chasm up to the home of the immortals, where doubt never enters,
where night never comes.   Weary mortal, groping amid the deeper
shadows of moral darkness, do you long for the morning dawn?
Do you long to know what undiscovered country lies in the far beyond?   The geologist would point to a rock and make the truth of science a lie.   The speculator would picture a dream, beautiful in fancy,
but wild and baseless as the mirage of the desert.   The philosopher
would light a taper, and in its feeble shimmer, deny the light of the
noonday sun, and with finite reason attempt to measure the mysteries,
the powers and the transcendant glories of the eternal world.

Take away, if you please, all books, all science, all philosophy;
leave but the Bible, and by that unerring chart, the Christian pilgrim will solve the problem of life—"the only star that rose upon
the night of Time, by which man could navigate the sea of life and
gain the coast of bliss"—the shores of a land, where day is eternal,
and whose sunshine is the glory of the LORD.

The Peroration.

List! oh, mortal, to the voices of the past!   Realize the living
present!   Forget not the swift-coming future!   What a multitude
of thoughts come crowding upon us, as we muse on the certainties
gone, and glance at the probabilities—nay, the certainties before us!
Nor are they limited to our history as a nation, but we launch out on
the wide ocean of time itself, invade the land of eternity, and strive
to grasp the finished past and give shape to the dark, uncertain future.
But, however far we may travel back over the ages, or forward on
the pinions of imagination, philosophy or religion, ever and anon
we come home to ourselves and pause to read our personal relations
to the Past, the Present and the eternal years to come—to read the
lessons before us, in the handwriting of the Almighty, through the
innate power conferred when man became a living soul.   Here we are
to-day, a single generation, rushing on, close in the wake of thou-

sands gone, and crowded by coming millions. One by one, the countless ages come and go, and one generation succeeds another, as they rapidly march across a narrow plain, and then pass away forever.

To-day we are here—to-morrow a new generation will carelessly tread the earth above our heads nor care to know that the clods beneath their feet once lived and exulted in the warm sunshine of life, and that they, too, in a little while must yield to another.

An hundred years! And every heart that beats with rapture to-day, rejoicing in the triumphs of a finished century, will be cold and still. Every voice that joins the million-toned shout of joy to hail our grand Centennial year, or swells the glad hallelujahs of praise to our Fathers' God for the blessings of an hundred years, will be hushed in the everlasting silence of the grave. Not one of all the millions who bring the tributes of affection, or the garlands of honor to the shrine of the dead to-day—not one of all the millions that eagerly press the gates to see the gathered wonders of the world, will see the dawn of another Centennial anniversary. Long ere then, all those busy managers and stately actors in the imposing ceremonies,—the speakers, the Emperors, the Presidents, the musicians, the singers, and the tired policemen—with all the thronging millions, will lie down and die. The high and the low, the rich and the poor—all will find a common abode, down in a lone, narrow house. The lordly millionaire, who rides in stately grandeur through the lovely avenues of the most magnificent park in the world, will lie down at last and sleep beside the poor, who can only catch a glance of its splendors through the open gates. Centuries may roll away. Other Centennials of '76 may come and go, but they shall heed no more the wild huzzas the waving banners of assembled nations, the thunders of artillery, nor the pomp and show of a world combined.

A century hence, and all will have passed away forever! The inventors will crumble to dust and mingle with the moldering work of their hands. The mighty achievments of " hand and brain " that mark the age will pale before the more stupendous triumphs of the era to come, and the dust of oblivion will settle forever on the pride of skill and the glory of man, nor leave a memorial of the great Centennial Exposition.

We, too, shall mingle with the vast caravan marching down to the gates of Death, to join the generations gone before. The march goes silently on—not to the inspiring notes of the musicians before me, but to the noiseless beat of the pulse, silent as rose leaves fall from the stem, but the end is sure. The generations come and go, but *they never return!* *Our* march will soon be over. Where, oh! where shall our next encampment be?

Statesmen.

Distance does not always lend enchantment to the view. In looking at the daily proceedings of Congress, and noting the chicanery of the cunning politician, we are forced to the conclusion that no distance, however remote, can ever magnify our present public men into the semblance of statesmen. Our own State, Pennsylvania, in days gone by, has contributed more than one star to the galaxy that will ever illume our national history. Who have we now to arouse the ambition of the American boy and to command the admiration of the world? We sometimes hope that Senator Cameron, or some other son of Pennsylvania, may yet rise above the level of mere party politics and on the higher plane of statesmanship stand beside the immortal founders of the State, with all of the past, who have given luster to the American name.

We know there are seasons of depression in the elements of national greatness, as well as in the financial world. Such is the history of nations, and we are not an exception. England had her golden " age," when the powers of genius kindled a glory whose radiance will never die. Her philosophers, poets and statesmen are still the pride and boast of her sons and daughters, at home and abroad, as they exultingly point to the brilliant galaxy of immortal names that adorn her history—an age when the statesmen laid the massive foundations of her greatness, when philosophers reared the fair superstructure of her national institutions, around which her poets wove the garlands of unfading beauty.

We too have had a " golden age." It dawned upon us in the gathering storm that preceded the revolution, and illuminated with a new-born glory our pathway through the Red sea and the wilderness, until we rose to the very pinnacle of national greatness. " There were giants in those days." Not comparatively great, nor yet because they have passed beyond the reach of envy or green-eyed jealousy, nor yet because we have been taught to worship at the shrines of the dead : but they were great in their endowments, great in the work they accomplished, in the monuments they reared and in the priceless legacy they bequeathed to their countrymen and the world. " Distance " does not always lend enchantment to the view." The founders of our government and our early statesmen were no less great in their own day. They were no less revered by the wise and good of every civilized nation on the globe, when grappling with the mighty problems of popular government. no less than now, when they are embalmed in the grateful memory of their countrymen. Passing over the founders of the Republic, where are the peers of Clay, Webster, Calhoun, Cass, Benton and all the sons of Anak of less than half a century ago ? They were men of ideas. In their view, *party* was nothing, only the shallow device of demagogues. They were above the plane of party politics. They were in the higher region of substantial ideas, where reason prompted thought, and judgment, divorced from party bias, impelled to action. Sharp contests they had—but not on party differences, for that belongs to the pigmy tribe—but on constitutional questions as they rose in the progress of the grand political experiment. Even now, no living man can claim a higher honor than an approach to the character of these statesmen whose intellectual power, solid worth, sterling patriotism and practical wisdom mark the golden age of America.

INDEX.

www.ingramcontent.com/pod-product-compliance
Lightning Source LLC
Chambersburg PA
CBHW020508270326
41926CB00008B/789